# Television Series
# of the 1960s

# Television Series of the 1960s

## Essential Facts and Quirky Details

VINCENT TERRACE

ROWMAN & LITTLEFIELD
*Lanham • Boulder • New York • London*

Published by Rowman & Littlefield
A wholly owned subsidary of The Rowman & Littlefield Publishing Group, Inc.
4501 Forbes Boulevard, Suite 200, Lanham, Maryland 20706
www.rowman.com

Unit A, Whitacre Mews, 26-34 Stannary Street, London SE11 4AB

British Library Cataloguing in Publication Information Available

**Library of Congress Cataloging-in-Publication Data**

Names: Terrace, Vincent, 1948– author.
Title: Television series of the 1960s : essential facts and quirky details /
    Vincent Terrace.
Description: Lanham : Rowman & Littlefield, [2016] | Includes index.
Identifiers: LCCN 2016000781 (print) | LCCN 2016004669 (ebook) | ISBN
    9781442268340 (hardback : alk. paper) | ISBN 9781442268357 (electronic)
Subjects: LCSH: Television programs—United States—Plots, themes, etc. |
    Television programs—United States—Dictionaries.
Classification: LCC PN1992.3.U5 T46855 2016 (print) | LCC PN1992.3.U5 (ebook) |
    DDC 791.45/750973—dc23
LC record available at http://lccn.loc.gov/2016000781

Printed in the United States of America

# Contents

# Acknowledgments

The author would like to thank James Robert Parish, Steven Eberly, Bob Leszczak, Nicole Galiardo, and Madison Gorman for their kind assistance on this project.

# Introduction

This is *not* a book of opinions or essays about specific 1960s American (and British) television programs that aired in the United States. Rather it is a presentation of intriguing facts associated with each of the TV series that are included in this volume. This book covers programs that premiered from January 1, 1960, through December 31, 1969.

Readers will discover a wealth of fascinating information about these shows—details that, for the most part, cannot be found anywhere else. In some cases, the factual data detailed herein is the only such documentation that currently exists on these shows.

While all the basic information available about each television series has been included (e.g., story line and cast), the bulk of each entry focuses on the trivia aspects associated with every program examined. This encompasses such data as street addresses, names of pets, telephone numbers, character facts, program details, and other factoids you may have once known but have long since forgotten. In situations where a TV movie or a revised remake version of a 1960s series showcased here was aired later (like *The Munsters*, *I Dream of Jeannie*, and *Gilligan's Island*), that information has been included as part of the main entry. (Note: Stage and theatrical adaptations of 1960s TV series presented in this book have *not* been included.)

Each entry was created by acquiring and watching available episodes of the show. Each entry is as complete as possible based on currently accessible material. Not every series is a candidate for such detailed books as this. Just because a program may be well known does not mean it has a wealth of (or even sufficient) trivia facts to be included in this volume. Cases in point are such series as *Dr. Kildare*, *The Defenders*, and *Mission: Impossible*—all of which are known but lack enough detailed data to be included (obvious information, such as full names, can be accessed on websites like IMDb.com, but other, more obscure factoids, such as character backgrounds, address, relatives, pets, and so on, are simply not given within the show's episodes).

Did you know, for example, that on *The Addams Family*, Lurch's mother had wanted him to become a jockey? That Jethro's mother, Pearl Bodine (*The Beverly Hillbillies*), played piano for the silent movies shown at the Palace Theater? That John Steed (*The Avengers*) had a pet dog named Freckles? That Dawn Wells (Mary Ann on *Gilligan's Island*) was the first actress to wear short shorts on TV (not the held belief that it was Catherine Bach as Daisy Duke on *The Dukes of Hazzard*)? And that Patty and Cathy Lane (*The Patty Duke Show*) had a distant cousin named Betsy Lane (whom Patty called a "Confederate Cleopatra")?

What about the ZIP code for Hooterville on *Green Acres* (40516½), the name of the band for which Opie played on *The Andy Griffith Show* (Freedom), the poker hand that won Ben Calhoun a bankrupt railroad on *Iron Horse* (four queens), *Mister Ed*'s Social Security number (054-22-5487), or Lily's favorite charity on *The Munsters* (Bundles for Transylvania)?

These are just a thimbleful of the many thousands of intriguing trivia facts that can be found within the pages that follow.

All told, *Television Series of the 1960s* is a totally different perspective on a past era of what has been seen on American television. It is geared to bring back fond memories or to enlighten those too young to have lived through the era covered.

Note: Programs that premiered in the 1950s and that continued first-run production into the 1960s are *not* included here. Information on the following programs can be found in the volume *Television Series of the 1950s*:

*Bonanza*
*Bronco*
*Cheyenne*
*Dennis the Menace*
*The Donna Reed Show*
*Gunsmoke*
*Have Gun—Will Travel*
*Hawaiian Eye*
*The Jack Benny Program*
*Lawman*
*Leave It to Beaver*
*Make Room for Daddy*
*Maverick*
*Perry Mason*
*Rawhide*
*The Real McCoys*
*The Rebel*
*77 Sunset Strip*
*Sugarfoot*
*The Untouchables*
*Zorro*

# Adam 12
### (NBC, 1968–1974)

*Cast:* Martin Milner (Officer Pete Malloy), Kent McCord (Officer Jim Reed), William Boyett (Sergeant MacDonald), Gary Crosby (Officer Ed Wells).
*Basis:* Realistic day-to-day assignments of Pete Malloy and Jim Reed, Los Angeles police officers assigned to patrol car Adam 12.

## OVERALL SERIES INFORMATION

Peter "Pete" Malloy and James "Jim" Reed ride in a patrol car with the code "One Adam 12," which, although attached to the Central Division of the Los Angeles Police Department (LAPD), is seen working in association with the Rampart Division (which is outside of the actual "One" code of the series setting). The "One" in the code refers to the area where Pete and Jim are stationed, the "Adam" refers to a two-man patrol car, and the "12" is a designation for the car's main patrol area.

Standard Chrysler Corporation and American Motors cars were used and outfitted with props to appear like real police cars. A 1968 Plymouth Belvedere was used in the first season (a 1967 version of the car was seen in the pilot). The second season sported a 1969 version; the third season used a Plymouth Satellite, and the remaining seasons used a 1972 (then 1973) American Motors Matador.

Sharon Claridge, a real-life LAPD radio dispatcher, provides the voice of the dispatcher for the series (producer Jack Webb felt it would make the series more realistic). The building housing Central Division (as seen) is actually the Rampart Division of the LAPD.

In almost every episode, Pete is seen driving the patrol car. Pete's badge number is 2430; Jim's is 744. When the opportunity permits, Jim and Pete enjoy lunch at Duke's Longhorn, a diner owned by their friend Duke. Marilyn Wells (played by Christina Sinatra) is Pete's romantic interest, and Jean (Mikki

Jamison, then Kristen Nelson) is Jim's wife. Sergeant MacDonald is their superior, and Ed Wells is the glory-seeking officer who causes nothing but trouble for Pete and Jim. T. J. (Robert Donner) appeared on occasion as Jim and Pete's informant (a recovering heroin addict).

Pete was depicted as a veteran officer, while Jim was said to be a probationary officer, a recent police academy graduate. However, on the series *Dragnet* (the updated 1967–1970 version), the Jim Reed character appeared several times as a patrol car officer before the *Adam 12* spin-off occurred. While gunplay was a part of the series, Pete was considered an expert sharpshooter and Jim a sharpshooter. In the final episode, Jim is awarded the Medal of Valor for saving Pete's life.

*Note:* The series was revised for syndication in 1989 as *The New Adam 12*. Here, Ethan Wayne (as Matt Doyle) and Peter Parros (as Gus Grant) were officers with the LAPD who patrolled the streets in a car designated as Adam 12.

# *The Addams Family*
## (ABC, 1964–1966)

*Cast:* John Astin (Gomez Addams), Carolyn Jones (Morticia Addams), Jackie Coogan (Uncle Fester), Ted Cassidy (Lurch), Lisa Loring (Wednesday Addams), Ken Weatherwax (Pugsley Addams), Blossom Rock (Grandmama), Carolyn Jones (Ophelia Frump).

*Basis:* An odd family, living in a creepy Victorian mansion, attempt to cope with life in a world where they believe they are normal and everyone else is strange. Gomez and Morticia Addams are the parents; Wednesday and Pugsley are their children. Also living with them is their Uncle Fester; their zombielike butler, Lurch; Gomez's mother, Grandmama; and Thing, a human right hand.

## OVERALL SERIES INFORMATION

*Family Address:* Given as 000 Cemetery Lane, 001 Cemetery Lane, and 001 North Cemetery Drive in the town of Cemetery Ridge.

*Family Pets:* Kit Kat, a cowardly lion; Zelda, the vulture; and Tristan, the piranha.

*Oddities:* In addition to the "Beware of Thing" sign posted on the spiked, wrought-iron gate that surrounds the home, one will find a large two-headed sea turtle, the head of a swordfish with a human leg sticking out (the leg belonging to Cousin Ferook), an Eskimo totem pole, a suit of armor, a harpsichord, an iron maiden, a torture rack, a bed of nails, and Pierre, the moose head that hangs over the fireplace.

## GOMEZ ADDAMS

*Ancestry:* Mixed, including American, Egyptian, and Spanish.

*Personality:* Wealthy but eccentric.

*Occupation:* Defense lawyer (although he has put more people in jail than any other defense lawyer in U.S. history).

*Claim to Fame:* That the second *d* in his name distinguishes him "from that embarrassingly famous and historic John Adams and family."

*Hobby:* Dabbling in the stock market.

*Favorite Stock:* Consolidated Fuzz.

*Investments:* A nut plantation in Brazil, an elephant herd in Africa, and a salt mine and an animal preserve in Nairobi (for family vacations and its subterranean bat caves).

*Relaxation:* Running his Lionel "O-Gauge" electric trains for the thrill of crashes and explosions.

*Enjoyment:* Gloomy weather, thunderstorms, moon bathing, exploring caves, and smoking cigars. He keeps his Garcia Vega cigars in a cigar store Indian that, when pulled out, are automatically lit.

*Polo Pony:* A polka-dot wooden pony named Kelso.

*Nicknames for Morticia:* "Tish," "Cara Mia," and "Caita."

*Constant Companion:* Thing, a human right hand he has had since he was a child. It now functions as the family servant.

*Expertise:* Gomez claims to be an excellent swordsman (both in battle and in sword-swallowing amusement).

*Affiliation:* Member of the Zen Yoga Society.

*Favorite Food:* Fried eyes of newt, fried yak, and barbecued turtle tips.

*Relatives:* Aunt Millicent (Elvia Allman). Other relatives that were mentioned but not seen were Uncle Droop and Aunt Drip, Uncle Tick (has two left feet), Aunt Trivia, Great Grandfather Blob, Cousin Kurdle, Cousin Bleek (has three eyes), Grandpa Slurp, Cousin Cackle, Great Uncle Grizzly, Aunt Blemish, and Uncle Crimp. Gomez mentions his earliest known relation as Maumud Kali Pashu Addams, who in the year AD 270 set the Egyptian Library at Alexandria on fire.

*Note:* In the 1998 update, *The New Addams Family*, Glenn Taranto played Gomez Addams.

## MORTICIA ADDAMS

*Maiden Name:* Morticia Frump.

*Ancestry:* Dates back to the witch burnings of seventeenth-century Salem, Massachusetts.

*Occupation:* Housewife (she prides herself on keeping the house "nice and bleak").

*Enjoyment:* Smoking (she has the ability to emit a mist from her body), thunderstorms, gloomy weather, and lightning.

*Hair Color:* Black.

*Wardrobe:* Long, sexy and tight black dresses (when Gomez first saw her in one, he became obsessed with her, and she said she would never wear another).

*Favorite Color:* Black ("It's so soothing and mysterious").

*Favorite Doll as a Kid:* Anne Boleyn (a wife of Henry VIII; the doll is also minus her head).

*Pet Plant:* Cleopatra (an African Strangler that loves zebra and giraffe burgers).

*Abilities:* Excellent cook (famous for her Dwarf Hair Pie), playing the bagpipes, and speaking French (which drives Gomez wild and makes him romantic).

*Favorite Holiday:* Halloween. She relishes in the fact that her house may be haunted.

*Hobbies:* Animal impersonations (especially the bullfrog), painting, and maintaining her backyard of deadly nightshade, poison sumac, assorted weeds, and quicksand.

*Nickname for Gomez:* Bubula.

*Book:* Morticia wrote her own children's book: *A Treasury of Mean Witches, Evil Giants, Wicked Goblins, and Other Bedtime Stories.*

*Note:* In the 1998 update, *The New Addams Family*, Ellie Harvie played Morticia Addams.

## UNCLE FESTER

*Relationship:* An eccentric who is first said to be Gomez's brother (making him Fester Addams), then Morticia's uncle (making him Fester Frump).

*Hobby:* Playing with dynamite caps and collecting hangman's nooses.

*Education:* While a school was not named, Fester mentioned that in a production of George Washington for his grammar school, he played the cherry tree.

*Quirk:* Thrives on electricity and needs to be recharged when he runs low. He relieves headaches by placing his head in a vise and tightening it until the pain "pops out." His right ear produces DC (direct current), his left ear AC (alternating current). He sleeps on a bed of nails and enjoys relaxing in the playroom (the dungeon).

*Job:* Worked as an advice-to-the-lovelorn columnist (but quit when people began suing him).

*Claim:* To know everything there is about women "Because I had a mother."

*Ability:* Mechanically inclined but never succeeded in inventing anything of use.

*Enjoyment:* Thunderstorms, lightning, fog, cloudy days, moon bathing, and exploring the tunnels beneath the house.

*Dislikes:* Strangers coming to the house (he threatens to "Shoot 'em in the back" with Genevieve, his Revolutionary War rifle).

*Note:* In the 1998 update, *The New Addams Family*, Michael Roberds played Uncle Fester Addams.

## WEDNESDAY ADDAMS

*Character:* A preteen version of her mother.

*Education:* Sherwood Elementary School.

*Enjoyment:* All that is morbid, especially thunderstorms and gloomy weather. Bright and sunny days make her feel sad.

*Favorite Doll:* A headless Marie Antoinette.

*Pet Spider:* Homer.

*Note:* In the 1998 update, *The New Addams Family*, Nicole Fugere played Wednesday Addams.

## PUGSLEY ADDAMS

*Character:* Wednesday's younger brother who sees a world beyond his macabre existence and would like to experience it (which horrifies Gomez and Morticia). Pugsley likes to dig tunnels, and, according to Wednesday, "Most people think he is part gopher."

*Education:* Sherwood Elementary School.

*Fault:* Overweight.

*Pets:* Aristotle (octopus), Lucifer (lizard), and Fang (jaguar).

*Ability:* Able to invent things (such as disintegrating ray guns and antigravity machines).

*Favorite Snack:* Licorice.

*Favorite Pastime:* Reading comic books, playing in the dungeon, and playing with dynamite caps.

*Note:* In the 1998 update, *The New Addams Family*, Brody Smith played Pugsley Addams.

## OPHELIA FRUMP

*Relationship:* Morticia's attractive but flaky sister.

*Personality:* The total opposite of Morticia. Although raised by the same mother, Ophelia despises gloom and doom. She loves bright and sunny days and anything that makes her feel good.

*Hair Color:* Blonde.

*Wardrobe:* Although seen most often in flowing white dresses, Ophelia loves clothes that are bright and colorful.

*Quirk:* Enjoys picking flowers and displaying them in full bloom (the opposite of what Morticia does: cuts the blooms off and displays the stems).

*Obsession:* Water. Ophelia can't get enough of water ("She is always jumping in fountains, brooks, and even tubs and sinks").

*Passion:* Cooking (but she does it only so she can wash dishes).

*Favorite Perfume:* Quagmire 13.

*Relatives:* Ophelia and Morticia's mother, Esther Frump (Margaret Hamilton).

*History:* Gomez and Ophelia were part of a prearranged marriage set up by their mothers (their fathers are never seen or mentioned). That marriage, however, never occurred. On that fatal day, Gomez saw Morticia for the first time and knew she was the woman for him (especially when she spoke French and it cleared up a sinus condition he had for 22 years). Fate stepped in. Ophelia saw Gomez's Cousin Itt (covered with hair from head to toe), and it was love at first sight. They eloped, allowing Gomez and Morticia to marry.

## LURCH

*Position:* Family butler. His mother wanted him to become a jockey.

*Height:* 6 feet, 9 inches tall.

*Affiliation:* Member of the Butler's Association.

*Musical Ability:* Plays the harpsichord.

*Hit Record:* Mizzy Records (named after the show's theme composer, Vic Mizzy) signed Lurch to a recording deal when Gomez thought it would be good for Lurch "to spread his wings." His unnamed song was a hit with teenagers and consisted of his grunts and groans.

*Catchphrases:* "You rang?," "Mail's in," "Follow me," and "Yes, Mrs. Addams."

*Greatest Fear:* Attending the Butler's Ball (as he can't dance).

*Relatives:* Mother Lurch (Ellen Corby).

*Note:* In the 1998 series update, *The New Addams Family*, it is revealed that Morticia found Lurch in a cemetery (dug him up) and that, when he tried to smile, his face broke. Joe DeSantis played Lurch here.

Front row, left to right: Lisa Loring, Carolyn Jones, John Astin, and Ken Weatherwax; back row, from left: Jackie Coogan, Blossom Rock, and Ted Cassidy.
*ABC/Photofest © ABC*

**OTHER CHARACTERS**

Grandmama Addams is Gomez's grandmother. She is a graduate of Swamp Town High School and first voted in 1906—even before woman suffrage ("It didn't stop me," she says). Her hobby appears to be making love potions to spark romances. In the 1998 update, *The New Addams Family*, Betty Phillips played Eudora "Grandmama" Addams.

Thing, Gomez's childhood friend and companion, lives in a series of small boxes that appear all over the house. He is a human right hand and now acts as a family servant. There is a warning posted on the iron gate that surrounds the house: "Beware of Thing" (Gomez also enjoys sharpening the pointy iron spikes that adorn the fence). Thing also found love when he fell for Lady Fingers, the human left hand maiden of Gomez's Aunt Millicent.

Cousin Itt (Felix Silla, Roger Arrovo) is the family intellectual. He has an IQ of 320 ("and that is with his shoes on"), is covered with blonde hair from head to toe, speaks a language all his own (the actor's voice played backward), and considers himself a ladies' man. He held a job as a zookeeper (although he was often mistaken for one of the exhibits), and when at the Addams home, the chimney and broom closet are his favorite places of relaxation. When Gomez became curious about Itt's hair, he asked what was under it. Itt replied, "Roots." Morticia claims that Itt is from both sides of the family (Addams and Frump), "but he hasn't found himself yet." Nat Perrin provided Itt's voice.

# *The Andy Griffith Show*
## (CBS, 1960–1968)

*Cast:* Andy Griffith (Andy Taylor), Don Knotts (Barney Fife), Ronny Howard (Opie Taylor), Frances Bavier (Aunt Bee Taylor), George Lindsey (Goober Pyle), Jim Nabors (Gomer Pyle), Betty Lynn (Thelma Lou), Howard McNear (Floyd Lawson).

*Basis:* Life in the small town of Mayberry, North Carolina, as seen through the eyes of Sheriff Andy Taylor and his deputy, Barney Fife.

**ANDREW "ANDY" JACKSON TAYLOR**

*Address:* 322 Maple Road (also given as 14 Maple Street and 332 Maple Street) in Mayberry (neighboring towns are Mount Pilot and Raleigh). Mayberry has a population of 2,000 people.

*Marital Status:* Widower.

*Son:* Opie.

*Squad Car License Plate:* JL 327 (in certain scenes, it looks like JL 322). The car is a Ford Galaxie, and its license plate is first seen as DC 269.

*Emergency Equipment:* A rake and shovel in the trunk of the squad car.

*Education:* Mayfield Union High School, Class of 1945 (orange and blue are the school colors). The school is also called Mayfield Central High School in another episode.

*Nickname:* "Anj" (as called by Barney) and "The Sheriff without a Gun" (as set in stone in the *National Sheriff's Magazine*); Andy does, however, keep a gun in the house (on top of the hutch in the dining room. The sheriff's office also reflects a rack of six rifles on the wall).

*Abilities:* Able to sing and play the guitar.

*Favorite Eatery:* The Junction Café (where he and Barney often dine; Juanita Beasley is the often-talked-about but never-seen waitress; Catfish Casserole is the Friday Special).

*Girlfriends:* Eleanor "Ellie" Walker (Elinor Donahue) and Helen Crump (Aneta Corsaut). Andy called Eleanor "Miss Ellie," and she worked as a pharmacist at the Walker Drug Store (which was owned by her uncle Fred Walker). Helen is the town's fourth- (then fifth-) grade schoolteacher whom Andy later marries; they later have a son named Andy Taylor Jr.

*Rowboat:* Gertrude (docked on the shore of Meyer's Lake).

*Notoriety:* Hollywood made a feature film about Andy called *The Sheriff Without a Gun.*

*Favorite Meal:* Leg of lamb.

## BERNARD "BARNEY" FIFE

*Middle Name:* Varies. Given as Milton, Milton P., and Oliver.

*Address:* 411 Elm Street.

*Marital Status:* Single.

*Education:* Mayfield Union High School.

*Relationship to Andy:* Cousins. Barney has been Andy's deputy for five of the 12 years that Andy has been the sheriff. It is later said that Barney has been with Andy for 10 years.

*Weight:* 132 pounds.

*Birthstone:* Ruby.

*Characteristic:* Easily excited and not taken seriously by lawbreakers.

*Casual Dress:* Out of uniform, Barney wears a red bow tie with a salt and pepper–colored coat and a white straw fedora.

*Nickname:* "Barn" (as called by Andy).

*Musical Ability:* Plays the harmonica. He also believes he is a great singer; Andy says, "He knows just how to sing a note off key to make your skin crawl."

*Weapon:* A gun that Andy allows him to carry but with no bullets. He carries one bullet in his shirt pocket and is allowed to load his gun only if there is a real emergency. He keeps his citation booklet in his police cap.

*Duties:* Besides upholding the law, Barney helps children cross the street, issues parking tickets, and replaces lids on garbage cans. He is also in charge of swatting flies in the office, and when he is permitted to use his gun, he does so to start the potato race at the Mason's Picnic.

*Girlfriend:* Thelma Lou. He is also known to have dated Miss Rosemary and Juanita Beasley at the same time he has known Thelma Lou. Thelma Lou's last name or occupation is never revealed. Mayberry 596 is Thelma Lou's phone number. Karen Moon played Thelma Lou's cousin, Mary Grace Gossage. Before he knew Thelma Lou, Barney dated Hilda May.

*Fifth-Year Anniversary Gift:* After serving as a deputy for five years, Barney received a stainless-steel watch with "5" engraved on the back.

*Character:* Barney fears the day that "Mayberry is going to turn into a sin town." When a better opportunity comes his way (1965), Barney leaves Mayberry for a job in nearby Raleigh in traffic control with its police department (he is later promoted to the position of detective). He was replaced by Jack Burns as Deputy Warren Ferguson, a by-the-books character (1965–1966).

*Relatives:* mother (Lillian Culver); Virgil, cousin (Michael J. Pollard).

## BEATRICE "AUNT BEE" TAYLOR

*Relationship:* Andy's aunt (lives with Andy and Opie and tends house and cooks).

*Place of Birth:* Morgantown, West Virginia.

*Birthday:* March 17.

*Education:* Sweet Briar Normal School (where she was a member of the basketball team).

*Ability:* Fabulous cook. She is noted for her homemade pies and pickles.

*Dessert Specialty:* Apple pie and butterscotch and pecan pie.

*Affiliations:* Member of the Garden Club, the Mayberry Community Church Choir, and the Greater Mayberry Historical Society and Tourist Bureau.

*Accomplishments:* Won a trip to Mexico with her cooking knowledge from the Tampico Tamale Contest, won assorted prizes on the TV game show *Win or Lose*, and hosted a TV cooking show preparing her favorite meals called *The Mayberry Chef* on WZAZ-TV, channel 12. She cowrote (with her friend Clara Edwards [Hope Summers]) the sentimental town song "Mayberry My Home Town" and appeared as the TV spokesperson for Foster's Furniture Polish.

*Business:* A restaurant called Aunt Bee's Canton Palace (a Chinese eatery that replaced the failed Spare Ribs Tavern restaurant).

*Catchphrase:* "Oh fiddle faddle."

*Flying Lessons:* Aunt Bee took flying lessons at Mac Donald's Flying School (she flew a 1958 Cessna 182A with the ID number N5955B).

*Note:* Mary Treen played Andy's original housekeeper, Rose, and was replaced by Aunt Bee when Rose left to marry Wilbur (Frank Ferguson).

## OPIE TAYLOR

*Pets:* Gulliver (dog), Oscar (lizard), and Dinkie (parakeet).

*Invisible Best Friend:* Blackie the black horse.

*Education:* Mayberry School.

*Affiliation:* Member of the Boy Scouts (Troop 44) and the school history club, the Mayberry Mountaineers.

*Jobs:* Selling newspapers; a get-rich-quick scheme selling jars of Miracle Salve, a cure-all for pain; and helper at the Walker Drug Store.

*Favorite Fishing Hole:* At Meyer's Lake (where he and Andy are seen heading in the opening theme).

*Quirk:* When guests stay over, they use Opie's room, as Opie enjoys what he calls "adventurous sleeping" (sleeping on the ironing board between two chairs).

*Musical Ability:* Plays piano and guitar.

*Band:* Member of a group called Freedom.

*Sport:* Quarterback on the Mayberry School football team.

*Nickname for Andy:* Pa.

## GOOBER PYLE

*Place of Birth:* Mayberry, North Carolina.

*Age:* Goober first mentions he is 36 years old in the 1967 Christmas episode (thus making his birth year 1931); he later says he was five years old in 1946 (knocking his birth year up to 1941).

*Phone Number:* Mayberry 371.

*Education:* Mayberry High School (where he was a member of the football team). He then attended school in nearby Raleigh, where he studied to be a car mechanic.

*Military Service:* The National Guard.

*Marital Status:* Single. He is shy and awkward around women.

*Job:* Mechanic at Wally's Filling Station. Goober originally worked there with his cousin, Gomer Pyle (who left to join the Marines), and later (after working there for 11¾ years) purchased the gas station. He raised $2,000 for the down payment. It was also learned that Goober's father owned a gas station. In 1963 episodes, gas can be seen selling for 30 cents a gallon.

*Pay:* $1.25 an hour.

*Hobbies:* Hunting, fishing, playing checkers, and reading comic books.

*Talent:* Impersonations of movie stars (although he is very bad at doing them). His first impression seen by viewers was that of Cary Grant's "Judy, Judy, Judy" catchphrase.

*Transportation:* A red pickup truck with the license plate M379054.

*Catchphrase:* "Yo."

*Favorite Foods:* Pancakes (he won a food-eating contest, downing 57 pancakes) and corn on the cob.

*Favorite Toy as a Kid:* Buster (a teddy bear).

*Favorite Movie: The Monster That Ate Minnesota* (which he mentions as seeing 10 times).

*Awards:* In addition to the pancake-eating win, Goober also won turkey shoots and arm-wrestling contests.

*Pets:* Spot (a dog without spots), a canary (Louise), and an unnamed skunk.

*Affiliations:* A member of the Regal Order of the Golden Door to Good Fellowship, manager of the Mayberry Little League team (the Giants), and singer in the town choir.

*Duties:* Goober has been deputized to guard the cannon at the park on Halloween "to prevent kids from putting orange peels, taters, and rotten tomatoes in it."

## FLOYD LAWSON

*Place of Birth:* Mayberry, North Carolina.

*Occupation:* Barber (owns the one-chair Floyd's Barber Shop). He has been in business for 30 years, and his shop also serves as a hangout where the men folk can gather, play checkers, and chat. Floyd practiced cutting hair on cats (Andy says, "The county has the baldest cats").

*Personality:* Wears glasses and has black hair, blue eyes, and a dark mustache.

*Dream:* To own a two-chair shop.

*Prices* (from the First Season): Haircut ($1), shave (35 cents), and shoeshine (25 cents). Over the years, the haircut became $1.75 and a shave 50 cents, and for $3 men could get a special scalp treatment.

*Hobbies:* Raising prized pansies, fishing, playing the trombone, and bowling (he is a member of the Mayberry Bowlers team).

*Affiliation:* Member of the Regal Order of the Golden Door to Good Fellowship, secretary of the Downtown Businessman's Club, and volunteer town deputy. He has been deputized to carry the flag in the annual Veteran's Day Parade.

*Favorite Drink:* Coffee, Huckleberry Smash soda, and Nectarine Crush soda (the sodas are apparently sold only at Wally's Filling Station).

*Barbershop Rent:* $50 a month (the building was originally owned by the Robinson family, then Howard Sprague [Jack Dodson], the town clerk, who raised the rent to $57.50 a month). Floyd later closed the shop (after 38 years in business) and sold the location to Emmett Clark, who opened Emmett's Fix-It Shop.

*Hero:* Calvin Coolidge, as he believes everything he said is memorable.

## OTHER CHARACTERS

Gomer Pyle, Goober's cousin and attendant at a gas station called both Wally's Filling Station and Wally's Service Station. The station sells Acme Gasoline. Gomer left the series in 1964, when he joined the Marines (thus creating the spin-off *Gomer Pyle, USMC* [see entry]).

Emmett Clark (Paul Hartman) is the owner of Emmett's Fix-It Shop; Otis Campbell (Hal Smith) is the town drunk (has his own jail privileges: locks himself up when he gets drunk and lets himself out when he feels he is sober; Mayberry apparently has no bars or pubs, and Otis "does his drinkin'" in nearby Mount Pilot).

## ORIGINS

The pilot episode aired as a segment of *The Danny Thomas Show* (aka *Make Room for Daddy*) on February 15, 1960. Here, Andy was portrayed as the sheriff, justice of the peace, and newspaper editor (Barney did not appear). Andy and Opie were cared for by their unseen Aunt Lucy; Mary Treen played their housekeeper, Rose. Frances Bavier played the role of Henrietta Perkins, a townsperson, and Frank Cady played the role of Will Hoople, the town drunk.

## UPDATE

In the 1986 NBC TV movie *Return to Mayberry*, Andy and Helen return to Mayberry, where Andy puts in a bid to once again become sheriff; unknowingly, he finds himself running against Barney Fife, who, after 25 years, is still engaged to Thelma Lou. Opie is now married to Eunice (Karlene Crockett) and is the editor of the town newspaper, the Mayberry *Courier-Express* (originally called *The Gazette*). Gomer, completing his military service, and Goober now own their own gas station, the G&G Garage; Otis, the former town drunk, is now an ice cream truck driver; and Howard Sprague is now Opie's assistant.

# *The Avengers*
## (ABC, 1966–1969)

*Cast:* Patrick Macnee (John Steed), Diana Rigg (Emma Peel), Linda Thorson (Tara King), Honor Blackman (Catherine Gale).

*Basis:* British secret agent John Steed and his female partners (Cathy Gale [1962–1965], Emma Peel [1965–1968], and Tara King [1968–1969]) avenge crimes committed against the government.

## JOHN STEED

*Address:* 5 Westminster Mews, then 3 Stable Mews, in London.
*Telephone Number:* Whitehall 1819 (originally Whitehall 00-001)

*Occupation:* Ministry agent.

*Abilities:* Trained to withstand brainwashing and torture and an expert on poisons, firearms, and breaking codes.

*Place of Birth:* England.

*Education:* The Eton School.

*Military Service:* The Royal Navy during World War II (he enlisted in 1939 and soon became a lieutenant in command of a torpedo boat).

*Prior Jobs:* Captain of an ex–naval launch (mid-1940s) in the Mediterranean that dealt with illegal cigarette trafficking. Civil servant in London (after quitting his captain's job, as he felt it was becoming too dangerous). Economic adviser to a sheik in the Middle East (when Steed settled a dispute between two neighboring states that made the sheik rich through oil deals, Steed was given lifetime royalties from two of the oil wells owned by the sheik).

*Trademark:* His Edwardian-style wardrobe. He is debonair and a purveyor of Old World charm and courtesy. He carries an umbrella with him at all times (its handle conceals a sword) and wears a bowler hat lined with metal. He never carries a gun and uses every dirty trick in the book to get the best of the enemy.

*Talents:* Plays the piano and croquet and is a connoisseur of fine wine (and women).

*Favorite Newspaper:* The Royal Edition of the *Times of London*.

*Cars:* Steed first drives a yellow 1926 vintage Rolls Royce Silver Ghost, then a dark green vintage 1929 4.5-liter Bentley (plate YT 3942, later RX 6180 and VT 3942). He also has a white Rolls Royce "that I usually keep in mothballs, as it has some mechanical problems."

*Pets:* Early episodes feature Steed's dog, a Great Dane named Juno, then a Dalmatian named Freckles.

*Weakness:* The opposite sex.

*Coffee:* Black with three sugars.

*Catchphrase:* "Mrs. Peel, we're needed" (when he receives an assignment and requires Emma's assistance).

*Superiors:* One-Ten (Douglas Muir) during the Cathy Gale era and Mother (Patrick Newell) during the Tara King era.

*Character:* Steed, as he is most often called, is the scion of a wealthy family and paid more attention to acting than school work. *The Avengers* and the John Steed character first appeared on British television in 1961 (at which time he was partners with Dr. David Keel, played by Ian Hendry). Keel joined with Steed to help avenge crimes after Steed helped him find the drug dealer who killed his fiancée, Peggy (Catherine Woodville). Their relationship ended when David accepted an internship overseas. The following year (and to 1965), Steed was teamed with Catherine Gale. Although Steed did work with Catherine, he also worked with Venus Smith (Julie Stevens) in six 1962–1963 episodes. Venus was not an agent and worked as a nightclub singer who helped Steed (sometimes reluctantly). The Kenny Powell Trio and later the David Lee Trio provided the music for Venus as she sang. These episodes were first seen in the United States on A&E in 1991.

## CATHERINE GALE
*Place of Birth:* England.
*Birthday:* October 5, 1930.
*Birth Sign:* Libra.
*Measurements:* 34-24-36.
*Address:* 14 Primrose Hall.
*Car:* A Triumph motorcycle with the license plate 987 CAA.
*Education:* Oxford University (where she graduated with a PhD in anthropology).
*Occupation:* Curator at the British Museum.
*Marital Status:* Widow (her husband, an anthropologist, was killed in a Mau Mau raid in Kenya, Africa; it was at this time that Cathy was recruited by the British government).
*Abilities:* A skilled mechanic and expert photographer and highly knowledgeable in the use of firearms. She possesses scientific knowledge and martial arts abilities and, unlike Steed, finds it necessary to carry a gun.
*Hobby:* Stamp collecting.
*Affiliation:* The British Cultural Council.
*Trademark:* Sexy black outfits while on assignments.
*Character:* Called Cathy, she was Steed's first female partner. She is impetuous and plunges headfirst into situations without really thinking. As time passed, Cathy became more of a professional as she worked and learned from Steed.

## EMMA PEEL
*Place of Birth:* England.
*Address:* A penthouse flat in Hampstead, later at Primrose Hill in London.
*Maiden Name:* Emma Knight.
*Height:* 5 feet, 8½ inches tall.
*IQ:* 152.
*Nickname as a Child:* "The Little Terror with Pigtails."
*Occupation:* Emma was first said to be the daughter of a rich shipbuilder; later, she is the child of Sir John Knight, the owner of Knight Industries (located in the Knight Building in London). She later became the head of her family company when she turned 21 (at which time her father died; no mention is

made of her mother or if Emma still has a vested interest in the company). Emma appears to be wealthy and is living either off a trust fund or from money her company generates.

*Marital Status:* Widow (she was married to Peter Peel, a test pilot who perished in the Amazon).

*Talents:* Skilled karate expert with an interest in anthropology and science (she has a minilab in her rooftop penthouse in Hampstead).

*Hobbies:* Rock sculpting (which she does in her living room) and playing bridge (she published an article called "Better Bridge through Applied Mathematics" in *The Bridge Players International Guide*).

*Cars:* Emma drives a white 1964 Lotus Elan S 2 (license plate SJH 4990, later a light blue 1966 Elan E 3, license plate HNK 9996, then SJH 4999D).

*Firearm:* A Beretta 7.65 pistol (which she actually uses).

*Preferred Clothing:* Sexy jumpsuits called "The Emma Peeler" for assignments.

*Character:* Emma is the replacement for Cathy (but no mention is made regarding Cathy's sudden disappearance; Steed however, does acknowledge Cathy when he receives a Christmas card from her). She is a beautiful emancipated woman who, although never sworn in as a Ministry agent, assists Steed in his battle against crime (Emma is loyal to the government and helps Steed for the sheer love of adventure). Through dialogue, it is learned that Emma and Steed met over a minor traffic accident. She became fascinated by his Old World charm and attached herself to him. Emma left Steed in 1968, when her husband, Peter, was found alive in the Amazonian jungle. Her parting words to Steed: "Always keep your bowler on in times of stress and a watchful eye open for diabolical masterminds!" His response: "I'll remember."

## TARA KING

*Place of Birth:* England (the daughter of a prosperous farmer).

*Education:* Tara had everything she wanted growing up and attended a prestigious finishing school where she acquired the sophistication of the young international set.

*Abilities:* Tara has survival skills and can ski and fly an airplane. She does not have any particular fighting skills but does know judo and will use whatever is handy as a weapon to protect herself.

*Address:* 9 Primrose Crescent in London.

*Bosom:* 39 inches.

*Preferred Clothing:* Tight sweaters and miniskirts.

*Car:* A red Lotus Europa (plate PPW 999F).

*Hobbies:* Music and auto racing.

*Character:* A beautiful and shapely Ministry agent who teams with Steed after Emma returns to her husband. Tara is the most affectionate of Steed's part-

Patrick Macnee and Diana Rigg. *ITV/ABC/ Photofest © ITV/ABC*

ners (they give each other an occasional hug or kiss). She and Steed met by accident. Tara was Recruit 69 and tackled Steed during a rescue exercise. Tara had come to admire Steed (hearing about his adventures) but never met him. It was Steed's superior, the wheelchair-bound Mother (Patrick Newell), who felt they would make the perfect crime fighting team. Rhonda (Rhonda Parker), a gorgeous six-foot-tall blonde, assisted Mother (but never spoke). Emma and Tara are Steed's only partners who actually met each other (in the transition episode "Forget-Me-Not," where, as Emma exits

Steed's apartment in the final minutes of the show and descends the stairs, Tara is seen walking up to Steed's apartment, and the two meet. Emma gives a look that approves of Tara and tells her that Steed likes his tea "stirred anticlockwise."

*Note:* In the series update, *The New Avengers* (CBS, 1978–1979), John Steed (Patrick Macnee) teams with a girl known only as Purdy (Joanna Lumley) and Mike Gambit (Gareth Hunt).

# *Batman*
## (ABC, 1966–1969)

*Cast:* Adam West (Bruce Wayne/Batman), Burt Ward (Dick Grayson/Robin), Yvonne Craig (Barbara Gordon/Batgirl), Neil Hamilton (Commissioner Gordon), Stafford Repp (Chief O'Hara), Alan Napier (Alfred), William Dozier (Narrator).

*Basis:* Bruce Wayne, alias Batman, and Dick Grayson, alias Robin, the Boy Wonder, defend Gotham City from the evils of diabolical villains.

### BRUCE WAYNE

*Parents:* Thomas and Martha Wayne, millionaire industrialists.

*Residence:* Stately Wayne Manor in Gotham City.

*Servant:* Alfred Pennyworth.

*Alias:* Batman, the Caped Crusader.

*Cover:* Bruce Wayne, the millionaire head of the Wayne Foundation, an organization that sponsors worthwhile projects. He is also called "Millionaire Bruce Wayne" and is chairman of the Gotham City Boxing Commission.

*Offices:* Located in the Wayne Foundation Building in downtown Gotham City.

*Racehorse:* Waynebow (which Bruce enters each year in the Bruce Wayne Foundation Handicap).

*History:* When Bruce was 10 years old, his parents were killed by thugs, and he swore to avenge their deaths by battling crime. Using his vast family wealth and with Alfred's help, Bruce established a secret laboratory beneath Wayne Manor that would later come to be known as the Bat Cave (which he completed when he was 20 years old). He now felt it was time to begin his quest and become "a creature of the night; black, mysterious." He chooses the name Batman when he sees a bat, attracted by the light, outside his window. He then creates his costume and utility belt.

## BRUCE AS BATMAN

*Headquarters:* The Bat Cave, which houses the Bat Computer (capable of amazing feats, such as analyzing any substance, providing answers to virtually any question, and solving puzzles or riddles). The Bat Cave is located 14 miles from Gotham City. Beneath the cave lies a supply of nilanium, the world's hardest metal (after it is refined).

*Assistant:* Alfred, who appears to others as Bruce Wayne's butler.

*Car:* The Batmobile, a customized 1955 Lincoln Futura (black with red trim). It is powered by atomic batteries, uses turbines for speed, and has controls such as the Bat Ray Projector, the Bat Homing/Receiving Scope, the Bat Ram, the Bat Parachute (to stop the car at high speeds), and the Start-Decoy Button (which fires rockets if an unauthorized person tries to start the car).

*License Plate:* 2F 3567, later seen as BAT 1 and B-1. Batman also breaks virtually every traffic rule as he rushes to crime scenes.

*Helicopter:* The Bat Copter (ID number N3079, later N703).

*Decoy:* The Batman Dummy Double (to fool people; Bruce stores it at Wayne Manor in the Bat Dummy Closet).

*Catchphrase:* "To the Batmobile!"

*Secret Controls:* At Wayne Manor, the button used to gain access to the Bat Cave is located in the bust of Shakespeare in Bruce's den. When the button is pressed, a secret entrance is revealed that allows Bruce (and Dick) to descend their respective Bat Poles and enter the Bat Cave.

*Dislikes:* Batman can't abide being called a coward.

*Costume:* Gray/black bodysuit with a black cape and black hoodlike mask.

*Dance Creation:* As Batman, Bruce created a dance known as the Batusi.

*Police Contact:* Batman works closely with Police Commissioner Gordon and Police Chief O'Hara. Gordon has two ways of contacting Batman: the red Bat Phone in his office and the Bat Signal (which is flashed in the sky). When the phone rings at Wayne Manor, Alfred answers it with "Stately Wayne Manor." Alfred can also contact Batman via his Emergency Bat Buckle Signal Button (he also assists Batman in the field by donning various disguises). O'Hara is famous for his catchphrase, "Saints preserve us." The large map of Gotham City that is seen is actually a reversed image of the map of St. Louis.

## RICHARD "DICK" GRAYSON

*Relationship:* Bruce Wayne's teenage ward.

*Education:* Woodrow Roosevelt High School.

*History:* A circus high-wire act, the Flying Graysons, are performing when a rope snaps, and the ensuing fall kills young Dick's parents. Bruce, at the circus with a group of orphans, investigates as Batman and discovers that the act was sabotaged to get the circus owner to pay protection money. Batman tells Dick what happened and how it also reflects what happened to him. Wanting to avenge their deaths, Dick pleads with Batman to let him join him. Bruce feels that with his acrobatic skills, plus what he could teach him, Dick would make the perfect sidekick. Dick eventually becomes Bruce's ward and adopts the alias of Robin, the Boy Wonder.

*Costume:* Red and green with a gold cape and black mask.

*Cover:* The teenage ward of Bruce Wayne. When Batman and Robin work together, they are called the Dynamic Duo.

*Catchphrase:* "Holy . . . ," followed by a word or two (e.g., "Holy crucial moments"). The one phrase Burt Ward wanted to say, "Holy strawberries, Batman, we're in a jam," was not permitted.

## BARBARA GORDON

*Alias:* Batgirl.

*Father:* Police Commissioner James Gordon.

*Job:* Librarian at the Gotham City Library.

*Residence:* Apartment 8A in downtown Gotham City.

*Pet Bird:* Charlie.

*History:* After graduating from college, Barbara saw the evil that was a part of Gotham City and, even though it had Batman and Robin as its protectors, chose to begin her own crusade to battle it. She adapted the guise of the sexy Batgirl and originally fought crime alone; when she joins with Batman and Robin, they form the Terrific Trio.

*Mode of Transportation:* The Batgirl Cycle (which is concealed in a secret freight elevator in the back of her building).

*Costume:* A tight purple bodysuit, a gold and purple cape, and a dark purple hoodlike mask. She conceals her costume in a secret door behind her bedroom wall (a hidden button on her vanity table opens the door).

*Character:* Barbara is the chairperson of the Gotham City Anti-Littering Committee and as Batgirl received the first Gotham City Female Crime Fighter and Fashion Award, the Battie, for her crusade against crime in her sexy costume.

*Favorite Opera: The Marriage of Figaro.*

*Note:* In the unaired 1967 pilot episode, Batgirl is called a "Dazzling dare doll" and has a makeup compact that emits a deadly laser beam. Her Batgirl costume is contained in a hidden room in the library.

## THE PRINCIPAL VILLAINS

The Penguin (Burgess Meredith); the Joker (Cesar Romero); Catwoman (Julie Newmar, then Eartha Kitt; Lee Meriwether played the role in the 1966 feature film version); the Riddler (Frank Gorshin, then John Astin); Lola Lasagna (Ethel Merman); the Archer (Art Carney); Louie the Lilac (Milton Berle); Marsha, Queen of Diamonds (Carolyn Jones); Mr. Freeze (Eli Wallach, George Sanders, and Otto Preminger); Minerva (Zsa Zsa Gabor); Egghead (Vincent Price); the Mad Hatter (David Wayne); the Clock King (Walter Slezak); and King Tut (Victor Buono).

# The Beverly Hillbillies
### (CBS, 1962–1971)

*Cast:* Buddy Ebsen (Jed Clampett), Donna Douglas (Elly Mae Clampett), Max Baer Jr. (Jethro Bodine), Irene Ryan (Granny), Raymond Bailey (Milburn Drysdale), Nancy Kulp (Jane Hathaway).

*Basis:* A poor, backwoods family (Jed, Granny, Elly Mae, and Jethro) experiences a new life in Beverly Hills when oil is discovered on their property and they try to fit into a world that they have never known before.

## JEDEDIAH "JED" CLAMPETT

*Place of Birth:* The Arkansas Ozarks.

*Prior Home:* A run-down cabin near Blueberry Ridge.

*Address:* 518 Crestview Drive, Beverly Hills, California. The home was built in 1933 by actor John Barrymore. It has 32 (sometimes mentioned as 35) rooms (12 of which are bedrooms). The Clampetts call the swimming pool in the backyard "The Cement Pond" and believe the steps leading into the pool are for the wildlife when they come down from the hills for a drink. There is a stone figure of a woman pouring water in the pool they call "The Rock Lady." They call the pool table in the billiard room "The Big Eatin' Table" and the room in which it sits "The Fancy Eatin' Room." When Jed and his kin first saw the home, they believed it was a prison.

*Daughter:* Elly Mae.

*Late Wife:* Rose Ellen (maiden name Rose Ellen Moses).

*Favorite Meal:* Mustard greens and possum innerds ("They're just as good the second day").

*Catchphrase:* "Whee doggies."

*Net Worth:* $25 million, then $34,783,127.34 (in 1963), and finally $80 million.

*Dog:* Duke (a bloodhound).

*Education:* Oxford Grammar School in the Arkansas Ozarks.

the O.K. Oil Company. In the TV movie update, *The Return of the Beverly Hillbillies*, Jed had returned to his beloved home in the Ozarks.

*Character:* When Rose Ellen passed, Jed tried to raise Elly Mae as best he could (basically as a boy). He lived in a cabin with Elly Mae and his mother-in-law, Daisy Moses, fondly called Granny. Jed's cabin sits on a half acre of land that is overrun with coyotes, skunks, bobcats, and possum. Jed drinks homemade moonshine and uses kerosene lamps for light. Granny cooks on a wood-burning stove, washes clothes with homemade lye soap, and runs her own still. Elly Mae is untamed (so to speak), loves wild animals, rough-houses with boys, and is swiftly developing her figure (as Granny points out "them buttons popping off" her blouse). The outhouse is 50 feet from the cabin, and the family believes they are living in the lap of luxury.

One day while hunting for food, Jed misses his target (a rabbit) and strikes the ground near a swamp. Oil emerges, and Jed suddenly becomes a millionaire when the O.K. Oil Company pays him $25 million for the oil rights. Milburn Drysdale of the Commerce Bank of Beverly Hills handles the account and arranges for Jed, Elly Mae, Granny, and Jed's nephew, Jethro Bodine, to move to Beverly Hills.

Jed is a simple man and asks very little from life. He cares only for providing for his family, and while he appears simple, he is shrewd, and his common sense guides him through the many situations he encounters.

*Relatives:* cousin, Roy (Roy Clark).

## ELLY MAE CLAMPETT

*Place of Birth:* A log cabin near Blueberry Ridge in the Arkansas Ozarks.
*Year of Birth:* 1944.
*Parents:* Jed and Rose Ellen Clampett.
*Pets* (which she calls "Critters"): Earl, a rooster, who can play dead; Skipper and Beth, chimpanzees (Beth is also called Bessie and Maybelle); Jasper, a jaguar; Nikki, a squirrel; Rusty, a cat; Charley, a duck; and Fairchild, a bear who loves liquor.
*Education:* Elly Mae had some "schoolin'" in the Ozarks, and although Jed says, "Elly Mae would rather chase raccoons up a tree than attend school," she did attend an all-girls finishing school, the Willows Academie for Select Young Ladies, in Beverly Hills. She was also a member of the Biddle Bird Watching Club.

*Favorite Hiding Place:* "The big tree out front" on their mansion property.

*Character:* Elly Mae is a beautiful young woman who dresses like a boy (when she got her first bra at the age of 18 [when the series begins], she thought it was "a store-bought lace-trimmed double-barreled sling shot"). Elly Mae knew she was different "when the buttons started to pop off her blouse." She is fearful of dressing like a girl because the boys called her "sissy." Jed wanted her to become refined like her mother, but ever since she could walk, "she's been climbin' trees and cuddlin' creatures." When Elly is mistaken for a boy by the clothes she sometimes wears, she responds with, "Why thank you." Jed tried to teach Elly Mae about the birds and the bees but hasn't had much success, as Elly Mae sees them in a literal light ("Gee Pa, I'm fond of those little creatures").

## JETHRO BODINE

*Place of Birth:* Blueberry Ridge in the Arkansas Ozarks on December 4 (year not given).

*Mother:* Pearl Bodine (father not mentioned).

*Sibling:* Jethrene Bodine (Jethro's sister). Played by Max Baer Jr., voiced by Linda Kaye Henning.

*Education:* Oxford Grammar School in the Ozarks (where he was "crawdad eating champion"). He spent two years in the first grade and three years in the fourth grade and brags that he was "educated and graduated from the sixth grade." He is considered the school-educated one of the family. He furthered his education in Beverly Hills at the Millicent Schyler Potts School.

*Job Aspirations:* An astronaut ("to find moon maidens"), a streetcar conductor, a "double-naught spy" (influenced by James Bond films), a pig farmer, to "do brain surgerin" (influenced by the doctor shows on TV), and to become a folk singer and a movie star (he did acquire a job as a stunt double for film star Dash Riprock). He also ran a diner (the Happy Gizzard) and appeared in a TV commercial for Foggy Mountain Soap. When Jethro felt he needed to become a playboy, Milburn Drysdale set him up at the bank with the job title "Junior Executive Research Consultant"; Drysdale also set Jethro up with an office in the bank as "Jethro Bodine, Double O Spy" (Elly Mae was his secretary).

*Catchphrase:* When something pleases Jethro, he yells "Yee haw."

*Ultimate Life's Goal:* "To find me a sweetheart."

*Allowance:* 50 cents a week.

*Character:* Jethro delights in the excitement of Beverly Hills. Unfortunately, he is not too bright. Jethro loves Granny's cooking (which he calls "vittles") but is not permitted to indulge in Granny's moonshine until he gets married.

When he does something wrong, Jed is heard saying, "I gotta have a long talk with that boy."

## GRANNY

*Real Name:* Daisy Moses.

*Birthday:* Questionable. Although Granny mentions she was born "sometime in the 1850s" in Tennessee, it would make her at least 111 years old when the series begins. Granny next mentions that her family moved to the Ozark community of Sibley but does not state a year. She later says that she is not sure of her age (although she appears to be in her late seventies). She also mentions that when she was a child, her mother fell into a swamp and drowned. With her statement that she won a beauty contest in 1897 (see below), it would mean that Granny, at least 18 at the time, would have been 79 years old when the series begins (which seems more plausible).

*Pageant Award:* "The Miss Good Sport Award" title in the Bug Tussle Bathing Beauty Contest at the Expo of 1897. It was at this time that Daisy was still single and feared becoming a spinster. She did find a beau shortly after and married and had the daughter, Rose Ellen, who would become Jed's wife.

*Specialty:* "Doctorin'." Granny is a self-proclaimed doctor in the Ozarks and feels she knows a lot about healing sick people. She has an all-around cure for ailments called Granny's Spring Tonic and is famous for her homemade lye soap (with fumes so toxic "it can peel the bark off a tree and bring a full grown mule to its knees"). She has a still in the backyard for making her "rheumatiz medicine."

*Abilities:* Granny says she was "the best dancer that ever came out of the Tennessee Hills." She is the only one in the family who can hold a grudge and can also predict when it is going to rain by "twinges" ("aches in my bones").

*Favorite TV Show: Journey to Misery.*

*Musical Abilities:* Plays a 200-year-old lap organ.

*Life Savings:* $5,000 in Confederate money. She still believes Jefferson Davis is the president of the United States.

*Gun:* A double-barreled 12-gauge shotgun that she uses "to get rid of revenuers."

*Favorite Meal to Cook:* Possum stew and boiled buzzard eggs.

*Racehorse:* Ladybelle (which Jed purchased for her).

*Character:* Granny grew up poor and relishes the simple life, as it is the only life she has ever known. She was reluctant to move to Beverly Hills because "if the Lord wanted me in Californie, he would have put me in Californie." The only way Jed could get her to move was to remove her from the back porch of the cabin and load her and the rocking chair she sat on onto the back of the car.

## OTHER CHARACTERS

Milburn Drysdale: When Milburn acquires Jed's money, Jed became the biggest depositor the bank ever had. Milburn is a man of vision and is seeking to exploit the potential of the Clampett income. To Milburn, "Jed is my kind of people: loaded" (and Jed's money has propelled the Commerce Bank to the number three bank in the country). It was mentioned that Milburn's mother's family had feuded with Granny's family many years ago in Tennessee.

Milburn is married to the very spoiled socialite Margaret (Harriet MacGibbon) and is the stepfather of the even more spoiled Sonny (Louis Nye), whom Margaret babies, and who has been in college for 19 years ("I'm trying to find myself," he claims). He is fond of Elly Mae (even though she is not a blueblood) and, because of her shapely figure, "digs that crazy package she comes in." When he dates a girl, he presents her with a framed picture of himself as opposed to a box of candy or flowers.

Margaret has a pampered French poodle named Claude and has made it her goal to rid the neighborhood of the unsavory Clampetts. Charlie Ruggles played Lowell Reddings Farquhar, Margaret's father, and Eddy Eccles was Milby Drysdale, Milburn's nephew.

Jane Hathaway is Milburn's secretary who also has the added duty of catering to the Clampetts' every wish. When Jane first met the Clampetts, she mistook them for the family servants and when first seeing Jethro summed him up as "a magnificent skyscraper with an uncomplicated penthouse" (in a later episode she says, "He is a lighthouse. Strong, tall, and sturdy. Too bad his beacon isn't bright"). Jane is a graduate of Vassar College and enjoys bird watching. She calls Milburn "Chief."

Pearl Bodine is Jethro's mother, a recurring regular in early episodes until Bea Benaderet left the series in 1963 to star in *Petticoat Junction* (see entry). Pearl taught piano and was also employed as the piano player for the silent movies shown at the Palace Theater (she was billed as "The Wizard of the Keyboard"). Peal is famous for her ability to yodel (which Granny considered a punishment to hear) and believed she could sing (which caused the wolves and coyotes to howl).

*Note:* In the original unaired pilot, *The Hillbillies of Beverly Hills*, the story differs in the fact that Jed knew there was oil on his land (the hunting scene of the series was not used) and just sold the rights, as he considered the oil a nuisance. The money is deposited in the Bank of Beverly Hills.

In the 1981 CBS TV movie *The Return of the Beverly Hillbillies*, it is learned that Granny passed on and Jed had divided his vast estate between Elly Mae and Jethro. Jed moved back to his beloved "hills" while Elly Mae opened Elly's Zoo and Jethro became the head of the Mammoth Film Studios in Hollywood. Jane Hathaway, now an employee with the Energy Department in Washington,

D.C., has been experimenting with Granny's moonshine and discovers that it has the potential to double the output of the country's gasoline and oil. Imogene Coca is introduced as Granny's maw, a 104-year-old woman who guards the moonshine recipe.

# *Bewitched*
## (ABC, 1964–1972)

*Cast:* Elizabeth Montgomery (Samantha Stephens/Serena), Dick York, Dick Sargent (Darrin Stephens), Agnes Moorehead (Endora), Maurice Evans (Maurice), David White (Larry Tate), Erin and Diane Murphy (Tabitha Stephens), David and Greg Lawrence (Adam Stephens), Bernard Fox (Dr. Bombay), George Tobias (Abner Kravitz), Alice Pearce and Sandra Gould (Gladys Kravitz).

*Basis:* A beautiful young witch (Samantha), her marriage to a mortal (Darrin Stephens), and their efforts to live a normal life despite the problems a witch–mortal marriage causes when Darrin insists that Samantha not use her powers.

### SAMANTHA "SAM" STEPHENS

*Parents:* Endora and Maurice.

*Maiden Name:* Never mentioned, as her mother says, "You would never be able to pronounce it."

*Hair:* Blonde.

*Eyes:* Blue.

*Husband:* Darrin. They honeymooned at the Moon Thatcher Inn. She revealed to Darrin that she is a witch on their wedding night.

*Children:* Tabitha and Adam.

*Birthday:* June 6 (year not mentioned, but it occurred on the eve of the Galactic Rejuvenation and Dinner Dance Celebration).

*Address:* 1164 Morning Glory Circle, Westport, Connecticut. Also said to be 164 Morning Glory Circle. They purchased the home from the Hopkins Realty Company.

*Phone Number:* 555-2134 (then 555-2368 and 555-6161).

*Nickname:* Sam (as called by Darrin).

*Distinguishing Mark:* A mole in the middle of her back.

*Favorite Eateries:* Cerino's Restaurant and La Bella Dona Restaurant.

*Ability:* To evoke her powers by wrinkling her nose (the musical effect that is heard, called "Samantha's Twitch," is performed by theme composer Warren Barker).

*Catchphrase:* "Oh my stars." She also says, "Witchcraft got you into this mess, I see no reason why witchcraft can't get you out of it" (referring to when something goes wrong when Samantha uses her powers).

*Status:* Queen of the witches (which she apparently lost when she married a mortal).

*Faults:* Samantha "short-circuits" or has "a power failure" under certain atmospheric conditions or when she doesn't use her powers on a regular basis. Conditions include rhyming words, uncontrollable laughing or crying, developing horizontal stripes across her face, or an extreme weight buildup.

*Favorite Food Craving:* Ringtail pheasant.

*Favorite Animal:* Unicorn (as a child, Samantha would turn herself into a polka-dot unicorn). She first learned to fly when she was almost three years old.

*Family (Witch) Doctor:* Dr. Bombay, a womanizer whose remedies often fail to produce cures. To summon Dr. Bombay, Sam cries, "Calling Dr. Bombay, calling Dr. Bombay! Emergency. Come right away!" or "Paging Dr. Bombay, Paging Dr. Bombay!" Naturally, she gets him at the most inopportune times, such as when chasing his nurse.

*Relatives:* Aunt Agatha (Kay Elliott); Cousin Edgar, an elf (Arte Johnson); Cousin Henry (Steve Franken); Aunt Hagatha (Ysabel MacCloskey and Reta Shaw); Aunt Enchantra (Estelle Winwood); Aunt Hephzibah (Jane Connell).

## DARRIN STEPHENS

*Wife:* Samantha.

*Children:* Tabitha and Adam.

*Place of Birth:* Missouri.

*Parents:* Frank and Phyllis Stephens. Robert F. Simon and Roy Roberts played Frank; Mabel Albertson was Phyllis.

*Education:* University of Missouri (Class of 1950).

*Prior Address:* An apartment seen only with its door number: 417 (apparently where he and Sam lived before acquiring their series home).

*Job:* Account executive at McMahon and Tate Advertising Agency (located in the International Building in Manhattan). In the pilot episode, he is a vice president. Darrin mentions that he began working for the company in 1961.

*Chevy Malibu Convertible License Plate:* 4R6 558.

*Business Telephone Number:* 555-6059.

*Favorite Dinner:* Beef stew and scrambled eggs with chicken livers (he later says corned beef and cabbage, then Irish stew).

*Favorite Breakfast:* Blueberry pancakes.

*Favorite Hangout:* Joe's Bar and Grill (also called Mulvanney's Bar and the Happy Times Bar), where he goes to drown his sorrows after Samantha uses her magic against his wishes.

*Military Service:* Served in the army with Company D.

*Nickname for Dr. Bombay:* Witch Doctor.

*Nicknames for Darrin by Endora:* Dum Dum, Durwood, and Dumbo.

*Nicknames for Darrin by Maurice:* Dobbin, Duspin, Dustin, and Duncan.

*Relatives:* Cousin Robbie (Don Knight), Cousin Helen (Louise Glenn). Darren mentioned he has an aunt, Madge, who believes she is a lighthouse.

## ENDORA

*Relationship:* Samantha's mother, a powerful witch.

*Position:* Chairwoman of the Witch's Council (also called the Witch's Committee).

*Weight:* 118 pounds.

*Age:* Admits to being 1,000 (she claims to have sailed on the *Mayflower* with Christopher Columbus). Maureen McCormick played Endora as a girl.

*Favorite Breakfast:* Fried raven's eggs.

*Favorite Drink:* Wolfbane on the rocks.

*Favorite Pastime:* Casting spells on Darrin (e.g., turning him into a werewolf, making him shrink, making his ears grow bigger for lying, turning him into a boy [played by Billy Mumy], or placing a dislike spell on him).

*Craving:* When Endora was pregnant with Samantha, she craved hummingbird wings.

*Fault:* Endora can temporarily lose her powers if she mixes eye of newt with oysters or is exposed to Bavarian roses. Coming in contact with the extinct Macedonian dodo bird will cause her powers to be transferred to someone else. Endora also opposes her daughter's marriage but often accepts it to please Samantha.

*TV Role:* Spokeswoman for Autumn Flame, "a perfume for older chicks."

## MAURICE

*Relationship:* Endora's husband and Samantha's powerful warlock father. He and Endora live apart from each other and thus lead separate lives.

*Affiliation:* Member of the Warlock Club.

*Appearance:* Very distinguished (always wears a tuxedo or suit).

*Ability:* Can quote lines from Shakespeare (whom he apparently knew personally).

*Fault:* Dislikes Darrin and casts spells on him, such as transforming him into things (a donkey, a statue, a pair of galoshes, a raven, or a monkey) or making him unable to speak English or to slowly shrink or granting him wishes without his knowledge.

## SERENA

*Relationship:* Samantha's fun-loving cousin.

*Hair:* Brunette.

*Eyes:* Blue.

*Affiliation:* A Member of the Cosmos Club; chairperson of the Cosmos Cotillion.

*Distinguishing Marks:* Serena has a birthmark on her face that changes with each episode (but is usually seen on the left side of her face near her lower eyelid; it can be seen as a heart, a question mark, or the letter S [for Serena]).

*Abilities:* Skilled in karate.

*Favorite Wine:* Chateau Lafitte Rothschild.

*Accomplishment:* Wrote (and sang) the song "Kisses in the Wind."

*Fault:* Does not trust anyone more than 3,000 years old.

## OTHER CHARACTERS

Uncle Arthur (Paul Lynde) is Samantha's practical joke–playing warlock uncle (he is actually Endora's brother). He is famous for his tablecloth trick (pulling the cloth out from under the dishes without breaking them) and has only this to say about Endora: "When I think of you as a blood relative, I long for a transfusion." He approves of Samantha and Darrin's marriage and calls the Witch's Council "The Old Cronies," Endora "The Wicked Witch of the West," and Samantha "Sammie"; Serena calls him "Unkie Pooh."

Aunt Clara (Marion Lorne) is Samantha's elderly, bumbling aunt. She is a witch and is most famous for her doorknob collection. She was once a lady-in-waiting to Queen Victoria but now has trouble remembering things and casting spells (the wrong things usually happen, and only she can reverse what has happened by correctly reciting the spell).

Esmeralda (Alice Ghostly) is the shy witch who fears Darrin doesn't like her and "pops out" whenever she hears his voice. She is also very nervous and does not fully materialize when she teleports from one place to another (her shoe, hat, dress, or coat will be seen but not her).

Larry Tate, called "Peter Cotton Top" (for his white hair; he originally had red hair in his youth) by Serena, is Darrin's boss, the president of McMahon and Tate. He is married to Louise (Irene Vernon, then Kasey Rogers) and always takes credit for Darrin's ideas in front of clients. Mitchell Silberman plays his son, Larry Tate Jr.

Abner and Gladys Kravitz are Samantha and Darrin's neighbors. Abner is retired and keeps to himself, while Gladys is a busybody and likes to snoop on her neighbors, hence her numerous "hallucinations" when she witnesses strange things at the Stephens' house (Samantha's magic) and cannot convince Abner (or anyone else) that she saw something strange. Her numerous calls to the police have her tagged as being a kook.

Tabitha and Adam Stephens: Tabitha was first said to be born on January 13, 1966 (the episode that introduced Samantha's Cousin Serena), but her birth was later said to be on Mother's Day. Tabitha first showed evidence of being a witch at the age of one when she touched her nose and levitated a toy. Samantha purchases Tabitha's clothes at Hinkley's Department Store. Adam also demonstrates powers as being a warlock (much to Maurice's delight). Tabitha attends Towners Elementary School and was also a model for a client of McMahon and Tate (Robbins Truck Transmissions). Tabitha and Adam were born at Perkins Hospital.

*Note:* On April 24, 1976, Tabitha (played by Liberty Williams) became 24 years old, and a pilot for a series called *Tabitha* aired. Tabitha was the editorial assistant for *Trend*, a San Francisco fashion magazine. Bruce Kimmel played Adam, but the project did not sell. It was revised with Lisa Hartman as Tabitha in the 1977–1978 ABC series *Tabitha*, wherein Tabitha was a production assistant at KXLA-TV in Los Angeles.

# The Big Valley
## (ABC, 1965–1969)

*Cast:* Barbara Stanwyck (Victoria Barkley), Richard Long (Jarrod Barkley), Peter Breck (Nick Barkley), Linda Evans (Audra Barkley), Lee Majors (Heath Barkley), Charles Briles (Eugene Barkley).
*Basis:* A pioneering family, the Barkleys, owners of the Barkley Ranch during the 1870s, fight for what is right in an era of lawlessness.

### VICTORIA BARKLEY
*Position:* Matriarch of the Barkley Ranch. She is middle-aged and the mother of four children (Jarrod, Nick, Audra, and Eugene). Her fifth child, Heath, is the illegitimate son of her husband Tom.
*Ranch:* The 30,000-acre Barkley Ranch in the San Joaquin Valley in Stockton, California.
*History:* During the 1830s, Victoria and her husband, Thomas (called Tom), left Ohio to find a new life in California. A hazardous trek over many months brought them to the San Joaquin Valley, where they settled and established their ranch. Over time, the Barkleys became a proud family with a name that stood for justice (as Nick says, "We share other people's troubles. It's our duty").

Tom lost his life (married 25 years at this time) in the late 1860s, when he was killed fighting railroad officials seeking his land for expansion. There is a statue of Tom Barkley, seated on a horse, in town (the citizens' way of honoring the man who established the valley).

*Characteristic:* Victoria is strong-willed and does not take a backseat to ranch operations. She is as rugged as Nick and Heath and is not always depicted as the lady she is (a woman of leisure, elegantly dressed, and entertaining guests). Victoria has become a part of the Old West. She has killed (to save Audra's life) and been kidnapped, drugged, shot at, stranded in the desert, and beaten—and through it all remains a lady. She most enjoys it when the entire family is present at dinner (at which times ranch business is discussed).

*Horse:* Misty Girl.

*Hobby:* Playing chess.

*Philosophy:* Victoria believes that although she heads a prominent family, she must never forget the struggles she and Tom endured: "My husband left us a heritage of wealth, power, and land, and he also left us his obligations" (to always stand up for injustice).

## JARROD THOMAS BARCLAY

*Age:* 32. The eldest child of Victoria and Tom Barclay. He is the calmest of the siblings (even Audra) and tries to reason through a situation before charging into it without thinking first (like Nick).

*Occupation:* Attorney (offices in Stockton and San Francisco).

*Duties:* While not actively involved in physical ranch actions, he does oversee the massive Barkley holdings, including the ranch (whose crops include peaches, apples, olives, grapes, strawberries, and oranges), the Barkley-Sierra Railroad, the Barkley Lumber Company, and the Barkley Mine.

*Characteristic:* Jarrod has a strong sense of justice and will not compromise the name of Barkley under any circumstance. Although he is opposed to violence, he often finds using a gun or his fists the only way to achieve justice from those who oppose him. He enjoys a good cigar when time permits.

## NICHOLAS "NICK" BARKLEY

*Age:* 28. The second-born son of Victoria and Tom Barkley.

*Characteristic:* Tough, eager to use fists or guns to settle an argument (possibly stemming from his father's death at the hands of railroad officials).

*Childhood:* Nick received his first saddle when he was six years old (he wrote, "Nick, age 6—keep off" on it). Ten years later, he fell down an open mine shaft and was almost killed. At the age of 18, Nick fell in love for the first time with a girl named Jeannie Price (they met in a town called Willow Springs). Jeannie's father ran the general store, but Nick was too restless to settle down and left her, hoping to return one day. In 1877, he found that Jeannie, born in 1850, had died of typhoid fever in 1870.

*Specialty:* Horse expert (he is responsible for buying horses for the ranch and breaking wild ones).

Front row: Barbara Stanwyck and Linda Evans; back row: Lee Majors, Peter Breck, and Richard Long. *ABC/Photofest © ABC*

*Duties:* In addition to overseeing ranch operations, he is also responsible for the ranch hiring (ranch hands receive $30 a month plus bunk and food).

*Favorite Saloon:* The Empire Saloon (also called the Golden Eagle and the Wagon Wheel).

*Marriage:* Nick was the only Barkley child to marry, to grant the dying wish of a woman named Julia Jenkins (she had a young son named Tommy and wanted him to have a fresh start with a respectable name, not be known as a boy whose mother had a shady background).

*Horse:* Nick first rode Coco, later Big Duke

*Trademark:* Known for his black leather vest and black gloves. He is also very fast on the draw and enjoys a good cigar.

## AUDRA BARKLEY

*Age:* 19.

*Characteristic:* The only daughter of Victoria and Thomas Barkley. She is not the typical cowgirl but an elegant and beautiful young woman. She is proud of her birthright (the name of Barkley) and fiercely protects the land her father died for (see Victoria Barkley, above, for information). Audra says, "This is Barkley land—and I'm Audra Barkley" when she encounters trespassers. She buys her dresses in town at Nell's Seamstress Shop.

*Love:* Horses. When she was eight, she began showing horses at county fairs. She believes she can break wild horses "with the best of 'em," but Nick refuses to let her do so, fearing she will get hurt. He also disapproves of her riding half-broken stock.

*Pets:* As a child, Audra had a canary (Bo Peep) and a cat (Sassafras).

*Fault:* Audra has a tendency to fall for men with shady backgrounds.

*Jobs:* While Audra has no specific job, she does volunteer at the Children's Or-phanage (located next to the Old Mill), teaches Saturday Bible class at the community church, and is also the fund-raiser for the church (she oversees the monthly Church Dinner gathering that costs 50 cents a plate).

## HEATH BARKLEY

*History:* Heath is the illegitimate child of Tom Barkley (Tom and Victoria were already the parents of Jarrod and Nick). When a business trip to invest in mines brought Tom to the town of Strawberry, he was attacked by two thugs and left for dead behind a saloon. A girl named Leah Simmons found Tom and nursed him back to health. Tom had a brief affair with Leah but left her before he knew she was pregnant.

Tom was on his way to becoming rich and famous and couldn't afford a scandal if he stayed with Leah. Tom returned to Victoria but never told her what happened in Strawberry. They eventually had two other children: Audra and Eugene. Leah also had a child—Tom's son, whom she named Heath. Leah never contacted Tom and, with the help of two friends, Han-nah and Rachel, raised Heath. In 1876, when Leah passes, Heath learns from Hannah that Tom Barkley was his father. Determined to seek his true birthright, Heath first hires on as a hand at the Barkley ranch but immedi-ately encounters the wrath of Nick, who believes he is a railroad spy. After a confrontation, Heath reveals who he really is, and while Victoria accepts him as her son, Nick finds it difficult to believe what his father did but eventually welcomes him to the family.

*Characteristic:* Before Heath discovered he was a Barkley, he described himself as "a tumbleweed in the wind, going from town to town and job to job." He now assists Nick in running the ranch, although he is still bitter, full of painful memories, and angry at the world. Heath carries a rattlesnake's rattle for good luck and is famous for his bullfrog stew. He can be even-tempered or violent, depending on the situation.

*Horse:* Charger.

*Favorite Dinner:* Wild duck.

*Ability:* Can imitate 20 different kinds of birdcalls.

*Relatives:* The only other family Heath ever knew were his uncle, Matt Simmons (John Anderson), and his aunt, Martha Simmons (Jeanne Cooper), who were related to Leah.

*Note:* Eugene was the youngest member of the family and appeared only during the first season. There is virtually no background information given. He was shy and sensitive and was dropped when he went off to college. Napoleon Whiting plays Silas, the family's faithful servant (but who is treated more like a member of the family).

## *The Brady Bunch*
### (ABC, 1969–1974)

*Cast:* Robert Reed (Mike Brady), Florence Henderson (Carol Brady), Barry Williams (Greg Brady), Maureen McCormick (Marcia Brady), Eve Plumb (Jan Brady), Susan Olsen (Cindy Brady), Christopher Knight (Peter Brady), Michael Lookinland (Bobby Brady), Ann B. Davis (Alice Nelson).

*Basis:* Blended family concept wherein a widower (Mike) with three sons (Greg, Peter, and Bobby) and a widow (Carol) with three daughters (Marcia, Jan, and Cindy) marry and attempt to begin a new life together.

### OVERALL SERIES INFORMATION

*Address:* 4222 Clinton Avenue in Los Angeles (four bedrooms, two bathrooms). The address is also said to be 4222 Clinton Way.

*Telephone Number:* 762-0799 (later 555-6161).

*Family Station Wagon License Plate:* 746 AEH.

*Sedan License Plate:* TEL 635.

*Family Pets:* Tiger (dog) and Fluffy (cat).

*Miscellaneous:* Cindy and Bobby attempted to break the world's teeter-totter (seesaw) record but failed; the Brady kids collected 94 books of Checker Trading Stamps, which they used to purchase a color TV for the family (prior to this, it appeared the family did not have a TV); Greg and Peter were the only children who did not wear braces on their teeth (Marcia, Jan, Cindy, and Bobby wore them at one time or another); the Brady Kids band appeared at the Silver Platter (a teen club) and sang the song "Time to Change"; the family appeared in a TV commercial for a laundry detergent. Bobby and Peter had frogs named Croaker and Spunker; the Westdale High School colors are blue and yellow (the school mascot was a bear).

## MICHAEL PAUL BRADY

*Occupation:* Architect (company never named). Mike designed the house in which the family lives.

*Attribute:* A wise and understanding father who always puts his family first. He considers what he has to say before disciplining his children or teaching them a valuable lesson about life.

*Award:* Received the 1969 Father of the Year Award from the *Daily Chronicle*. As a kid, he was the checkers champion of Chestnut Street.

*Hobby:* Playing golf.

*Relatives:* Aunt Jenny (Imogene Coca); Hank Brady, grandfather (Robert Reed). Gene Hackman was the original choice to play Mike.

## CAROL ANN BRADY

*Maiden Name:* Carol Tyler; former married name Carol Ann Martin (thus, her full name is Carol Ann Tyler Martin Brady).

*Occupation:* Housewife and mother. She is also a freelance writer.

*Place of Birth:* Los Angeles.

*Education:* Westdale High School.

*Nickname:* Twinkles (given to her by a boy she dated in high school).

*Hobby:* Needlepoint.

*Attributes:* Excellent singer and fine cook.

*Affiliation:* Member of the PTA.

*Character:* Carol enjoys helping her children with their homework. She and Mike try to give their children the right advice as they approach adulthood but sometimes find that they are behind the times when it comes to the youth of the 1970s. Carol also wrote an article (name not mentioned) about her family for *Tomorrow's Woman* magazine. Joyce Bulifant was originally cast as Carol.

*Relatives:* Oliver, nephew (Robbie Rist); Henry Tyler, father (J. Pat O'Malley); mother (Joan Tompkins); Connie Hutchins, grandmother (Florence Henderson).

*Miscellaneous:* In the first series update, *The Brady Brides* (NBC, 1981), Mike is still an architect, and Carol has become a real estate agent for the Willowbrook Realty Company (a position she held in the second update, *The Bradys*, on CBS in 1990). Here, Mike had retired to become a Fourth District councilman. His middle name was also changed to Thomas.

## GREG BRADY

*Status:* Eldest brother.

*Education:* Fillmore Junior High School and Westdale High School (where he is a member of the basketball team, football team [jersey 23], and baseball team). He was also the football team photographer.

*Jobs:* Delivery boy for Sam's Butcher Shop and office boy at his father's company. He had hoped to make enough money to buy a surfboard.

*Ability:* Sings and plays the guitar. Believing that he had the necessary talent, he attempted to break into show business as a singer named Johnny Bravo.

*Band:* The Banana Convention. Greg later formed one with his siblings called the Brady Six (later changed to the Brady Kids).

*Film:* Greg tried his hand at filmmaking and used his family as Pilgrims in a production about the first Thanksgiving.

*Image:* While Greg appeared to be an all-American boy, he did get into mischief, the worst being (for the time) when he was caught smoking a cigarette by his parents.

*Signature Clothing:* A light blue ringer T-shirt.

*Affiliation:* As a child, Greg was a Frontier Scout.

*Pet:* Myron (a hamster).

*Note:* In real life, the Brady Kids did produce two albums: *Meet the Brady Bunch* and *The Brady Bunch Christmas Album*. In the NBC 1981 series update *The Brady Brides*, Greg is seen married to Nora (Caryn Richman). In the 1988 CBS TV movie *A Very Brady Christmas* and in the 1990 CBS series update *The Bradys*, Greg is working in the same hospital as Nora, a nurse. They are also the parents of Kevin (Zachary Bostrom). Jonathan Weiss later played Kevin.

## PETER BRADY

*Status:* Middle brother.

*Education:* Clinton Elementary School and Fillmore Junior High School (where he was a columnist for the school newspaper paper and was called "Scoop").

*Image:* Peter feels he is insecure and has no personality. He also feels he is dull and unattractive to girls. When he tried to change his appearance, he could be heard saying, "Pork chops and applesauce."

*Club:* A member of the neighborhood Tree House Club.

*Job:* Helper at Mr. Martinelli's Bike Shop.

*Favorite TV Show: Kartoon King* (wherein he attempted to win an ice cream eating contest as promoted on the program. He eventually lost).

*Hero:* George Washington.

*Miscellaneous:* Peter joined the air force in *The Brady Brides*. He became engaged to Valerie Thomas (Carol Huston) in the 1988 TV movie *A Very Brady Christmas*, and in *The Bradys*, he is married and assists his councilman father.

## BOBBY BRADY

*Status:* Youngest brother.

*Education:* Clinton Elementary School (where he is a safety monitor).

*Hero:* Old West outlaw Jesse James.

*Pet:* Bird (a parakeet).

*Fault:* Attempts get-rich-quick schemes (like selling Neat and Tidy Hair Tonic for $1 bottle; the end result: turns hair orange).

*Miscellaneous:* Bobby is a college student (in *The Brady Brides*) and is seen as a race car driver in *The Bradys*. He is also married to Tracy (Martha Quinn) and suffered a horrible racing accident that left him paralyzed from the waist down.

## MARCIA BRADY

*Status:* Eldest sister.

*Education:* Fillmore Junior High School (where she was class president and editor of its paper, the *Fillmore Flier*) and Westdale High School (where she was a cheerleader for the Bears football team). She also played Juliet in the Westdale production of *Romeo and Juliet.*

*Worst School Subject:* History ("I get confused with dates").

*Affiliation:* A member of the Sun Flowers Girl Scout Troop and the Frontier Scouts; she also takes ballet lessons at the Valley School of Dancing.

*Club President:* Marcia is president of the Davy Jones Fan Club (Davy was lead singer of the Monkees).

*Job:* Counter girl at Hanson's Ice Cream Parlor.

*Favorite Hangout:* The Pizza Parlor.

*Dream:* Marcia keeps a diary and in it wrote about her desire to become Mrs. Desi Arnaz Jr. (the son of Lucille Ball and Desi Arnaz from *I Love Lucy*).

*Character:* As Marcia became a young woman and found an interest in boys, she also found herself being spied on by Jan and Cindy, whom she called "The Nosey Bradys." Her most devastating moment occurred when she was hit in the face with a football that broke her nose (the saying, "Oh my nose!" became a part of the show's history; Peter was throwing the football to Bobby and accidentally hit Marcia). She also had a fascination with skiing.

*Miscellaneous:* Marcia marries the wacky Wally Logan (Jerry Houser) in *The Brady Brides*. Wally is a toy designer for the Tyler Toy Company (later called Prescott Toys). Marcia has become a fashion designer for Casual Clothes. They reside in the same house as Jan and her husband Philip. In *The Bradys*, Marcia (now played by Leah Ayres) and Wally are the owners of the Party Girls Catering Company. They are also the parents of Jessica (Jaclyn Bernstein) and Mickey (J. W. Lee).

## JAN BRADY

*Status:* Middle sister.

*Education:* Fillmore Junior High School (where each year she looks forward to the Junior Carnival) and Westdale High School (where she holds the title "Most Popular Girl in the Class").

*Personality:* Jan describes herself as "pretty, smart, and kind." But because she wears glasses, she feels "I'm not as beautiful as Marcia" (the term "Marcia, Marcia, Marcia" became associated with Jan [which she said when she became jealous]). She also tried but failed to lighten the freckles on her face with lemon juice.

*Hobby:* Playing practical jokes.

*Talent:* Ability to paint and write (most famous for her school essay "What America Means to Me").

*Boyfriend:* Jan is insecure around boys, and to prove to others that she liked them, she invented one named George Glass.

*Hair Color:* Blonde. However, she wore a brunette wig to become an individual so "I'm not a blonde Brady" (as her mother and sisters are also blonde).

*Job:* Counter girl at Hanson's Ice Cream Parlor.

*Favorite Snack:* Cinnamon spice cookies.

*Allergy:* Allergic to certain types of dog flea powder.

*Miscellaneous:* The 1981 *Brady Brides* finds Jan becoming an architect in her father's unnamed company and marrying Philip Covington III (Ron Kuhlman), a college chemistry professor. To save on expenses, they share a house with Marcia and her husband, Wally. Jan became the head of her father's company in the 1990 *Bradys* (where she and Philip have also become the parents of an adopted daughter named Patty).

The 1977 ABC series *The Brady Bunch Hour* finds the Brady family performing music, songs, and comedy skits. Geri Reischl played Jan Brady.

## CYNTHIA "CINDY" BRADY

*Status:* Youngest sister.

*Education:* Dixie Canyon Elementary School (also called Clinton Elementary School).

*Pet Rabbits:* Romeo and Juliet.

*Favorite Doll:* Kitty Karry-All.

*Hero:* Joan of Arc.

*Bad Habit:* Eavesdropping and tattling on her brothers and sisters.

*Favorite Game:* Jacks.

*Miscellaneous:* In *The Brady Brides* series update, Cindy has graduated from college and is now the host of her own radio program, *Cindy at Sunrise*, on station KBLA. Jennifer Runyon played Cindy in the 1988 *A Very Brady Christmas*.

## ALICE NELSON

*Relationship:* Family cook and maid (although she is treated like a member of the family). She never eats dinner at the same table with the Bradys.

*Temporary Job:* Waitress at the Golden Spoon Diner.

*Residence:* Lives in the Brady home and has a room to the right side of the kitchen. She began working for Mike in 1962 (his wife had died shortly after Bobby was born).

*Place of Birth:* California.

*Education:* Westdale High School.

*Hobbies:* Bowling, entering jingle-writing contests, and dancing (she especially likes the Charleston).

*Boyfriend:* Sam Franklin (Allan Melvin), a butcher (owner of Sam's Butcher Shop) she later marries.

*Claim to Fame:* Friends with Lucille Ball's housekeeper.

*Favorite TV Show: Perry Mason.*

*Relatives:* Cousin Emma, a former Marine sergeant (Ann B. Davis).

# *Branded*
## (NBC, 1965–1966)

*Cast:* Chuck Connors (Jason McCord).

*Basis:* Jason McCord, an army captain branded as a coward for deserting his troops during battle, roams the West of the 1870s seeking to begin a new life.

### JASON McCORD

*Place of Birth:* Washington, D.C.

*Education:* West Point.

*Schoolmate:* George Armstrong Custer.

*Military Experience:* Jason fought in the Battle of Shiloh and was a soldier in the Army of the Ohio (where he was stationed at Fort Ohio). In 1863, he met General Ulysses S. Grant at the Battle of Vicksburg (May 1863) and was a lieutenant with the Union army during the Civil War. He was later stationed at Fort Lincoln. He voted for Grant when he ran for president of the United States.

*Job Experience:* Jason gained knowledge as a geologist and now uses that ability to help him navigate life "as a coward."

*Plight:* In 1869, Jason served under the command of a general named Reed, the man responsible for establishing peace between the white man and Indian tribes in western Wyoming. At the Battle of Bitter Creek, Jason noticed that Reed was becoming incapable of commanding his troops (due to old age) and had to relieve him of command. "Something happened after that," Jason said. "I was knocked unconscious [by the attacking Comanche Indians], and when I woke up three days later, I was being treated by a farmer miles from the battle."

*The Court-Martial:* Jason was the only survivor of the battle and, when found, was arrested for deserting his troops. The farmer testified that Jason walked into his place on two good legs and was perfectly rational. "That may be so," Jason said at his trial, "but I can't recall anything for those three days. Maybe I did run." A trial was held, and Jason was accused of desertion. He was court-martialed, stripped of his rank, and left with only a broken sword, his sign of being a coward.

*The Aftermath:* Jason never testified at his trial that he took command to save the reputation of General Reed. Only Colonel Snow (Jon Lorimar) believed Jason was innocent, but his testimony was not enough. Jason has been branded "The Coward of Bitter Creek"; Horace Greeley (Burgess Meredith) wrote stories about Jason at his trial, and through his newspaper columns the name Jason McCord has become associated with cowardice. Jason is also called "Yellow Tail" and "Yellow Belly." The theme lyrics relate Jason's struggles: "What do you do when you're branded and you know you're a man? Wherever you go for the rest of your life, you must prove you're a man."

*The Present:* In 1871, Jason is summoned to the office of President Grant. In this episode, "The Mission," it is learned that Grant believes Jason is innocent and can do a great service for the country. "You've already been marked as a coward. How would you like to be branded a traitor as well?" Grant explains that he needs an undercover agent to help him deal with the problems he has—from people trying to assassinate him to smugglers supplying guns to the Indians. Grant's assignments also became a part of the series.

*Jobs:* Jason's surveying assignments took him from Seattle to Alaska. He and his partner Rufus I. Pitkin (J. Pat O'Malley) surveyed the Alaska wilderness for William Seward (Ian Wolfe) and the docks of Seattle for the governor. Rufus left Jason to become an undertaker (because his initials spelled RIP). He has a horse named Margaret, and he established a business in the town of Cutbank. Jason continued to work (but on his own), seeking to leave his past behind him and begin a new life.

*New Life:* Jason is seeking a job surveying for the railroad that is planning to lay track through the town of Panamint. It is here that Jason meets his old flame, Ann Williams (Lola Albright), the editor of the town newspaper, the *Banner.* In the episode "Cowards Die Many Times," Ann and Jason have become close, and a romance is blooming.

*The Final Episode, "Kellie:"* Jason and his grandfather General Joshua McCord (John Carradine) have established a business called McCord and McCord, Survey Engineers. Ann, still a part of Jason's life, has become guardian of an orphan girl named Kellie, and it is assumed that Jason and Ann will marry and care for Kellie. Suzanne Cupito, later known as Morgan Brittany, plays Kellie.

# *Burke's Law*
## (ABC, 1963–1965)

*Cast*: Gene Barry (Captain Amos Burke), Regis Toomey (Detective Lester Hart), Gary Conway (Detective Tim Tilson), Leon Lontoc (Henry), Eileen O'Neill (Sergeant Gloria Ames).

*Basis:* A millionaire police captain (Amos Burke) investigates crimes most often associated with the wealthy and glamorous people of Los Angeles.

## AMOS BURKE

*Age:* 44 (born in June 1919).

*Place of Birth:* Los Angeles.

*Address:* 109 North Melbourne in Beverly Hills.

*Occupation:* Police captain with the Homicide Bureau of the Metropolitan Division of the Los Angeles Police Department (LAPD). In the pilot episode, he is an inspector with Division 3 of the LAPD.

*Prior Position:* Police officer ("He started out pounding a beat and worked himself all the way up").

*Office Phone Number:* Madison 6-7399.

*Philosophy:* "I love solving crimes in general but murder in particular."

*Rolls Royce Silver Cloud Limo License Plate:* JZG 063 (also seen as HEK 388 and JE 8495; the car also doubles as his police car).

*Car Features:* A mobile phone (number WO-2356), air conditioning, a bar, a stereo music system, automatic windows, and radio and TV capabilities.

*Day Off:* Although Amos believes there is no day off from crime (at least for him), he is forced to take one day a week off (he chose Tuesday).

*Trait:* A ladies' man with a fine taste in women, wine, and food. He is wealthy and does not need to work but does so because he believes he has a knack for solving crimes. He goes strictly by the book when solving crimes and will not use unorthodox methods to achieve a goal.

*Expertise:* Treats and solves each case like a complex puzzle.

*Wealth:* Amos is very elusive as to how he acquired his money. He says, "My grandfather died and left me a fortune." He later contradicts that by saying he invested in the stock market and real estate. In the pilot episode, it said that Amos acquired his money the smart way—"He was born with it."

*Burke's Law:* The title refers to the "words of wisdom" Amos uses during cases. Some of his expressions are "Money is worthless unless you can enjoy it—Burke's Law," "Never make fun of an older woman. One day you'll be married to one—Burke's Law," "Murder is the only game you can never win—Burke's

Law," "When you come to a dead end, go back to the beginning—Burke's Law," and "If catching a killer were easy anyone could do it—Burke's Law."

*Catchphrase:* When Amos first meets a suspect he says, "I'm Captain Burke, Homicide."

*1965 Job:* Secret agent for U.S. intelligence. Amos resigned from the LAPD, and the show's title changed to *Amos Burke, Secret Agent* (it ran until 1966). Amos was the same type of character as in the prior series, although he was now involved with more danger, intrigue, and especially beautiful women. His superior was "The Man" (Carl Benton Reid). The revised format, influenced by the James Bond film craze, simply did not work, and the show ended after 17 episodes.

## OTHER CHARACTERS

Lester Hart (called Les) and Tim Tilson are the detectives who assist Amos. Lester is the wiser, older, and seasoned detective, while Tim is the cop still learning the tricks of the trade (most of which he learns from Les, whom he looks on as a mentor. Tim does have an encyclopedic knowledge of crime but lacks the real experience to implement it during investigations). By dialogue, it appears that Amos and Les have been friends for a long time, as he sometimes calls Burke "Amos." Les resides at 106 Essex Drive, and 676-4882 is Tim's home phone number. While Amos, Les, and Tim investigate the same crimes, it is most often Amos who prefers to question the most interesting suspects (as he would tell his associates with the words "Your Old Captain" [will handle this]). In the pilot episode, John Damler played Lester Hart, and Edward Platt played Detective Joe Nelson (the character of Tim did not appear).

Henry is Amos's houseboy and chauffeur; Gloria Ames is the sexy police station sergeant who often became an object of distraction for Amos.

*Note:* The original pilot episode, "Amos Burke: Who Killed Julie Greer?" aired on *The Dick Powell Show* and featured Dick Powell as Amos Burke.

## UPDATE

In 1994 (to 1995), CBS aired a revised version of the program again called *Burke's Law.* In the interim, Amos had apparently returned to the LAPD after his inability to succeed as a secret agent. At one point, he married a woman named Sarah, whom he met on the dance floor of the Coconut Grove Club in Los Angeles and with whom he had a son named Peter (Peter Barton). While not stated when, Amos has become the chief of police of the LAPD. He now works with Peter, a detective, and Lily Morgan (Bever-Leigh Banfield), a brilliant forensic detective, to solve highly complex crimes. Here, Amos owned a 1961 Silver Cloud Rolls Royce, and Danny Kamekona played the part of Burke's chauffeur, Henry.

*Note:* On the January 21, 1994, episode of the new *Burke's Law* ("Who Killed Nick Hazzard"), Anne Francis, who played Honey West (from the TV series of the same title), guest-starred as Honey Best in a takeoff on her 1965 ABC series. It is also interesting to note that *Honey West* was also a spin-off from the ABC version of *Burke's Law* (from the episode "Honey West: Who Killed the Jackpot?").

# Captain Nice
(NBC, 1966–1967)

*Cast:* William Daniels (Carter Nash), Ann Prentiss (Candy Kane), Alice Ghostley (Esther Nash), Byron Fougler (Harvey Nash).

*Basis:* A mild-mannered police department chemist (Carter Nash) develops a special liquid that enables him to fight crime as the mysterious Captain Nice.

## CARTER NASH

*Parents:* Esther and Harvey Nash (with whom he lives).

*Home:* Big Town, U.S.A. ("Somewhere in the midwestern part of North America"). It has a population of 112,000 people.

*Job:* Chemist with the Big Town, U.S.A., Police Department.

*Office:* Room 1908 in the City Hall Building.

*Reasons for Being Hired:* "He is a good chemist," and his uncle, Fred Finney (Liam Dunn), is the mayor of Big Town (and Esther's brother).

*Character:* Shy and timid; just ordinary and doesn't stand out (actually a Mama's boy). When Carter enrolled in a self-defense course, for example, "They said I should carry an axe"; when he tried to join the army, "They burned my draft card."

*Fears:* Girls (he tends to think of them "as round men").

*Hidden Desire:* Candice "Candy" Kane, a beautiful Big Town police officer on whom he has a boylike crush but hasn't the courage to ask her out on a date; he does say, "She is quite attractive and a credit to her uniform."

*Harvey's Nickname for Carter:* Spot (Harvey can't remember his son's real name and is never fully seen, as the newspaper he is reading, the Big Town *Chronicle*, obstructs his face).

*Invention:* Super Juice, a liquid that, when taken, transforms him into the heroic crime fighter Captain Nice.

*First Act as Captain Nice:* Rescuing Candy Kane from thugs.

*Name Creation:* Taken from the initials on his belt (C.N.). Carter told his mother about what he invented and was ready to destroy the formula when she convinced him to use Super Juice to battle evil. She then made him a red, white, and blue costume and mask and cape ("Captain Nice" appears across the front of the costume).

*Prior Superhero Names:* Before choosing "Captain Nice," Esther suggested "Muscle Head" and "Wonder Man."

*Captain Nice Abilities:* Incredible speed, strength, and the ability to fly.

*Captain Nice Quirks:* Must always be neat and tidy. Before Carter drinks Super Juice and changes into Captain Nice, he hangs up his suit so it will not wrinkle.

*Slogan:* "From now on, the forces of evil will have to watch out for Captain Nice!"

# *Captain Scarlet and the Mysterons*
## (Syndicated, 1967–1968)

*Voice Cast:* Francis Matthews (Captain Scarlet), Ed Bishop (Captain Blue), Donald Gray (Colonel White), Paul Maxwell (Captain Grey), Jeremy Wilkins (Captain Ochre), Gary Files (Captain Magenta), Cy Grant (Lieutenant Green), Jana Hill (Symphony Angel), Sylvia Anderson (Melody Angel), Liz Morgan (Destiny Angel and Rhapsody Angel), Shin-Lian (Harmony Angel), Charles Tingwell (Dr. Fawn).

*Basis:* Spectrum, a futuristic defense organization headquartered on Cloudbase, battles the never-seen Mysterons, inhabitants of the planet Mars who have waged a war of revenge against the planet Earth (mistakenly believing that an exploration of the planet was an unprovoked attack). The program uses marionettes and is filmed in Supermarionation.

## OVERALL SERIES INFORMATION

All male agents are named after the colors of the Spectrum. Women serve as pilots, called Angels. The Mysterons possess the power to re-create any person or object after first destroying it (as was the case with Captain Scarlet; their effort to kill him and make him their agent on Earth failed when he retained his human qualities). They also killed Spectrum agent Captain Black, who is now their agent on Earth (he failed to retain any human abilities) and an enemy of Spectrum.

## CAPTAIN SCARLET

*Position:* Spectrum's top agent.

*Ability:* To defy death.

*Background:* English and from a family of distinguished soldiers.
*Year of Birth:* 2036.
*Degrees:* Technology, history, and mathematics.
*Previous Service:* The World Army (where he served in field combat).
*On Duty:* A true professional agent, carrying out orders fast and efficiently.
*Off Duty:* Full of fun, carefree, and bursting with energy; he is popular with all the Spectrum agents and female Angels.

## COLONEL WHITE

*Position:* Supreme commander in chief of Spectrum.
*Background:* English.
*Abilities:* Highly educated with first-class honors in computer control, navigation, and technology.
*Prior Service:* The World Navy and the Universal Secret Service.
*Off Duty:* Loves to play "War Games" with Captain Scarlet.

## CAPTAIN GREY

*Position:* Field agent.
*Background:* American.
*Place of Birth:* Chicago.
*Prior Service:* The U.S. Navy and the World Aquanaut Security Patrol (where he was put in charge of the submarine *Stingray*).
*Abilities:* Cool handling of tough situations, quick thinking, alertness, fast reactions, and an uncanny anticipation of impending danger.
*Off Duty:* Enjoys swimming (in the Spectrum Swimming Pool) and developing new strokes and styles.

## CAPTAIN BLUE

*Position:* Field agent.
*Background:* American.
*Place of Birth:* Boston, Massachusetts. The son of a wealthy financier.
*Prior Service:* Test pilot for the World Aeronautic Society, later an agent in its security department.
*Abilities:* Brilliant scholar with first-class honors in economics, technology, applied mathematics, computer control, and aerodynamics. He preferred a thrilling life and thus abandoned the business world.
*Off Duty:* Enjoys an active outdoor life.

## CAPTAIN OCHRE

*Position:* Field agent.
*Background:* American.

*Interest:* Flying.

*Prior Service:* Earned his pilot's license at the age of 16; served with the World Government Police Corps (where he broke up one of the toughest crime syndicates in the United States).

*Abilities:* He does not have outstanding academic qualifications, but his loyalty to his own convictions (flying) led to his being recruited by Spectrum. He is quick-witted and a brilliant conversationalist but prone to be the victim of practical jokes.

*Off Duty:* Enjoys hanging out with the opposite sex and is a devoted model plane builder.

## CAPTAIN MAGENTA

*Position:* Security agent.

*Background:* Irish. His parents immigrated to America, and he was raised in a poor New York suburb in an atmosphere of poverty and crime. While he had leaned toward becoming a criminal (he was an excellent pickpocket), his mother encouraged him to work hard in school.

*Education:* Yale University.

*Degrees:* Physics, electrical engineering, and technology.

*Prior Life:* Although well educated, Magenta became involved with daredevil extremists and turned to a life of crime, becoming the ruthless mastermind that controlled two-thirds of New York's criminal empire. Spectrum realized that such a man was crucial to their organization (respected and trusted in the underworld) and recruited him to work from the inside and get to the heart of criminal activity.

*Off Duty:* Noted for his charm and wit, he loves to interact with other agents, especially the Angels.

## LIEUTENANT GREEN

*Position:* Colonel White's right-hand man.

*Background:* Spanish.

*Place of Birth:* Port of Spain, Trinidad.

*Prior Service:* The World Aquanaut Security Patrol, the Submarine Corps, and sole commander of communication installations at the Marineville Control Tower (at which time he was recruited by Spectrum).

*Degrees:* Music, telecommunications, and technology.

*Abilities:* Alert, calm, and never flustered or annoyed.

*Off Duty:* Enjoys relaxing with the music of the West Indies.

## DR. FAWN

*Position:* Supreme medical commander.

*Background:* Australian. He is the son of a prominent Australian specialist.

*Degrees:* Biology and medicine.

*Prior Service:* The World Medical Organization.

*Achievements:* Responsible for remarkable advances in medicine and the development of robot doctors.

### SYMPHONY ANGEL

*Position:* Spectrum pilot.

*Background:* American.

*Place of Birth:* Cedar Rapids, Ohio.

*Degrees:* Possesses seven degrees in mathematics and technology.

*Abilities:* Superior intelligence (able to complete a five-year school course in two years) and obsessed with flying. She is also sympathetic and quick-witted.

*Prior Service:* The Universal Secret Service (as a pilot), later owner of a private (unnamed) air charter company.

*Off Duty:* Enjoys creating new hairstyles for herself and the other Angels.

### MELODY ANGEL

*Position:* Spectrum pilot.

*Background:* American.

*Place of Birth:* Atlanta, Georgia, where she was raised on a cotton farm.

*History:* With four brothers and Melody being the only girl, she grew up to become a tomboy. This led her to become a professional motor car racer after graduating from high school. Her parents felt she needed further education and sent her to a Swiss finishing school. It was here that she developed a love of flying. Melody, however, was quite unruly and was expelled from school.

*Prior Service*: The World Army Air Force.

*Abilities:* Amazing courage and nerves of iron, which lead to her recruitment by Spectrum.

### RHAPSODY ANGEL

*Position:* Spectrum pilot.

*Background:* British.

*Place of Birth:* Chelsea, England.

*Heritage:* Aristocratic parentage.

*Education:* London University.

*Degrees:* Law and sociology.

*Inspiration:* Lady Penelope Creighton-Ward, Britain's top secret agent (with F.A.B.—Federal Agents Bureau).

*Prior Service:* Rhapsody took over command of F.A.B. when Lady Penelope joined International Rescue (see the entry *Thunderbirds*). She later resigned to become the chief security officer for an airline company, then started her own airline service.

*Off Duty:* She loves playing chess and is as charming on duty as she is off and is totally dedicated to Spectrum.

## HARMONY ANGEL
*Position:* Spectrum pilot.
*Place of Birth:* Tokyo, Japan.
*Heritage:* Daughter of a wealthy flying taxi cab company owner. She grew up in a world of high-speed jets.
*Education:* The finest schools in Japan and London.
*Prior Activities:* A member of the Tokyo Flying Club (flew around the world nonstop, breaking every existing record). After inheriting her father's company, Spectrum recruited her as an agent.
*Off Duty:* Exudes Eastern charm and femininity and enjoys sports and teaching her Angel copilots judo and karate.

## DESTINY ANGEL
*Position:* Pilot and leader of the Angels.
*Place of Birth:* Paris, France.
*Education:* The finest universities in France and Rome.
*Prior Service:* The World Air Army Force (where she became a member of the Intelligence Corps) and the commanding officer of the Women's Flight Squadron. She later started her airline contracting firm.
*Off Duty:* Very feminine, charming, and sophisticated (as compared to her on-duty persona of being utterly ruthless and totally efficient). She enjoys designing and making her own clothes.

# Car 54, Where Are You?
## (NBC, 1961–1963)

*Cast:* Fred Gwynne (Officer Francis Muldoon), Joe E. Ross (Officer Gunther Toody), Paul Reed (Captain Martin Block), Al Lewis (Officer Leo Schnauser), Beatrice Pons (Lucille Toody), Charlotte Rae (Sylvia Schnauser).
*Basis:* The patrolling assignments of Francis Muldoon and Gunther Toody, officers attached to the 53rd Precinct of the New York Police Department in the Bronx (located on Tremont Avenue) and assigned car 54.

## CHARACTER OVERVIEW
Francis Muldoon, tall and thin, and Gunther Toody, short and stocky, were first teamed and assigned to car 54 (license plate 54) on August 16, 1952, as the only police officers who could ride with each other. Muldoon rarely speaks and

makes other partners uneasy ("It's like riding with a spook," they say). Toody is just the opposite and constantly talks, making other partners crazy. They are members of the 53rd Precinct's Brotherhood Club and Singing Whippoorwills. They jointly coach the Wildcats and are members of the PAL (Police Athletic League) basketball team, and nailing Benny the Bookie was the first arrest they made together.

## FRANCIS MULDOON

*Address:* 807 East 57th Street (also given as 175th Street) in the Bronx.
*Badge Number:* 723 (787 in the pilot). He is a third-generation police officer. His grandfather was a deputy police commissioner and his father a captain.
*Education:* Holy Cross High School (where he was also a member of the basketball team). He was also said to attend Bryant High School and New Town High School.
*Height:* As Francis says, "I'm six feet, five inches tall, and it's all face."
*Weight:* 183¾ pounds.
*Nickname:* Called My Big Baby Boy by his mother. In grammar school, the kids called him Horse Face.
*Ability:* Francis has a mind like a computer and can recall any police regulation. He is also a writer of sorts and wrote a play called *Tempest in the Tropics* (later called *Coppers Capers*) for the Policeman's Benefit.
*Hobby:* Stamp collecting (he is a member of the Bronx Stamp Club).
*Bank Account:* The Bronx Home Savings Bank.
*Relatives:* mother (Ruth Masters); Peggy Muldoon, sister (Helen Parker); Cathy Muldoon, sister (Nancy Donohue). Francis lives with his mother and sisters. Nancy is attending Columbia University in Manhattan; Peggy is an aspiring actress (she appeared in the Broadway play *Waiting for Wednesday*).

## GUNTHER TOODY

*Wife:* Lucille. They have been married for 15 years.
*Address:* While an exact address was not given, they live in a five-room, rent-controlled apartment in the Bronx. Their rent is $45 a month.
*Badge Number:* 432 (camera angles also make it look like 1432 and 453).
*Height:* 5 feet, 8 inches tall.
*Birthday:* August 15.
*Education:* Fairview High School (where he had the nickname Bull as a member of the school's football team).
*Prior Jobs:* Garbage collector with the New York City Department of Sanitation.
*Army Service:* Private stationed at Fort Dix in New Jersey (where he was called Lover Lips by girls when he attended camp dances).

*Ambition:* To become a police detective (he "studies" crime detection by watching then-current TV shows *Dragnet, Checkmate,* and *Perry Mason.* "I've gotten so good that I can solve the crime by the third commercial").

*Rookie School Experience:* Told by his lieutenant that if he (Toody) ever graduated, he would shoot himself. Toody graduated, and the lieutenant is fine.

*Catchphrase:* "Ooh, ooh, jumpin' Jehosiphat!" (which he says when something excites him).

*Ability:* Although he comes from a family of famous singers (the Singing Toodys), Gunther has a gravelly voice and believes he has followed in the family tradition.

*Bank Account:* The Bronx Home Savings Bank.

*Newspaper:* Gunter reads the *News Journal.*

## LUCILLE TOODY

*Husband:* Gunther Toody.

*Maiden Name:* Lucille Hasselwhite.

*Occupation:* Housewife.

*Education:* Fairview High School (where she met Gunther) and Hunter College.

*Nickname* (by Francis): Boo Boo (as he treats her like a sister).

*Trait:* Forever yelling at Gunther for all the stupid things he does (she lets off steam by yelling out the apartment house window, "My husband is a nut!").

## LEO SCHNAUSER

*Wife:* Sylvia (she and Leo have been married for 20 years when the series begins).

*Badge Number:* 1062.

*Apartment:* 6A (address not given).

*Position:* Patrolman.

*Prior Job:* Mounted policeman (rode a horse named Sally for 12 years before being assigned to the 53rd Precinct).

*Birthday:* Said only to be "Friday the 13th." He believes on that day a black cat crossed his path for all the bad luck he has.

*Siblings:* Six sisters (never seen), but Leo is considered to be the prettiest one in the family.

*Activities:* Coach for a basketball team called the Tigers.

*Dislike:* Night duty "because I get home in time to see Sylvia getting out of bed."

## SYLVIA SCHNAUSER

*Husband:* Leo.

*Occupation:* Housewife.

*Maiden Name:* Sylvia Schwarzcock.

*Prior Jobs:* Actress, ballet dancer, and failed artist.

*Activity:* Working on a book based on Leo's experiences called *Precinct Place* (a takeoff of the novel *Peyton Place*).

*Trait:* Very argumentative (she and Leo constantly argue about everything). Sylvia is also extremely jealous. She believes that when Leo joins with Toody and Muldoon for a get-together, he is having a secret affair with Marilyn Monroe.

*Nickname:* Leo calls her Pussycat.

*Note:* In the pilot episode, Al Lewis played Al Spencer, a building contractor.

## OTHER CHARACTERS

Martin Block is the stern captain of the 53rd Precinct. He feels his life has been plagued since the day Toody was assigned to his precinct. He considers Toody and Muldoon to be "like Tinkerbell and Peter Pan returning to Never Never Land" when they come off patrol. He believes Muldoon is intelligent but knows Toody is "gullible, stupid and simple-minded." In high school, Martin (also called Paul) starred in a play called *Vagabond King*. Louise Kirtland, then Patricia Bright, played his wife Claire (also called Elsie).

Mr. Eisenberg (not seen) is the notorious Bronx jaywalker, Charlie the Drunk (Larry Storch) has become the number one project of the Helping Hand Committee of the 53rd Precinct to sober up, and Mrs. Bronson (Molly Picon), first as the elderly lady befriended by Toody and Muldoon (when she refused to move out of her condemned building) and later when she opened the Wedding Bells Matrimonial Agency (wherein she matched elderly Bronx citizens with famous movie stars).

# *The Champions*

(Syndicated, NBC, 1968)

*Cast:* Stuart Damon (Craig Stirling), Alexandra Bastedo (Sharron Macready), William Gaunt (Richard Barrett), Anthony Nicolls (W. L. Tremayne).

*Basis:* Craig Stirling, Sharron Macready, and Richard Barrett, human beings endowed with special powers, battle evil on behalf of Nemesis, an international organization attached to the United Nations and based in Geneva, Switzerland.

## OVERALL SERIES INFORMATION

While on an assignment in Tibet to retrieve deadly bacteria specimens from scientists, Richard, Sharron, and Craig are spotted by the enemy, and in an attempt to escape, their plane is hit by gunfire. Richard, unable to maintain flight, figures their best chance for survival is to land in the forbidding Himalayan Mountains. The plane, however, crash-lands, and the Nemesis agents appear to have been killed. Unknown beings from a lost city find the agents and take them to their world, where they are revived and endowed with superhuman abilities (advanced sight, hearing, and mental capabilities) for the benefit of humankind (battle evil). The agents vow to keep secret the location of the lost people and never reveal what actually happened to them. W. L. Tremayne is their superior at Nemesis.

## CRAIG STIRLING

*Place of Birth:* New York City.
*Birthday:* December 1, 1939.
*Address:* 487 Hampton Drive.
*Military Service:* Pilot in the U.S. Air Force.
*Position:* Special agent for Nemesis (which he joined in 1965).
*Ability:* Possesses a black belt in karate and can outwit the enemy by quickly assessing a situation and acting on it.
*Trait:* Intelligent and well versed in the martial arts. He likes to take his time when it comes to a plan but often finds that he must come up with an on-the-spot plan when situations become critical.

## SHARRON MACREADY

*Place of Birth:* England.
*Address:* 36 Bristol Court.
*Occupation:* Special agent for Nemesis.
*Prior Occupation:* A scientist and doctor (although she is never addressed as a doctor). She is a recent widow and at one point in time worked as an investigator for the C.I.D. (Criminal Investigative Division) of New Scotland Yard.
*Trait:* Intelligence and her knowledge in medical procedures has given her the ability to withstand physical and mental punishment.
*Wardrobe:* While very sexy and alluring, Sharron states that she prefers not to wear miniskirts as part of an assignment. She is, however, seen in a miniskirt and using it as a distraction to allow Richard and Craig to complete an assignment.

## RICHARD BARRETT

*Occupation:* Special agent for Nemesis.
*Place of Birth:* Salisbury, England.
*Year of Birth:* 1938.
*Address:* 101 Barrington Place.

*Expertise:* Martial arts and code breaking.

*Position:* The (unofficial) head of the team.

*Trait:* Nothing fazes Richard, and he will risk his life to accomplish a mission. He is a snappy dresser and believes that clothes make the man. He is also a gourmet cook and frequents only the finest restaurants.

# The Courtship of Eddie's Father
## (ABC, 1969–1972)

*Cast:* Bill Bixby (Tom Corbett), Brandon Cruz (Eddie Corbett), Miyoshi Umeki (Mrs. Livingston), Kristina Holland (Tina Rickles), James Komack (Norman Tinker).

*Basis:* A young boy (Eddie) attempts to find the perfect girl to become his new mother when he feels enough time has elapsed after his mother's passing and his father (Tom) needs to start dating again.

## THOMAS "TOM" CORBETT

*Marital Status:* Widower.

*Son:* Eddie.

*Late Wife:* Helen.

*Tom's Nickname for Eddie:* Sport.

*Address:* 146 South Beverly Boulevard, Apartment C, in Los Angeles.

*First Woman Tom Dated after His Wife's Passing:* Lynn Bardman (played by Diana Muldaur). Lynn, however, was not ready to give up her single life for that of a housewife and mother.

*Occupation:* Editor of *Tomorrow Magazine*, a newspaper supplement. Cissy Drummond (played by Tippy Hedren) is the editor in chief.

*Magazine Slogan:* "Today's Magazine Supplement."

*Business Location:* The number 221 appears on the unidentified building.

*Tom's Passion:* Books (he is trying to pass his love of books on to Eddie).

*Classes:* Tom and Eddie take karate lessons.

*Relatives:* father, Harry Corbett (Will Geer); sister-in-law, Kate Landis (Francine York).

## EDWARD "EDDIE" CORBETT

*Age:* 6 years old when the series begins.

*Education:* Selmar Grammar School. He is in the first grade, but the setting looks more like a kindergarten classroom.

*Job:* Playing matchmaker for his father by bringing "strays" home. Tom's thoughts about that: "Stop trying to find girls for me."

*Philosophy:* "Most kids have a father father. But I have a father who's my best friend" (hence the theme song, "Best Friend"). He tells women his father is "kind, generous, and handsome." While Eddie's matchmaking efforts were a part of the series when it began, it gradually decreased to focus on a father–son relationship.

*Favorite Breakfast:* Crunchy Flakes cereal.

*Bedtime Snack:* Cookies (too many Tom believes).

*Bedtime Memories:* Eddie's most cherished memory of his mother was her singing the song "Little Cowboy" as he fell asleep.

*Morning Job:* Bringing Tom his cup of coffee and trying not to spill any.

*Pajamas:* When Eddie is sick, he wears his special pajamas with dive-bombers on them.

*Piggybank:* Eddie keeps his money in a rocket ship–shaped glass bank.

*About Women:* He doesn't fully understand them and calls their makeup "gloop and glop."

*Difficulty:* Using chopsticks (he uses his fingers instead).

## OTHER CHARACTERS

Mrs. Livingston is Tom's housekeeper. She is Japanese and attending night school to improve her English. She calls Tom "Mr. Eddie's father." She often offers motherly advice to Eddie when she feels he needs it. She possesses a college degree (not stated in what) and is an expert in what Tom calls "royal cuisine." In early episodes, Eddie sees Mrs. Livingston as a substitute mother. Sunday is her day off.

Tina Rickles is Tom's secretary (who replaced his former secretary, Etta, played by Karin Wolfe). Tina is a bit clumsy and ditzy but pretty, and Tom says, "They threw away the mold when they made you." Tom also confides in her when he has a problem with Eddie.

Norman Tinker is Tom's friend, the magazine's art director (although he is mostly seen taking photographs). He is Eddie's "adoptive uncle" and a bit irresponsible. He also considers himself a ladies' man and believes 26 is a lucky number.

# The Dick Van Dyke Show
(CBS, 1961–1966)

*Cast:* Dick Van Dyke (Rob Petrie), Mary Tyler Moore (Laura Petrie), Larry Matthews (Richie Petrie), Morey Amsterdam (Buddy Sorrell), Rose Marie (Sally Rogers), Richard Deacon (Mel Cooley), Carl Reiner (Alan Brady), Jerry Paris (Jerry Helper), Ann Morgan Guilbert (Millie Helper).

*Basis:* Incidents in the home and working life of Rob Petrie, head writer for the fictitious TV series *The Alan Brady Show.*

## ROBERT "ROB" PETRIE

*Address:* 148 Bonnie Meadow Road (also given as 485 Bonnie Meadow Road) in New Rochelle, New York (Rob paid $27,990 for the home). The doorbell sounds in the keys of E and G-flat; there are 382½ roses on Rob and Laura's bedroom wallpaper.

*Wife:* Laura.

*Son:* Richie (Richard Rosebud Petrie; the middle name stems from Rob's efforts to please relatives who wanted to name the baby Robert Oscar Sam Edward Benjamin Ulysses David). Buddy suggested "Exit" as a name ("If the kid becomes an actor, it'll be in every theater in the country"). Sally suggested "Valentino" ("I was saving it for a parakeet, but you can have it"). Mel suggested "Allen," "Allan," or "Alan." Laura wanted "Robert" or "Roberta," and Rob wanted "Laura" or "Laurence."

*Place of Birth:* Danville, Ohio.

*Middle Name:* Simpson.

*Oddity:* When connected, all but one freckle on his back (the other being a scar) forms the Liberty Bell.

*Job:* Head writer of *The Alan Brady Show.* His office is on the 28th floor of an unnamed building in Manhattan.

*Education:* Danville High School (where he was called the "Devil of Danville High" for his fastball as pitcher on the school baseball team). He also starred in a school production of *Romeo and Juliet* opposite classmate Janie Layton (Joan O'Brien).

*Nickname as a Teenager:* Bones.

*Army Career:* Private, then sergeant, stationed at Camp Crowder in Missouri (flashback episodes place him in both Company A and Company E). It was at this time that he met, fell in love with, and married Laura Meeker, a beautiful dancer with the USO (United Serviceman's Organization). Shortly after his marriage to Laura, Rob was transferred to a small army base in Anchor, Texas.

*First Job:* Disc jockey for WOFF in Ohio, the number two radio station in a two-radio-station town (WDDX is number 1). Rob broke the world record for broadcasting without sleep by staying awake for 100 hours. It was here that Rob and Laura lived after Rob's service discharge before moving to New Rochelle.

*Song:* Wrote the lyrics to a song called "Bupkis" (which means "Nothing").

*Favorite Dinner:* Franks and beans with sauerkraut.

*Favorite Breakfast:* Leftover spaghetti and meatballs.

*Shoe Size:* 10D.

*Allergies:* Allergic to chicken feathers and cats.

*Wallet:* Rob carries a wallet with a picture of actress Paula Marshall inside (it came with the wallet and has a calendar on the other side, but Rob never removed it).

*Politics:* Rob ran for the position of 9th District councilman but lost (3,694 to 3,619) to his opponent Lincoln Goodheart (Wally Cox).

*Petrie Family Heirloom:* The grotesque Empress Carlotta necklace (which is cumbersome and shaped like a map of the United States; it has a jewel designating the birthplace of each family member).

*Cemetery Plots:* Rock Meadows Rest (located on the 15th hole of a golf course).

*Mentor:* Happy Spangler (Jay C. Flippen), a comedy writer who called him Stringbean.

*Relatives:* brother, Stacey Petrie (Jerry Van Dyke); mother, Clara Petrie (Carol Veazie and Isabel Randolph); father, Sam Petrie (Will Wright, Tom Tully, and J. Pat O'Malley); uncle, George (Denver Pyle); grandfather, Edward Petrie (Cyril Delevanti); great uncle, Hezekiah Petrie (Dick Van Dyke); Hezekiah's half brother, Alfred Reinbeck (Herb Vigran).

*Note:* In the 2004 CBS series update, *The Dick Van Dyke Show Revisited*, Rob and Laura have moved to Manhattan. Rob has retired (he hasn't written for Alan since the show was canceled 40 years ago); Laura now runs a dance studio from their apartment.

## LAURA PETRIE

*Maiden Name:* Laura Meeker (also said to be Laura Meehan).

*Weight:* 112 pounds.

*Hair Color:* Brunette (although she attempted to dye it blonde when she felt being blonde would make Rob more romantic).

*Occupation:* Housewife and mother.

*Prior Occupation:* Professional dancer.

*Education:* Questionable. It is indicated that Laura is a high school (and possibly a college) graduate, but in the flashback episode where Rob and Laura first meet, Laura was 17 years old (Laura never mentioned she was underage, and it later came out that Rob married a minor; they then remarried legally). The age discrepancy is not really discussed (did Laura drop out of high school to become a dancer, or did she graduate early and then pursue her career?). With their son Richie being born one year later, it also makes Laura's college education doubtful.

*Pageant Title:* At Camp Crowder, Laura's beauty won her the title "Bivouac Baby." It is here that she and Rob performed the song "You Wonderful You" together. It is also during the song that Rob, wearing combat boots, stepped on Laura's foot and broke her toes.

*Regrets:* Concealing her true age from Rob; posing for a clothed portrait of herself called "October Eve" as a present for Rob that became a nude painting when the artist envisioned—and painted—Laura without clothes; and revealing on the mythical TV interview program "The Ray Murdoch X-Ray Show" that Alan Brady was bald.

*Achievement:* Writing a children's book called *Be Yourself: The Seven Days of Danny* under the pen name Samantha Q. Wiggins.

*Catchphrase:* "Oh Rob," her sobering expression, which she says when something goes wrong.

*First Boyfriend:* Joe Coogan (she hides his old love letters to her behind a loose brick in the basement of her home next to the furnace).

*Favorite Meal:* Moo goo gai pan.

*Favorite TV Show:* The soap opera *Town of Passion*.

*Relatives:* father, Ben Meehan (Carl Benton Reid); mother, first name not given (Geraldine Wall); cousin, Thomas Edison (Eddie Firestone); cousin, Donna Palmer (Lyla Graham); uncle, Harold (Willard Waterman).

## BUDDY SORRELL

*Real Name:* Maurice Sorrell.

*Wife:* Fiona, called Pickles because, where Fiona comes from, "all the girls named Fiona are called Pickles" (Barbara Perry and Joan Shawlee).

*Pickles's Former Husband:* Floyd B. Bariscale (Sheldon Leonard), a forger.

*Pet Dog:* Larry, a German shepherd.

*Ability:* To make a joke out of any word in the English language. He can also play the cello and does so at parties.

*Job:* Cowriter of *The Alan Brady Show.*

*Prior Jobs:* Host of his own TV series (*Buddy's Bag*) and writer on *The Billy Barrows Show.* He also worked with Sally Rogers as the comedy team Gilbert and Solomon at Herbie's Hiawatha Lodge.

*Famous For:* "Baldy jokes" about show producer Mel Cooley.

*Buddy's Favorite Drink:* Tomato juice.

*Pickles's Favorite Dessert:* Strawberry-on-a-stick ice cream.

*Relatives:* brother, Blackie Sorrell (Phil Leeds).

## SALLY ROGERS

*Occupation:* Cowriter of *The Alan Brady Show.*

*Marital Status:* Single. She is looking to marry and settle down (but unable to find the right man).

*Boyfriend:* The mother-dominated Herman Glimshire (also called Woody Glimshire; played by Bill Idelson).

*Education:* Herbert Hoover High School.

*Prior Job:* Writer for *The Milton Berle Show.*

*Ability:* Uses her sense of humor and quick wit to conceal her loneliness.

*Shoe Size:* 6½B.

*Pet Cat:* Mr. Henderson.

*Habit:* Accentuating her hair with a pearl necklace.

*Discovery:* Sally introduced Randy Isenbauer, who created a dance called the Twizzle (a cross between the Twist and the Sizzle that is performed wearing tennis shoes).

*Note:* In *The Dick Van Dyke Show Revisited* special, Sally is seen living in Manhattan with her husband, Herman Glimshire.

## ALAN BRADY

*Character:* The overbearing, temperamental, easily exasperated, always-yelling star and executive producer of *The Alan Brady Show* (which ranks 17 in the ratings; airs at 8:30 p.m. opposite *Yancy Derringer* and is the highest rated show in Liberia). Alan is married to the never-seen Margaret and lives at the Temple Towers on East 61st Street in Manhattan. Alan firmly believes he should be held in admiration when he is in public and considers his viewers "the little people" and "his adoring public." Alan is perceived by most as outwardly crude, but he believes he has a soft, caring heart. Alan is very sensitive to the fact that he is bald and calls his hair pieces "fellas."

Front: Mary Tyler Moore and Dick Van Dyke; back row: Richard Deacon, Rose Marie, and Morey Amsterdam. *CBS/Photofest © CBS*

## OTHER CHARACTERS

Jerry and Millie Helper are Rob and Laura's neighbors. Jerry is a dentist and Millie a homemaker. They have an iron jockey on their front lawn and a pet mynah bird named Herschel. Rob pays Jerry $37.50 a year so that he can tar the back wall of his house (the rock in Rob's basement causes Jerry's basement to flood); Millie keeps a siren pen for protection in the porcelain bull on the fireplace mantle. Jerry and Rob owned a boat called *The Betty Lynn* (although Rob wanted to call her *Shangri-La*, and Jerry wanted the name *Challenger*). Peter Oliphant, then David Fresco, played their son, Freddie Helper.

Richie Petrie, Rob and Laura's son, has virtually no factual information. Other than attending New Rochelle Grammar School, having two pet ducks (Stanley and Oliver), saying a "bad word" (not revealed), and having been attacked by a woodpecker (who wanted his hair for a nest), he is just a typical sitcom kid—used only when needed. His favorite TV program is the mythical "Uncle Spunky Show," and his one enjoyment is asking his father what he got him when he comes home from work (the simplest of things, like a paper clip, would make him happy).

*Show Note:* Rob is paid by Alan's company, the Ishimoto Motorcycle Company; Buddy and Sally were originally paid by Alan's Dean Martin and Jerry Lewis coloring book company, Tam-O-Shatner, Ltd. When it folded, Alan's mother-in-law's company, Barracuda, Ltd, paid them. The show's band is paid by Brady Lady, Alan's wife's company.

*Note:* In the original pilot, *Head of the Family*, Carl Reiner played Rob Petrie; Barbara Britton, Laura Petrie; Morty Gunty, Buddy Sorrell; Sylvia Miles, Sally Rogers; Jack Wakefield (Alan Sturdy, host of *The Alan Sturdy Show*); and Gary Morgan, Richie Petrie.

# The Doris Day Show
## (CBS, 1968–1973)

*Cast:* Doris Day (Doris Martin), Denver Pyle (Buck Webb), Philip Brown (Billy Martin), Todd Starke (Toby Martin), McLean Stevenson (Michael Nicholson), John Dehner (Cyril Bennett).

*Basis:* A widow (Doris Martin) and the mother of two children attempts to reconstruct her life following the death of her husband.

## DORIS MARTIN
*Marital Status:* Widow.
*Children:* Billy and Toby.
*Father:* Buck Webb.
*Maiden Name:* Doris Webb.
*Family Dog:* Lord Nelson.
*Prior-to-the-Series Occupation:* Singer (performs in San Francisco).

*1968–1969 Occupation:* Housewife and mother.

*1969–1971 Occupation:* Executive secretary to Michael Nicholson at *Today's World* magazine ("The Now Magazine").

*1971–1973 Occupation:* Reporter for *Today's World* magazine with Cyril Bennett as her boss.

*1968–1969 Address:* 32 Mill Valley Road (a farm owned by Buck).

*1970–1971 Address:* 965 North Parkway (Apartment 207 over Palucci's Italian Restaurant).

*Rent:* $140 a month.

*Landlords:* Louie Palucci (Bernie Kopell) and his wife, Angie Palucci (Kaye Ballard).

*Palucci's Dog:* Sophie.

*Neighbor:* Willard Jarvis (Billy DeWolfe), a set-in-his ways bachelor who feels his life is now plagued by "The Martin Gang."

*1971–1973 Address:* Assumed to be the same at 965 North Parkway. Here, Doris Martin is depicted as a single woman (her children, her dog, and her landlords are dropped).

*Doris's Car License Plate:* 225 NOZ.

*Cyril's Car License Plate:* 495 CCF.


*Note:* Doris Day sings the theme, "Que Sera, Sera" ("Whatever Will Be Will Be"), which became associated with Doris from her role in the Alfred Hitchcock film *The Man Who Knew Too Much.*

# *F Troop*
## (ABC, 1965–1967)

*Cast:* Ken Berry (Captain Wilton Parmenter), Forrest Tucker (Sergeant Morgan O'Rourke), Larry Storch (Corporal Randolph Agarn), Melody Patterson (Wrangler Jane), Frank DeCova (Chief Wild Eagle), Don Diamond (Crazy Cat).

*Basis:* A newly commissioned army captain (Wilton Parmenter), sent to Kansas (1860s) and placed in charge of F Troop, attempts to deal with the antics of his misfit troops while also struggling to keep the peace between the white man and the Indian.

## WILTON PARMENTER

*Rank:* Captain.

*Previous Rank:* Private with the Union army's Quartermaster Corps.

*Position:* Officer in charge of laundry.

*Reputation:* The "scourge of the West." He earned the name when an excess of pollen affected his sinuses and he sneezed, blurting out what sounded like "Charge!" Soldiers on standby were led into action that foiled a Confederate plan and brought victory to the Union.

*Award:* Medal of Honor.

*Birth Month:* June.

*Reassignment:* Fort Courage in Kansas.

*Replaced:* Captain "Cannonball" Bill McCormick (Willard Waterman), who had retired.

*Troop:* The army's worst collection of misfit cavalry soldiers called F Troop (principally, Morgan O'Rourke and Randolph Agarn).

*Duty:* Maintain peace between the army and the Apache, Chiracahua, and Hewaki Indians. Unknown to Wilton, the Hekawi are friendly, but he believes they are a constant threat and may go on the warpath at any time.

*Relatives:* Daphne Parmenter, accident-prone sister (Patty Regan). She was famous for making Toll House Cookies (although the name and recipe weren't invented until 1930). Mrs. Parmenter, mother (Jeanette Nolan). In one episode, Ken Berry played his evil double, Kid Vicious. Other mentioned family members are General Thor X. Parmenter (father), Colonel Jupiter Parmenter (uncle), Achilles Parmenter (cousin), and Hercules Parmenter (cousin).

## MORGAN SYLVESTER O'ROURKE

*Ancestry:* Irish.

*Rank:* Sergeant (it took him 10 years to accomplish it).

*Prior Service:* 25-year career army officer and a nine-year veteran.

*Secret Business:* Head of O'Rourke Enterprises, a business that he operates without Wilton's knowledge from his barracks in Fort Courage.

*Other Enterprises:* O'Rourke also owns the town saloon (the Fort Courage Saloon) and the International Trading Company (which deals in Indian souvenirs, whiskey, and anything else that will make money, all of which are made by the Hewaki Indians).

*Liquor Served at the Saloon:* Apache Ale, Comanche Cognac, Hewaki Fire Water, Shoshone Sherry, and Blackfoot Bourbon. The saloon is called Pete's Place in dialogue.

*Ability:* O'Rourke is the only soldier able to read Indian smoke signals.

*Relatives:* Morgan O'Rourke Sr., father (Forrest Tucker).

## RANDOLPH AGARN

*Rank:* Corporal (which took him six years to earn).

*Middle Name:* None (as Agarn insists, "No middle name!").

*Position:* Vice president of O'Rourke Enterprises.

*Prior Position:* While nothing specific is mentioned, it appears he served with O'Rourke in the past.

*Horse:* Barney.

*Failed Business Venture:* Formed a "rock" band called the Bedbugs (an 1860s version of the Beatles that played similar music. But audiences appeared not to like them and Agarn sent them off to make it on their own).

*Club Association:* He and O'Rourke are members of the Hewaki Playbrave Club (an 1860s Playboy type of club).

*Relatives:* Agarn has a weird assortment of relatives all played by Larry Storch: El Diablo, his thieving Mexican cousin; Lucky Pierre, his French cousin, a trapper; and his Russian cousin, Dimitri Arganoff, a soldier.

## WRANGLER JANE

*Full Name:* Jane Angelica Thrift.

*Nickname:* Wrangler Jane (for her cowgirl-like abilities, including trick horse riding and her ability to handle a gun).

*Boyfriend:* Wilton Parmenter (although Wilton constantly tries to avoid her pursuit, as he feels he is not ready for marriage).

*Occupation:* Owner of Wrangler Jane's (comprises the general store, post office, and hay and feed store).

*Birth Month:* November.

*Dress Size:* 10.

*Horse:* Pecos.

*Musical Ability:* Plays the tambourine and can sing. When O'Rourke formed the "rock" group the Termites, Jane sang the songs "Lemon Tree" and "Mr. Tambourine Man."

## WILD EAGLE

*Position:* Chief of the Hewaki Indian tribe (situated on a reservation one mile from Fort Courage). He is money-hungry and has taken his tribe to a point where they have become soft and can no longer live off the land; they need the money generated by making souvenirs.

*Assistant:* Crazy Cat (who is seeking to become the tribal chief).

*Business:* Making the items, including "fire water" (whiskey) for the International Trading Company.

*Tribal Customs:* The monthly Moon Festival and the annual Hewaki Festival of the Succotash (O'Rourke fears Agarn celebrating such occasions as he gets carried away and yells, "Kill the paleface").

*Tribal Medicine Man:* Roaring Chicken (played by Edward Everett Horton).

*History:* The Hewaki are called such after two Indians fell off a cliff and one asked, "Where the heck are we?"

*Wild Eagle's Name for Wilton:* Great White Pigeon.

*Relatives:* son, Bald Eagle (Don Rickles); sister, Whispering Dove (Cathy Lewis); daughter, Silver Dove (Laurie Sibbald); nephew, Johnny Eagle Eye, an expert with a rifle (Paul Petersen); cousin, the fierce Geronimo (Mike Mazurki).

## OTHER CHARACTERS

Private Hannibal Shirley Dobbs (James Hampton), the inept company bugler, who is from Texas and mentions he was a Texas independence fighter (wounded at the Alamo); Private Vanderbilt (Joe Brooks), the almost blind tower lookout; Private Duffy (Bob Steele), a survivor of the Alamo who rambles relentlessly about his experience with Davy Crockett; Private Hoffenmeuller (John Mitchum), the German soldier who is unable to speak English; and Private Duddleston (Ivan Bell), the lazy soldier that loves to eat (as Agarn would constantly tell him, pointing to his uniform, "Gravy stains, Duddleston, gravy stains"). Nydia Westman played Hannibal's mother, Mother Dobbs.

# *Family Affair*
## (CBS, 1966–1971)

*Cast:* Brian Keith (Bill Davis), Sebastian Cabot (Giles French), Kathy Garver (Cissy Davis), Anissa Jones (Buffy Davis), Johnny Whitaker (Jody Davis).

*Basis:* A swinging bachelor (Bill Davis) tries to readjust his life to care for his orphaned nieces (Cissy and Buffy) and nephew (Jody) when their parents (Bill's brother and sister-in-law) are killed in a car accident.

## OVERALL SERIES INFORMATION

Bill Davis and his brother, Bob, where born in Terre Haute, Indiana. Bill seemed destined to remain a bachelor as he took an interest in engineering and world traveling; Bob settled down and married his high school sweetheart, Mary Patterson. Bill became a successful engineer; Bob and Mary remained in town and began a family. Cissy and twins Buffy and Jody became their children. Four years after the twins' birth, Bob and Mary are killed in an automobile accident. The children are separated and placed in the homes of relatives who are reluctant to care for them. Cissy, Buffy, and Jody become Bill's responsibility when the relatives literally drop them off on his doorstep. Unable to abandon the children and seeing that they should remain together, Bill begins the loving task of rearing three children. While not the typical "swinging bachelor," Bill has changed his life to accommodate the children. Bill still entertains the ladies but is careful not to let that overshadow his newly acquired responsibilities.

## WILLIAM "BILL" DAVIS

*Full Name:* William Lloyd Davis.

*Address:* 600 East 62nd Street, Penthouse Apartment 27A in Manhattan.

*Occupation:* Engineer. He is internationally famous, and his picture has appeared on the cover of *World* magazine for completing an extremely difficult construction job (a dam) in India.

*Company:* Davis and Gaynor Construction Company (also called Davis Engineering).

*Education:* Indiana State University (where he acquired a degree in engineering).

*Note:* In the *Family Affair* update (WB, 2002), Bill (played by Gary Cole) is part owner of Davis-Hartwell-Newberg Industries (first called Davis-Hartwell Engineering). His address is given as Apartment 18A at 85 Park Avenue in Manhattan.

## CATHERINE "CISSY" DAVIS
*Age:* 15.

*Education:* Lexington High School (nicknamed Lexy High) in Manhattan. Bill had originally planned to send her to the Briarfield School in Connecticut but changed his mind when he saw how Buffy and Jody missed her.

*Place of Birth:* Terre Haute, Indiana.

*Parents:* Bob and Mary Davis (deceased). Cissy was originally sent to her Aunt Jenny and Uncle Doug in Ohio after the car accident.

*Personality:* Typical teenage girl with no set goals in life. She did work as a candy striper in the local hospital and had thoughts of becoming a nurse. In last-season episodes, Cissy attends an unnamed college and is dating Gregg Bartlett (Gregg Fedderson), a gas station attendant at the Mid-Town Service Station.

*Note:* In the *Family Affair* update, Cissy (played by Caitlin Wachs) has the real name Sigourney Elizabeth Davis. Here, Cissy is portrayed as a teenager who yearns to become an actress. She attends the High School for the Lively Arts at 79th Street and Broadway (the school is also called the Performing Arts High School) and performed in a production of *Pygmalion*. She was a member of the Antionettes, a social club for young ladies, and could write poetry, sing, dance, and act. In the episode "A Family Affair Christmas" (December 5, 2002), Kathy Garver appears in the role of a passenger at the airport. Her parents were said to be Ken and Laura (not Bob and Mary).

## BUFFY AND JODY DAVIS
*Relationship:* The twin sister and brother of Cissy.

*Place of Birth:* Terre Haute, Indiana.

*Age:* 6.

*Real Names:* Ava Elizabeth "Buffy" Davis and Jonathan "Jody" Davis.

*Education:* Dove Tail School.

*Room:* Buffy and Cissy share a bedroom; Jody has his own room.

*Buffy's Doll:* Mrs. Beasley (which she cherishes, as it was her mother's doll when she was a child). Buffy doesn't like people to call Mrs. Beasley a doll: "She's my friend." Mrs. Beasley suffered some "horrific" incidents, such as being lost, falling off a building, and, the most devastating of all, losing an arm when Buffy and Jody fought over her (a local doll hospital repaired the damage). While Mrs. Beasley is seen wearing eyeglasses, she did not wear them in the pilot episode.

Kathy Garver, Anissa Jones, Brian Keith, Sebastian Cabot, and Johnny Whitaker. *CBS/Photofest © CBS*

*Buffy's Hairstyle:* Blonde hair in curly twin pony tails.
*Jody's Pet Turtle:* Dinky.
*Sports:* Jody and Buffy love to play stickball (for the 63rd Street Tigers), and
  Jody is the quarterback on the neighborhood football team, the Spartans
  (he wears jersey 24).

*Favorite TV Show:* Buffy and Jody enjoy *Captain Hippopotamus.*

*Clubs:* Jody was a member of the Dare Devils Club, Buffy the more genteel Mod
Maidens Club.

*First Crush:* While Buffy accepted boys, Jody did not really like girls until he
"discovered" one his own age—Geraldine Haskins (Lisa Gerritsen), a girl
who didn't know what to make of his misguided attempts to impress her.

*Note:* In the *Family Affair* update, Sasha Pierese played Buffy, and Jimmy
Pinchak was Jody. Here, the twins shared the guest room (as opposed to having separate rooms) and were a bit more mischievous and rambunctious than
originally portrayed.

## GILES FRENCH

*Relationship:* Bill's "gentleman's gentleman" and often called Mr. French. He
is most proud of his beard. Before the children arrived, he considered his
employment as "the ideal bachelor existence." The kids think of him as "the
alarm clock for school."

*Place of Birth:* England.

*Prior Employment:* The Duke of Glenmore.

*Business Venture:* Attempted to open his own restaurant, Our Mr. French's.

*Expertise:* Excellent gourmet cook and fastidious housekeeper. He also cares for
the children when Bill is away on long business trips. He would often read
passages from Buffy and Jody's favorite book, *Winnie the Pooh,* to them at
bedtime.

*Spokesperson:* Mr. French was chosen to represent a jam product called Marma-
lade.

*Replacement:* When Sebastian Cabot became ill, his brother, Niles French
(John Williams), took over his duties as gentleman's gentleman for a
short time.

*Note:* Tim Curry played the role of Mr. French in the *Family Affair* update. The
character remained basically the same.

# *The Flintstones*
## (ABC, 1960–1966)

*Voice Cast:* Alan Reed (Fred Flintstone); Jean Vander Pyl (Wilma and Pebbles
Flintstone); Mel Blanc (Barney Rubble); Bea Benaderet, then Gerry Johnson (Betty Rubble); Don Messick (Bamm Bamm Rubble and Dino).

*Basis:* It is the year 1,000,056 BC, and two modern-day cave families (the Flintstones and the Rubbles) living in the town of Bedrock attempt to cope with the numerous problems of everyday life.

## FRED FLINTSTONE

*Place of Birth:* Bedrock.
*Wife:* Wilma.
*Daughter:* Pebbles.
*Address:* 345 Stone Cave Road (also said to be Cobblestone Lane).
*Job:* Dino operator for the Slaterock Gravel Company. It is also seen as the Rockhead Quarry Construction Company, the Bedrock Quarry Gravel Company, the Bedrock Gravel Company, and the Rockhead Quarry Cove Construction Company. His boss is George Slate (also called Howard Slate and George Slaterock).
*Prior Occupation:* Bellboy at the Honeyrock Hotel.
*Lodge:* A member of the Loyal Order of the Water Buffalo (originally called the Loyal Order of Dinosaurs).
*Sports:* Fred is a member of the Bedrock Quarry baseball team and enjoys bowling at the Bedrock Bowling Alley. The Bedrock Boulders is Fred's favorite baseball team.
*Education:* Fred attended Rockville Center High School (where he was a member of the football team. He wore jersey 22 and was called "Fireball Freddy." As a member of the baseball team he was called "Five Ball Freddy").
*Scout Troop:* As a child, Fred was a member of the Saber Tooth Tigers Troop.
*Favorite Dinner:* Bronto Burgers and pterodactyl pie.
*Catchphrase:* "Yabba dabba doo."
*Family Pet:* Dino, a snarkasaurus (purple with black spots on his back).

## WILMA FLINTSTONE

*Husband:* Fred.
*Daughter:* Pebbles.
*Place of Birth:* Bedrock.
*Birth Sign:* Capricorn.
*Maiden Name:* Wilma Flaghoople.
*Specialty:* Fixes the best roast dodo bird in Bedrock.
*Occupation:* Housewife and mother.
*Prior Occupation:* Waitress at the Honeyrock Hotel (where she first met Fred. They have been married for 16 years when the series begins). Singer on the

TV show *The Rockingbird Happy Housewives Show* (for the sponsor, the Bedrock Radio and TV Company).

*Ability:* Being patient and putting up with Fred and all his nonsense (seeking get-rich-quick schemes).

*Animated First:* Wilma became the first animated figure to become pregnant on TV.

## BERNARD "BARNEY" RUBBLE

*Relationship:* Fred and Wilma's neighbor.

*Address:* 343 Stone Cave Road.

*Wife:* Betty.

*Son:* Bamm-Bamm (adopted).

*Place of Birth:* Granite Town.

*Prior Address:* 142 Boulder Avenue.

*Occupation:* Dino operator for the Pebble Rock and Gravel Company, then for the same companies as listed above for Fred.

*Prior Occupation:* Bellboy (with Fred) at the Honeyrock Hotel.

*Education:* Bedrock High School (where he was a member of the Beta Slatta Gamma fraternity).

*Sports:* Coaches the Giants Little League baseball team. He is a member of the Bedrock Quarry baseball team and bowls with Fred at the Bedrock Bowling Alley.

*Favorite Breakfast:* Rock Toasties cereal.

## BETTY RUBBLE

*Husband:* Barney.

*Son:* Bamm-Bamm (adopted). She and Barney wished for a child (apparently unable to have their own) on a falling star. The following morning, they found an orphan on their doorstep with a note attached asking them to care for their little Bamm-Bamm (who has incredible strength).

*Maiden Name:* Betty Jean McBricker.

*Occupation:* Housewife.

*Prior Occupation:* Waitress at the Honeyrock Hotel (where she worked with Wilma).

*Family Pet:* Hoppy (a hoparoo).

## OVERALL SERIES INFORMATION

In the opening theme, the film seen on the theater marquee is *The Monster*. The population of Bedrock is 2,500. Arnold (voice of Don Messick) is the newspaper boy who delivers the *Bugle*; John Stephenson provides the voice for Mr. Slate. The program is actually an animated version of *The Honeymooners*.

# *The Flying Nun*
(ABC, 1967–1970)

*Cast:* Sally Field (Sister Bertrille), Madeleine Sherwood (Reverend Mother Plasceato), Marge Redmond (Sister Jacqueline), Alejandro Rey (Carlos Ramirez), Linda Dangcil (Sister Ana), Shelley Morrison (Sister Sixto).

*Basis:* A young Catholic nun (Sister Bertrille) uses her gift of flight to help the less fortunate people of the town of San Tanco in San Juan, Puerto Rico.

## SISTER BERTRILLE

*Real Name:* Elsie Ethrington.

*Residence:* Chicago.

*Family:* Her father, a doctor; her mother, a surgical nurse; her brother, a second-year medical student; and her sister, Jennifer, an obstetrician with the Peace Corps (it is later said Jennifer is a doctor at Manhattan General Hospital in New York City).

*Age:* 18.

*Weight:* 90 pounds.

*Height:* 5 feet, 2 inches tall.

*Education:* Westside High School in California (where she was voted "Most Far-Out Girl of 1965").

*1966 Rock Band:* The Gorries (this and Westside High are references to Sally Field's prior series *Gidget* that were used for *The Flying Nun*).

*1966 Summer Job:* Counselor at Camp Laughing Rock.

*Inspiration:* Her aunt, who worked as a missionary and instilled in Elsie the ambition to become a nun. Elsie was expected to follow in the family tradition and become a doctor.

*Order:* The Sisters of San Tanco.

*Habits Colors:* Blue and white (in some episodes, the habits look to be eggshell white or antique white).

*Convent:* The Convent San Tanco. The convent was established in 1572 on land given to the Sisters by King Philip of Spain. The Sisters pay $1 a year in rent (on a 99-year lease). On-screen, it is seen as Convento San Tanco.

*Convent Pet Cat:* Delfinia.

*San Tanco Population:* 3,956.

*Ability:* Flight. Her white coronets (headgear) have sides that resemble wings. San Tanco is an area affected by trade winds. Due to Sister Bertrille's light weight, strong gale winds lift her off the ground and enable her to fly (landings are difficult, but she does gain control of her flying by manipulating her coronets). "When lift plus thrust is greater than load plus drag, objects fly," as Sister Bertrille explains.

*Temporary Job:* Newspaper advice columnist (as "Dear Aggie") for the San Tanco *Tribune.*

*Activities:* Coaches the San Tanco Orphanage team, a baseball team sponsored by Casino Carlos.

*Talent:* Plays the guitar and sings.

*TV Debut:* Sister Bertrille sang the song "The World Inside You" on the local kids television series *Claudio the Clown* (Paul Winchell played Claudio).

*Teaching Assignment:* English, music appreciation, and sewing.

*Relatives:* sister, Jennifer Ethrington (Elinor Donahue); uncle, Reggie (Dick Gautier).

## OTHER CHARACTERS

The Reverend Mother Plasceato is Sister Bertrille's superior; Sister Jacqueline assists the Reverend Mother (as a kid, Jacqueline was the tennis champion of the Maple Street Bloomer Girls and worked as a file clerk for an advertising firm before deciding to become a nun).

Carlos Ramirez is the playboy owner of a discotheque called Casino Carlos A-Go-Go (also seen as the gambling and nightclub Club Carlos) in San Juan (which is five miles from the convent). It is often Carlos who helps the nuns out when they are in financial difficulty. Henry Corden was Carlos's uncle, Antonio, and Frank Silvera was Carlos's uncle, Thomas.

Pamelyn Ferdin plays Carlos's niece, Linda Shapiro, a young girl called "The Little Nun," who admires Sister Bertrille and yearns to follow in her footsteps. June Whitley and Laurence Haddon played Linda's mother and father.

Vito Scotti is the fumbling local police officer, Gaspar Formento, and Don Diamond is his superior, Chief Galindo.

# *The Fugitive*
### (ABC, 1963–1967)

*Cast:* David Janssen (Dr. Richard Kimble), Barry Morse (Lieutenant Philip Gerard), Bill Raisch (Fred Johnson).

*Basis:* Richard Kimble, falsely convicted for the murder of his wife and sentenced to death, escapes authorities and begins a search for the real killer—a mysterious one-armed man (Fred Johnson) he saw leave the scene of the crime on the night of the murder. (Richard was returning home, caught a glimpse of Johnson running from his home, and found his wife, Helen, killed by Johnson as he attempted to rob the house. Johnson had hit her with the base of a lamp when she caught him by surprise.)

## DR. RICHARD KIMBLE

*Parents:* John and Elizabeth Kimble.

*Birthday:* March 27, 1927.

*Place of Birth:* Stafford, Indiana.

*Wife:* Helen Kimball (maiden name Helen Watkins).

*Education:* Cornell University.

*Internship:* Fairgreen County Hospital in Stafford.

*Residency:* Chicago's Memorial Hospital (later opened his own practice).

*Specialty:* Pediatrics and obstetrics.

*Height:* 6 feet.

*Weight:* 175 pounds.

*Crime:* Wanted for the murder of his wife and interstate flight. (Life was progressing smoothly for Richard and Helen until Helen became pregnant but lost the baby [a stillbirth]. Helen was diagnosed with an inability to have children, and she and Richard argued constantly over the prospect of adoption [Helen was opposed, feeling it would be living with a lie]. It was these arguments that led authorities to believe Kimble killed his wife.)

*Hair:* Salt and pepper (as a fugitive, he dyes it black).

*Indiana Court Case:* 33972. (Found Richard guilty of the murder of his wife. His defense, that he found Helen dead and saw a one-armed man running from the scene of the crime, was dismissed when no evidence could be found to substantiate his claim.)

*Booking File Number:* KB 7601863.

*Finger Print Classification:* 19M 9400013 L24001.

*Court Verdict:* Found guilty and sentenced to death.

*Officer Assigned to Kimble:* Lieutenant Philip Gerard.

*Relatives:* Donna Taft, sister (Jacqueline Scott); Ray Kimble, brother (Andrew Prine); Leonard Taft, Donna's husband (James B. Sikking, then Richard Anderson); Dr. John Kimble, father (Robert Keith); Helen Kimble, wife, flashbacks (Diane Brewster); Marie Gerard, Philip's wife, maiden name Marie Lindsey (Barbara Rush); name also given as Ann Gerard and played by Rachel Ames; David Taft, Donna's son (Bill Mumy); Billy Taft, Donna's son (Clint Howard, then Johnny Jensen).

## OVERALL SERIES INFORMATION

Kimble, being escorted by Gerard to the "death house," frees himself when the train on which they are traveling derails. Although Gerard has sworn to capture his escaped prisoner and relentlessly pursues him, Kimble begins a seemingly impossible mission to find the mysterious one-armed man who killed Helen. He often faces arrest when his strong sense of helping injured or sick people takes priority over his own safety, making for compelling and suspenseful stories.

David Janssen. *ABC/Photofest © ABC*

*Note:* A revised version of *The Fugitive* appeared on CBS in 2000. It follows the same overall concept but changes the facts.

*CBS Cast:* Tim Daly (Dr. Richard Kimble), Mykelti Williamson (Lieutenant Philip Gerard), Stephen Lang (Fred Johnson).

At the conclusion of the trial, *State of Illinois v. Dr. Richard Kimble*, Richard is found guilty of the murder of his wife (Helen) and sentenced to death (by lethal injection at the Joliet State Prison). "I didn't kill my wife," Richard insisted, claiming he returned home one night to find Helen, lying in a pool of blood. As he tried to help Helen, he encountered the culprit, a one-armed man who escaped when Richard chose to help Helen rather than chase the man (later discovered to be Fred Johnson). That night, Richard and Helen discussed the prospect of buying a new house. On his way home from the hospital, Richard stopped to buy Helen flowers; "If I didn't, she might still be alive," he says.

Richard, police file 760813, was assigned to Lieutenant Philip Gerard for transport to Menard a police van (number 598). En route, the van swerves to avoid hitting a car and overturns. Richard escapes but is relentlessly pursued by Gerard, who is determined to recapture him.

Although both versions feature Richard receiving help from the various people he meets, the CBS version uses the latest technology with Richard creating a website (www.richardkimble.com) that asks people for help and money for his defense (authorities believe Richard murdered Helen to collect her $20 million inheritance).

The ABC version ended with Richard being cleared when a witness to the crime came forward to reveal that it was the one-armed man who killed Helen. The CBS edition ended in an unresolved cliffhanger with Richard finding Johnson (but not being able to get a confession out of him) and Gerard closing in on both of them.

# Get Smart
## (NBC, 1965–1969; CBS, 1969–1970)

*Cast:* Don Adams (Maxwell Smart), Barbara Feldon (Agent 99), Edward Platt (Chief), Bernie Kopell (Siegfried), Dick Gautier (Hymie).

*Basis:* A bumbling secret agent for CONTROL (Maxwell Smart) and his beautiful, levelheaded partner, Agent 99, attempt to thwart the evils of KAOS, an organization bent on world domination.

## CONTROL

*Address:* 123 Main Street in Washington, D.C. It is accessed by entering a pay telephone booth inside the building. As the floor lowers, the agents must pass through a series of eight iron gates before entering headquarters.

*Telephone Number:* 555-3734.

*Agency Head:* A man identified only as Thaddeus but called Chief.

*Chief's Cover:* Howard Clark, owner of the Pontiac Greeting Card Company.

*Former Head of CONTROL:* Admiral Harold Harmon Hargrade (played by William Schallert).

*Dog Agent:* Fang (Agent K-13).

*Security Debugging Device:* The seldom-working Cone of Silence.

*Robotic Agent:* Hymie (a former KAOS robot that was captured and reprogrammed for good; its major fault is that it takes everything literally).

*CONTROL Computer:* Aardvark.

*Enemy:* KAOS and its evil leader Siegfried (in the pilot episode, the leader was a man called Big).

*KAOS Symbol:* A vulture standing on top of the world.

## MAXWELL SMART

*Address:* Apartment 86 at the Cherry Arms Apartments.

*Agent Number:* 86. He is sometimes called 86, and being a spy is the only thing he has ever known.

*Cover:* Maxwell Smart, salesman for the Pontiac Greeting Card Company.

*Fault:* A bumbling klutz.

*Fears:* Lightning and gollywoggles.

*Attributes:* He believes his constant vigilance and razor-sharp instincts are his weapons for defeating KAOS (in particular, the German-accented Siegfried, who believes Maxwell is a threat and has put out the word to all evil agents: "Get Schmart").

*Height:* Max first claims he is 5 feet 9 inches tall, then 5 feet 11 inches tall.

*Weight:* 150 pounds.

*Birth Sign:* Scorpio (it was mentioned only that Max was born in 1930).

*Jacket Size:* 40 regular.

*Phone:* Standard-issue shoe phone.

*Salary:* $35,000 a year.

*Red Sunbeam Car License Plate:* 6A7 379 (also seen as 9G 893). In the pilot, Max drove a Ferrari 250GT (the car was red in the first two seasons, blue in seasons three and four, and bronze in the final season).

*Password for His Booby-Trapped Apartment:* Bismarck.

*Catchphrases:* "Sorry about that Chief," "I asked you not to tell me that," and "Would you believe . . ."

*Idol:* Legendary spy Herb Gaffer, Agent 4.

*Relatives:* uncle, Albert (Charles Lane); aunt, Bertha (Maudie Pritchett). Both regret having Max as a family member and are not sure which side of the family he comes from.

*Note:* In one episode, "Ice Station Siegfried," Max didn't appear (Don Adams was said to be suffering from exhaustion) and was replaced by Bill Dana as Agent Quigley.

## AGENT 99

*Real Name:* Top secret and never revealed (although she does use aliases; because stations are editing program content for more commercials, key dialogue regarding that aspect is often cut, leading viewers to believe her real name is being said).

*Character:* Very little information is revealed about Agent 99 (also called 99). She is very bright and relies on her years of spy training and intuition to solve cases despite the problems that Max's constant bumbling cause. She has no specific cover name (other than working with Max at the Pontiac Greeting Card Company), and eventually she and Max fall in love and marry (in episode 95). They set up housekeeping in Max's apartment and

Barbara Feldon and Don Adams. *ABC/Photofest © ABC*

toward the end of the series became the parents of twins. Max calls her only 99 (he calls her mother 99's Mother and Mrs. 99). Shortly after becoming husband and wife, their work together earned them the title "Spy Couple of the Year" in 1968. It was revealed that 99's father was a spy, and 99 followed in his footsteps.

*Relatives:* mother (Jane Dulo).

**OTHER CHARACTERS**

Agent 13 (Dave Ketchum) is the agent who can go undercover in virtually anything (from a washing machine to a grandfather clock), Charlie Watkins (Angelique Pettyjohn) appears as a gorgeous and shapely woman who Max has a hard time believing is a man in disguise, Larabee (Robert Karvelas) is Chief's dim-witted assistant, Schtarker (King Moody) is Siegfried's bumbling assistant, and Joey Forman is Harry Hoo, the famous Oriental detective (a spoof of Charlie Chan).

**UPDATES**

In the 1989 ABC TV movie *Get Smart Again*, it is revealed that CONTROL was deactivated in 1974 and its records stored in a warehouse at 96427 43rd Street in Washington, D.C. It is 1989 when CONTROL must be reactivated when KAOS threatens the world with a stolen weather machine. Commander Drury (Ken Mars) of U.S. Intelligence reassembles the CONTROL team to stop KAOS.

Maxwell Smart (Don Adams) is now a protocol officer for the State Department; 99 (Barbara Feldon), still not identified with a name, is writing her memoirs in a book called *Out of Control*; Hymie the robot (Dick Gautier) has been working as a crash dummy for the National Car Testing Institute; and Agent 13 (Dave Ketchum) has been engaged in various undercover government assignments. Hover Cover (agents speaking on a roof over the noise of helicopters) has replaced the Cone of Silence.

The series revival *Get Smart* (Fox, 1995) finds Maxwell Smart (Don Adams) as the new Chief of CONTROL. 99 (Barbara Feldon) is a congresswoman and, while she is still without a name, explains, "I don't like to be called Mrs. Smart. That makes me feel like 100. Call me 99." Max and 99's son, Zack (Andy Dick), has become an agent for CONTROL, and his cover is that of executive vice president of the Pontiac Greeting Card Company. Agent 66 (Elaine Hendrix) is Zack's assistant, a beautiful woman also without a real name (although, she says, "It's tattooed on my body somewhere, but nobody is seeing it"). Agent 66 (99's name upside down) wears a "Bullet Bra" (a round in each cup) that doubles as her "bra phone." Siegfried (Bernie Kopell) is still the head of KAOS but is now assisted by his beautiful but evil daughter Gretchen (Leah Lail).

# *The Ghost and Mrs. Muir*

### (NBC, 1968–1969; ABC, 1969–1970)

*Cast:* Hope Lange (Carolyn Muir), Edward Mulhare (Captain Daniel Gregg), Kellie Flanagan (Candy Muir), Harlen Carraher (Jonathan Muir), Charles Nelson Reilly (Claymore Gregg), Reta Shaw (Martha Grant).

*Basis:* A widow (Carolyn Muir) with two children (Candy and Jonathan) attempts to make a new life for herself in a small New England town in a home haunted by the ghost of its former owner (Captain Daniel Gregg). Based on the feature film of the same title.

## CAROLYN MUIR

*Parents:* Emily and Brad Williams.

*Place of Birth:* Philadelphia.

*Year of Birth:* 1931.

*Marital Status:* Widow.

*Children:* Candace (Candy) and Jonathan.

*Occupation:* Freelance writer. She later acquires a position with the town newspaper, the Schooner Bay *Beacon.*

*Address:* Gull cottage in the town of Schooner Bay, Maine. Carolyn finds Gull Cottage to be "a dear, gentle, lovely little cottage" and Schooner Bay the perfect town to raise children. She has made Captain Greg's former bedroom ("The Captain's Cabin") her bedroom.

*Favorite Eatery:* The Lobster House.

*Organization:* Member of the local Community Theater.

*Custom:* On Tuesday afternoons, Carolyn meets with the captain in the Wheelhouse at 2:00 p.m. for a glass of Madeira.

*Relatives:* mother, Emily Williams (Jane Wyatt); father, Brad Williams (Leon Ames); uncle, Arnold (Jack Gilford).

## CAPTAIN DANIEL GREGG

*Year of Birth:* 1828.

*Place of Birth:* Schooner Bay, Maine.

*Home:* Gull Cottage (which he originally built as a home for retired sailors).

*Occupation:* Daniel grew up amid the fishing industry and eventually became a fisherman, then the captain of his own ship.

*Trait:* As he calls himself, "A scoundrel; a notorious ladies' man with a girl in every port."

*1868:* Captain Gregg planted the Monkey Puzzle Tree, which still stands on the grounds of Gull Cottage (which he built himself).

*Tragedy:* One night in November 1868, a southwest gale approached the town, and Daniel closed his bedroom windows. While sleeping, "I kicked the blasted gas heater with my blasted foot" and was killed by the escaping fumes. The coroner's jury brought in a verdict of suicide "because my confounded cleaning woman testified that I slept with my windows open."

*Retraction:* It took 100 years, but the local paper reversed its original story on the captain's death and reported that it was not a suicide but an accident.

*Personality:* Balks at having to share his home, but he does see that Carolyn loves the house and allows her to stay. Carolyn is the first woman he has ever allowed to share his "ship" (as he calls the house) and he watches over her from the porch above Carolyn's bedroom. He now considers the Wheelhouse (the attic) his only retreat from Carolyn and her kids.

*Catchphrase:* "Blast" and "Blasted." He calls Carolyn "Madame" (and Carolyn can predict when the captain becomes angry by the barometer on the living room wall; it reads "Stormy Weather"). Martha Grant, the housekeeper, calls Daniel "The Old Barnacle."

*Enjoyment:* Watching Candy and Jonathan playing—although he will never admit it. He would also like peace and quiet but rarely gets it.

*Literary Achievement:* Attempted to write a book about a female stowaway on a ship called *Maiden Voyage*.

*First and Only Love:* An enchanting girl named Vanessa, whom he met in the 1840s but never married, as the sea was his life.

*Endorsement:* A photograph of Captain Gregg appears as the label of Yankee Skipper Clam Chowder.

*Note:* In one episode, Edward Mulhare played his look-alike, Sean Callahan, an Irish writer and author of a book about the captain called *The Great Ghost Gregg*.

## OTHER CHARACTERS

Claymore Gregg, Daniel's wimpy descendant (although Daniel insists he is not related to him. "I am the only son of an only son. I've never met Claymore's grandmother. I've been trying to tell him that for years, but every time he sees me, he faints"). In some episodes, Daniel does call Claymore his nephew. Claymore owns Claymore Gregg Real Estate Sales and Services (it was Claymore who rented Gull Cottage to Carolyn when it became his inheritance). Claymore is also the town justice of the peace and notary public.

Noorie Coolidge (Dabbs Greer) owns the Lobster House restaurant; Ed Peevy (Guy Raymond) is the town's handyman (charges $1.75 an hour). Jonathan and Candy attend the Schooner Bay School. Scruffy is the Muir family dog.

# *Gidget*
## (ABC, 1965–1966)

*Cast:* Sally Field (Frances "Gidget" Lawrence), Don Porter (Russell Lawrence), Lynette Winter (Larue), Betty Conner (Annie Cooper), Peter Deuel (John Cooper).

*Basis:* A 15½-year-old girl, Frances Lawrence, and her experiences as she discovers the world of surfing.

## FRANCES "GIDGET" LAWRENCE

*Father:* Russell Lawrence. Her mother is deceased.

*Sibling:* Annie, her older sister.

*Best Friend:* Larue.

*Address:* 803 North Dutton Drive, Santa Monica, California.

*Telephone Number:* GRantite 5-5099, later 477-0599. She has her own pink princess phone in her bedroom.

*Day of Transition:* June 23, 1965: "The day I fell in love with two things: My Moondoggie [boyfriend] and surfing."

*Nickname:* Gidget (called as such by her surfer friends—"A girl who is neither tall or a midget, a Gidget").

*Education:* Westside High School.

*School Activities:* President of the Civics Club and writer of the "Helpful Hannah" advice column for the school newspaper, the *Westside Jester.*

*Rock Band Affiliation:* The Young People (later called Gidget and the Gorries).

*Preferred Nail Polish Color:* Perpetual Emotion Pink.

*Boyfriend:* Jeff Matthews (Stephen Mines), a student at Princeton University and nicknamed Moondoggie (as he is a surfer).

*After-School Hangout:* The Shaggy Dog, the shake shop; Pops (all hamburger joints); and the Spring Street Theater (for movies).

*Jobs:* Delivery girl for Buds 'n' Blooms (a flower shop) and waitress at Kicks, a teen club.

*Beach Swimwear:* A conservative bikini.

*Philosophy:* "Why can't we be born with maturity and lose it as we grow older and don't need it?"

*Catchphrase:* "Toodles" (which she says for "good-bye").

## LARUE

*Age:* 16 (five months older than Gidget). She attends the same school and hangouts as Gidget. Her last name is never mentioned.

*Passion:* Horses (has an old gelding named Snowball).

*Self-Opinion:* While Gidget is bright and bubbly, Larue is her complete opposite and considers herself a "Limpnick" ("a left-footed, lopsided jerk. I can't walk right or even sit right"). Deep down, Larue really doesn't care "because when the people I like are happy, I'm happy. I really don't care what other people think." Russ offers his own opinion: "You're a rare bird, a genuinely happy, unselfish person."

*Quirk:* She and Gidget enjoy a snack before dinner.

*Allergies:* Roses and direct sun (she has to wear "cover-up clothes [like large hats] and has an "ox" reputation [the surfers can't understand why Gidget hangs out "with an ox like that"]). Gidget knows Larue is pretty but self-conscious and wants to "blow that wall and demolish it out of existence" (which she tries to do with makeovers).

## OTHER CHARACTERS
Russell Lawrence, called Russ, is Gidget's father, an English professor at UCLA. He often calls Gidget "Gidge," and, other than being a widower, nothing else concerning his background is given. Annie Cooper, Gidget's sister, is married to John Cooper, a graduate student pursuing his degree in psychology. He and Annie live in Apartment 17 (address not given), and Gidget believes that John is a bit "whacko, and it is going to be a contest to see whether they'll let him practice or put him away." Annie believes Russ is too permissive with Gidget and worries "so much about my little sister" that she has become like a parent to her ("I know Annie means well," says Gidget, "but I wish she would stop being my mother").

*Note:* The series is based on the Sandra Dee feature film of the same title. In the 1986 syndicated series update *The New Gidget*, Caryn Richman plays Gidget as Frances "Gidget" Griffin (as she is now married to Jeff Griffin [Dean Butler], a Los Angeles city planner). Larue has been given a last name (Powell) and works with Gidget at her company, Gidget Travel. Gidget and Jeff live at 656 Glendale Avenue, and they care for Danni Collins (Sydney Penny), Annie and John's daughter (who are away on business). William Schallert now portrays Gidget's father, Russell Lawrence.

# *Gilligan's Island*
## (CBS, 1964–1967)

*Cast:* Alan Hale Jr. (the Skipper), Bob Denver (Gilligan), Tina Louise (Ginger Grant), Jim Backus (Thurston Howell III), Natalie Schafer (Lovey Howell), Dawn Wells (Mary Ann), Russell Johnson (the Professor).

*Basis:* Following a shipwreck, seven survivors (the Skipper, Gilligan, Ginger, Thurston and Lovey Howell, Mary Ann, and the Professor) seek a way off the island on which they are now stranded (located at 140 degrees latitude and 10 degrees longitude). In the series, the passengers engaged in a three-hour tour; in the original pilot, it was a six-hour tour.

## THE SKIPPER
*Real Name:* Jonas Grumby.
*Occupation:* Captain of the Hawaii-based sightseeing boat SS *Minnow*. It was during a three-hour tour that his ship became engulfed by a tropical storm and was beached on an uncharted island 300 miles southeast

of Hawaii. It was the Skipper's quick thinking that saved the lives of his crew and passengers. Jonas lost everything when his boat was destroyed, but he plans to use the insurance money to start over again (although in a later episode he says he wants to reenlist in the navy when they are rescued).

*History:* Jonas saw action in the South Pacific during World War II as a navy man and earned the rank of captain. He played football in high school and is an excellent poker player.

*Height:* 6 feet, 3 inches.

*Weight:* 221 pounds (then 199 pounds).

*Favorite Steak Sandwich:* "A filet between two top sirloins."

*Quirks:* He is superstitious and concerned about voodoo curses (as he witnessed a number of peculiar happenings in his dealings with native tribes).

*Shirt Color:* Always seen in a blue shirt.

*Favorite Vegetable:* String beans.


*Note:* In the hut that the Skipper and Gilligan share, they have a bunk bed–like setup: Gilligan sleeps in the top hammock; the Skipper on the bottom.

Carroll O'Connor was the first choice to play the role. The *Minnow* was named after then chairman of the Federal Communications Commission, Newton Minow, who tagged television as a "vast wasteland."

## GILLIGAN

*Occupation:* Jonas's bumbling first mate (whom he calls Little Buddy). Gilligan met Jonas during a hitch in the navy (Gilligan saved Jonas's life when he pushed him out of the way of a depth charge that had come loose on the ship on which they were stationed).

*Place of Birth:* Pennsylvania. He mentioned that he was president of his grammar school camera club.

*Pet:* Herman (a turtle). On the island, he has a pet duck named Gretchen.

*Best Stateside Friend:* Skinny Mulligan.

*Prior Job:* Gas station attendant before joining the navy.

*Favorite Island Food:* Coconut, papaya, and tuna fish pie.

*Lucky Charm:* A not-so-lucky rabbit's foot (as Gilligan is very mishap prone, and his antics always cost the castaways a way off the island). His image is carved in wood on the top of a totem pole (he resembles the former native inhabitants' king).

*Residence:* He shares a hut with the Skipper.

*Hobby:* Fishing and listening to kid shows on the radio from the salvaged battery-powered radio that is the only means of communication the castaways have with the outside world.

*Shirt Color:* Always seen in a red shirt.
*Favorite Vegetable:* Spinach.

*Note:* Jerry Van Dyke was the first choice to play the role. Although Gilligan never had a first name (Bob Denver insisted that Gilligan was his character's first name), producer Sherwood Schwartz mentioned that Willy was to be the first name but was never used.

## GINGER GRANT
*Occupation:* Movie actress.
*Place of Birth:* California.
*Measurements:* 38-27-35 (also given as 36-25-36, 36-22-36, and 37-25-36).
*Nickname* (in Hollywood): Miss Hour Glass ("They said I had all the sand in the right places").
*Feature Film Credits: Belly Dancers from Bali Bali, Mohawk over the Moon, The Rain Dancers of Rango Rango, San Quentin Blues,* and *A Song of Sing Sing.*
*Television Role:* A nurse on the ABC series *Ben Casey.*
*First Show Business Job:* A stage act with Merlin the Mind Reader.
*Favorite Radio Program: The Hollywood Gossip Report.*
*Favorite Snack:* Dates ("Not the kind you date; the kind you eat," as Ginger says).
*Character:* With her gorgeous features, Ginger changed her style to embrace those of legendary sex symbol Marilyn Monroe. She became a popular star of romantic comedies but believed she could have been a major star with her role of Cleopatra in the Broadway production of *Pyramid for Two* (the role she was offered before the shipwreck). Ginger has virtually no wardrobe (she originally had only the gown she wore on the cruise; she later makes a skintight dress from the ship's sail and as the series progressed suddenly had a varied and often sexy wardrobe). Despite the deplorable conditions on the island, Ginger remains alluring and sexy, shares a hut with Mary Ann, and has learned to fend for herself, cooking, gathering firewood, and doing the laundry.

*Note:* Jayne Mansfield was the first choice to play the role. In the original pilot, Ginger (played by Kit Smith) was a bright and pretty secretary. In the first two TV movie updates, *Rescue from Gilligan's Island* (1978) and *The Castaways on Gilligan's Island* (1979), Judith Baldwin played Ginger. Constance Forsland became Ginger in the final TV movie, *The Harlem Globetrotters on Gilligan's Island* (1981).

## THURSTON HOWELL III
*Wife:* Lovey Howell.
*Nickname:* The Wolf of Wall Street.

*Company:* Howell Industries (one subsidiary, the Thurston Howell Battery Company, is mentioned).

*Education:* Thurston first says SMU (Super Millionaires University), then Harvard University.

*Status:* Retired (he says he doesn't need to work because "dear daddy left me everything").

*Security Blanket:* Teddy (his teddy bear).

*Favorite Clubs:* The New York Stock Exchange and the Oyster Bay Yacht Club.

*Favorite Reading Matter:* The Social Register.

*Favorite Stock:* Amalgamated.

*Favorite Sports:* Fox hunting and polo.

*Convictions:* Convicted six times on antitrust suits and is constantly being investigated by the Internal Revenue Service for tax evasion.

*Practice Polo Pony:* Bruce (made out of bamboo by the Professor).

*Relaxation:* Playing golf and listening to the stock market reports on the radio.

*Favorite Vegetable:* Artichokes.

## LOVEY HOWELL

*Real First Name:* Eunice.

*Maiden Name:* Eunice Wentworth.

*Education:* Harvard University (where she met Thurston and married him in 1944).

*Heritage:* Dates back to the days of Christopher Columbus. The diamond broach she is seen wearing has been in her family since Queen Isabella presented it to Columbus.

*Beauty Pageant Title:* Queen of the Pitted Prune Parade.

*Trait:* Lovey, who inherited her wealth, considers herself one of the world's most socially active women.

*Favorite Perfume:* Gold Dust No. 5.

*Favorite Vegetable:* Sugar beets.

*Character:* Thurston and Lovey share a hut and for unexplained reasons packed a fabulous wardrobe and a considerable amount of cash for a three-hour tour (they even have bottles of wine and champagne, and Lovey has every imaginable type of makeup there is). They are known to associate with royalty, and Lovey most misses the social season.

## MARY ANN SUMMERS

*Place of Birth:* Horners Corners, Kansas (she later says Winfield, Kansas).

*Occupation:* Farmer (helps her parents run a farm) and clerk in the town's general store.

*Expertise:* Knowledgeable in plants and crops (thus supplementing the castaways' diet of fish and fruit).

*Band:* Mary Ann, Ginger, and Lovey formed a singing group called the Honey Bees.

*Favorite Radio Program:* The soap opera *Young Dr. Young* (later *Old Dr. Young*).

*Favorite Vegetable:* Carrots.

*Character:* Pretty, gentle, kind, and down-to-earth. She shares a hut with Ginger, and, while as sexy as Ginger, she downplays her sexuality (although her tight shorts and stomach-revealing blouses make her appear sexy). She most misses life on the farm.

*Miscellaneous:* When it comes to girls wearing short shorts on TV, it is believed that Catherine Bach (as Daisy Duke on the 1970s TV series *The Dukes of Hazzard*) was the first girl to do so. Dawn Wells mentioned in a TV interview that Mary Ann was actually the first female to wear short shorts (she helped design the shorts with a wider waistband to cover her navel, which was considered taboo at the time). In this time frame (1964) and before, her statement appears to be correct, as no evidence of other girls wearing short shorts could be found, although Connie Hines (Carol Post on *Mister Ed*) comes very close when she appears in tennis shorts. Episode scenes featuring other popular adult and teenage actresses of the time, such as Joi Lansing (*Love That Bob*), Debbie Watson (*Karen*), Candy Moore (*The Lucy Show*), Jeannine Riley, Pat Woodell, and Linda Kaye Henning (the Bradley Sisters on *Petticoat Junction*), were also checked, and although they wore shorts, they could not compare to what Dawn Wells or Connie Hines wore.

*Note:* Raquel Welch was the first choice to play the role. In the original unaired pilot, Mary Ann did not appear; there, Nancy McCarthy was Bunny, a blonde, slightly ditzy secretary.

## THE PROFESSOR

*Real Name:* Roy Hinkley (known as the Professor for his extensive knowledge).

*Place of Birth:* Cleveland, Ohio.

*Occupation:* High school science teacher.

*Age:* 35.

*Degrees:* Master's degrees in psychology, botany, and chemistry.

*Languages:* English and the languages of Hawaiian and African tribes.

*Activities:* Boy Scout troop leader and, as a child, the youngest Eagle Scout in Cleveland.

*Accomplishments:* Chess champion and author of the book *Rust: The Red Menace*. He was in Hawaii doing research for his next book (*Fun with Ferns*) when he decided to relax and take a cruise.

*Discoveries:* Five different mutations of ragweed on his first week on the island. Roy's knowledge made life tolerable on the island. Yet, with all his wisdom, he could not figure out how to make a raft out of bamboo that would stay afloat. Roy keeps a diary of his experiences on the island, and he is the only castaway to live in his own hut. He has devised a way, through coconut shells, metal, and seawater, to recharge the batteries for their only contact with the outside world: a portable AM radio.

*Favorite Meal:* Halibut with kumquat sauce.

# The Girl from U.N.C.L.E.
### (NBC, 1966–1967)

*Cast:* Stefanie Powers (April Dancer), Noel Harrison (Mark Slate), Leo G. Carroll (Alexander Waverly).

*Basis:* April Dancer and Mark Slate, agents for U.N.C.L.E. (United Network Command for Law Enforcement), battle the evils of THRUSH, an organization bent on world domination. Alexander Waverly is their superior.

## OVERALL SERIES INFORMATION

*U.N.C.L.E. Headquarters:* Based in Manhattan with the Del Floria Taylor Shop on Second Avenue and 40th Street as the front for its operations.

*U.N.C.L.E. Sections:* 1. Policy and Operations. 2. Operations and Enforcement. 3. Enforcement and Intelligence. 4. Intelligence and Communications. 5. Communications and Security. 6. Security and Personnel. 7. Propaganda and Finance. 8. Camouflage and Deception.

## APRIL DANCER

*Place of Birth:* Maine (she received an international education, as her father was a constantly uprooted serviceman). She settled long enough in Maine to graduate from a prestigious New England university. She joined U.N.C.L.E. Academy shortly after (1965) and was teamed with Mark Slate on graduation.

*Height:* 5 feet, 5 inches tall.

*Languages:* English, French, Italian, Japanese, Spanish, and Polish.

*Wardrobe:* Very conservative; careful not to show too much cleavage or leg.

*Abilities:* April is trained in unarmed combat, and her fashion accessories are also her weapons. Her coat buttons double as explosives; her makeup case conceals gas capsules, and her lipstick can be used as a tranquilizer dart gun and a communicator (April also contacts headquarters with the standard-issue communicator pen). She carries a gun but is reluctant to use it (only if absolutely necessary).

*Trait:* Although April is a spy, she is also a very typical girl. She becomes easily frightened and is not above making mistakes.

*Sports Car License Plate:* LJH 681.

**MARK SLATE**

*Place of Birth:* England.

*Education:* College educated (university not named). He joined the Royal Air Force after graduating from college and became a pilot. After resigning, he joined the London branch of U.N.C.L.E. Shortly after, he applied for a transfer to New York and was teamed with April Dancer, a recent graduate.

*Abilities:* Mark has technical ability (from his experiences with the air force) and is an expert marksman. He is trained in unarmed combat and can speak several languages. He is also a ladies' man and loves fast cars (but not so much a fast life).

*Character Trait:* He enjoys singing and playing the guitar (but not at every opportunity), and, while flirtatious, he never makes a pass at April (he looks on her as his little sister).

*Height:* 5 feet, 11 inches tall.

*Wardrobe:* He is often seen wearing some sort of hat, usually a battered old woolen cap.

See also *The Man from U.N.C.L.E.*

# Gomer Pyle, USMC
## (CBS, 1964–1969)

*Cast:* Jim Nabors (Gomer Pyle), Frank Sutton (Vince Carter).

*Basis:* A dim-witted young man (Gomer Pyle) from a small town attempts to adjust to life outside his sheltered upbringing as a serviceman with the U.S. Marines.

**GOMER PYLE**

*Place of Birth:* Mayberry, North Carolina.

*Job:* Service attendant at Wally's Filling Station.

*Home:* A room in the back of the filling station.

*Ambition:* Hoping to become a doctor.

*Pet as a Kid:* Spot (dog).

*Favorite Meal:* Limburger and onion sandwiches.

*Catchphrases:* "Shazam!" (which he says when something excites him), "Goll-lly," "Surprise, surprise, surprise," and "Hey."

*Career:* U.S. Marine recruit.

*Inspiration:* The lyrics to the *Marine Hymn* ("From the halls of Montezuma to the shores of Tripoli . . .") that he learned from the back of a calendar distributed by Nelson's Funeral Parlor. When he learned he was expected to serve a term of military service, he joined the Marines.

*Quirk:* Eating Welch rarebit gives Gomer strange dreams. According to Grandma Pyle, when Gomer loses weight, it first goes to his face.

*Camps:* First stationed at Camp Wilson at the Wilmington Naval Base in North Carolina, then Camp Henderson in Los Angeles (Second Platoon, B Company). Attempting to conquer the rope course was Gomer's biggest problem in training.

*Camp Henderson Booby Prize:* The Lead Combat Boot.

*Rank:* Private, then private first class. In real life, the U.S. Marines honored Jim Nabors with an honorary promotion to lance corporal (2001), and in 2007 he was given the honorary title of corporal.

*Nickname:* Crazy Legs Gomer (called so for winning the platoon's footrace).

*Awards:* In season 4, Gomer was awarded the Marine Good Conduct Medal, a National Service Medal, and an Expert Marksman Badge.

*Girlfriend:* Lu Ann Poovie (Elizabeth MacRae), a singer at the Blue Bird Café. She has a pet cat named Boots.

## VINCENT "VINCE" CARTER

*Place of Birth:* Wichita, Kansas.

*Rank:* Gunnery sergeant with the U.S. Marines.

*Base:* Camp Wilson at the Wilmington Naval Base in North Carolina, then Camp Henderson in Los Angeles (Second Platoon, B Company).

*Trait:* Stern and by-the-book ("It will do you well to remember that name [Sergeant Carter] because it is the only name that is going to matter from now on").

*Catchphrase:* "I Can't Hear You!" (said when he address his recruits and gets a faint response).

*Awards:* The Navy Presidential Unit Citation, Bronze Star, Purple Heart, Korean Service Medal (he served four campaigns during the Korean War), Marine Corps Good Conduct Medal, Expert Marksman (rifle and pistol), National Defense Service Medal, and World War II Victory Medal (indicating that Carter also served in that war).

*Film Career:* Starred in the Marine documentary *A Day in the Life of a Sergeant.*

*Girlfriend:* Bunny Olson (Barbara Stuart). She and Vince often frequent the dance club Way Out A-Go-Go.

*Note:* The marching band seen in the opening theme (with Gomer unable to keep pace) was filmed at the Marine Corps Recruit Depot in San Diego, California. Jim Nabors mentioned that he has a difficult time watching that opening because some of the marines he marched with lost their lives in the Vietnam War.

# Green Acres
## (CBS, 1965–1971)

*Cast:* Eddie Albert (Oliver Wendell Douglas); Eva Gabor (Lisa Douglas); Pat Buttram (Mr. Haney); Frank Cady (Sam Drucker); Hank Patterson (Fred Ziffel); Barbara Pepper, then Fran Ryan (Doris Ziffel); Tom Lester (Eb Dawson).

*Basis:* "City slicker" Oliver Wendell Douglas and his glamorous wife, Lisa, attempt to become farmers on a run-down rural farm called Green Acres in the town of Hooterville.

## HOOTERVILLE HISTORY

Hooterville was founded by Horace Hooter in the 1840s. Horace, born in Sacramento, California, came east to find land free of gold prospectors. His journey led him to establish Hooterville, and Oliver now lives in the historic house that Horace called home and that was later owned by the conniving Mr. Haney. The house is literally falling apart, the land is virtually unsuitable for farming, but Oliver sees it as his dream and is determined to make a living as a farmer.

Another episode states that "the great state of Hooterville" was founded by Rutherford B. Skrug and that the home in which Oliver now lives was the birthplace of Rutherford. Hooterville has an elevation of 1,427 feet, and its ZIP code is 40516½.

## OLIVER WENDELL DOUGLAS

*Place of Birth:* A farm in upstate New York near Sarasota Springs (which he feels instilled in him the desire to become a farmer, not a lawyer as his parents wanted).

*Occupation:* Private-practice Manhattan attorney (Oliver Wendell Douglas, attorney-at-law). He was named by his father after associate justice of the Supreme Court Oliver Wendell Holmes.

*Prior Occupation:* Lawyer with the firm of (as printed on the door): Judson Carter Felton, Bart Turner O'Connell, Vincent Roland Clay, Carter James Blakely, John Wilson Harmon, Brian Albert Dillon, and Michel Fenton Pastor. In very small letters below these names appears "O. W. Douglas." He was dismissed from his job for growing crops in his desk drawers.

*Dream:* "To buy a farm, move away from the city, plow my own fields, get my hands dirty, sweat, and strain to make things grow. To join with other farmers, the backbone of the American economy."

*Education:* Law degree from Harvard University (he had the nickname Dimples at the time).

*Military Service:* Air force fighter pilot (a lieutenant; his biggest regret was destroying farmlands).

*Address:* In New York, Oliver sought apartments with the best sunlight for the crops he grew on his balcony (corn, lettuce, tomatoes, string beans, and carrots)—from East 62nd Street, East 54th Street, East 37th Street, Sutton Place, Madison Avenue, and Central Park South. In the first episode, he and Lisa reside in a penthouse apartment at 255 Park Avenue in Manhattan.

*Occupation:* Farmer and owner of the former 160-acre Haney farm in Hooterville (the farm is four miles outside of town). He believes the rocky soil is good for planting corn and wheat.

*Motivation:* After continually failing to grow vegetables in his office desk drawer and on the balcony of his apartment, Oliver purchased, sight unseen, the Haney farm from the conniving Eustace Haney (commonly called Mr. Haney) after seeing an ad in *Farm Gazette* magazine. Lisa is reluctant to relocate but agrees to try "farm living" for six months.

*Work Clothes:* Oliver does his farming in a three-piece suit (he has 12 suits, and each has a specific purpose: plowing, planting, harvesting, and so on). Lisa also dresses elegantly for her duties as a farm wife.

*Farming Equipment:* An ancient Hoyt-Clagwell tractor. He uses a generator for electricity and has a phone with a wire too short to reach the house (he must climb the nearby telephone pole to answer the phone and make calls).

*Association:* A member of the Hooterville Volunteer Fire Department Band and the Hooterville School Board.

*Coffee:* Black with sugar.

*Hobby:* Collecting and writing folk songs.

*Transportation:* While Oliver has his own car, an 1890s train, the Hooterville Cannonball (owned by the C. & F. W. Railroad), services the community (Hooterville and the neighboring towns of Pixley and Crabtree Corners).

*Relatives:* mother, Eunice Douglas (Eleanor Audley).

*Flashbacks:* Eddie Albert as Oliver's father and Jackie Jones as Oliver as a boy.

## LISA DOUGLAS

*Ancestry:* Hungarian.

*Maiden Name:* Lisa Gromyith.

*Pets:* Mignon (dog), Eleanor (milk cow), and the "Girls" (chickens; Alice is Lisa's favorite).

*Name for Town:* With Lisa's accent, "Hooterville" becomes "Hootersville."

*Special Ability:* The only one who can hear a fife playing when Oliver tells why he chose to become a farmer (as listed in "Dream" for Oliver above).

*Fault:* Cannot cook. Her "hotscakes" (pancakes, made with Hal's Hotcake Flour) are like rocks, and how Oliver (or even Lisa) manages to survive is a mystery, as everything Lisa cooks appears nonedible.

*Education:* Budapest University (in Germany) and Hooterville High School (an economics class to improve her cooking skills).

*Problem:* Understanding the electrical system in the house. Each appliance is numbered, and plugging in anything over a 7 short-circuits the generator.

*Coffee:* Cream with sugar.

*Relatives:* mother (Lilia Skala); uncle, Fedor (Leo Fuchs).

## OLIVER AND LISA'S HISTORY

Like Hooterville's founding, Oliver and Lisa share an inconsistent relationship. Flashbacks first reveal that during World War II, Lisa was with the Resistance (a sergeant in the Hungarian Underground whose mission was to distract the Germans and blow up their tanks); they met when Lisa rescued Oliver after his plane was hit by enemy gunfire and he parachuted into enemy territory. Lisa is next said to be a Gypsy and the daughter of a wealthy family in Budapest (where she and Oliver met and were married). The cruise ship SS *Titanic* ("not the one you think") provided the initial meeting when Oliver, a member of the ship's band (played guitar), and Lisa, the wealthy daughter of the ship's owner, fell in love. Finally, Oliver was a salesman peddling women's unmentionables when he and Lisa met on a train.

## MR. HANEY

*Character:* The conniving salesman with mostly only junk to sell (Oliver is his biggest but most reluctant customer). He is a member of the Hooterville Chamber of Commerce and chairman of the Bringing Outside Money into Hooterville Committee.

## SAM DRUCKER

*Character:* The owner of the general store (called Sam Drucker's and seen as Sam Drucker's General Store). He is also the postmaster, notary public, head of the Hooterville Fire Department, and publisher of the valley's only newspaper, the *Hooterville World Guardian*.

## FRED AND DORIS ZIFFEL

*Character:* Husband-and-wife farmers who plant crops and raise pigs. One of their pigs, Arnold, was raised as if it were their own son (Fred is seen with other pigs, two of which he calls by name—Alice and Myrtle—but they appear to be just ordinary pigs).

Fred dresses as the typical farmer, but it is actually Doris who wears the pants (she plows, cooks, feeds the animals, and cares for the house). Fred and Doris were born in Hooterville and not able to have children; thus, Arnold became their only "child." Fred takes great pride in Arnold and hopes he will become a veterinarian when he grows up. Arnold is quite intelligent and is respected by the community as Fred and Doris's son. When Doris's lumbago acts up, Fred knows to plant corn for the season.

On the series *Petticoat Junction*, where the character of Fred Ziffel was first seen (1963), Fred's wife was originally named Ruthie (but did not appear). Fred called her "the ugliest woman the Lord ever let loose." In episode 38 (1964), Barbara Pepper played the role, but when the character appeared in second-season episodes, she was called Doris and remained so for the entire run of *Green Acres*.

## ARNOLD ZIFFEL

*Education:* Hooterville Elementary School (where he is in the third grade). He is even seen in the classroom with children and carries his own lunchbox with him.

*Languages:* English, French, and Japanese (although heard as pig grunts but translated in subtitles for viewers).

*Volunteer Job:* The Hooterville Volunteer Fire Department's mascot (the company does not have a dog).

*Favorite Soda Flavor:* Lime.

*Favorite Activity:* Joining Lisa Douglas for tea and biscuits.

*Abilities:* Arnold can write his own name and predict the weather with his tail and enjoys playing practical jokes.

*Favorite Movie Actor:* John Wayne.

*Favorite TV Program:* The *CBS Evening News with Walter Cronkite*.

*Acting Career:* Starred as Columbo, the crime-solving pig in the Hooterville Theater production of *Who Killed Jacques Robin*.

*Bedroom Color:* Arnold has his own room in the Ziffel house and painted (by himself) his room orange.

*Fault:* Arnold gets the "shies" in front of beautiful women.

*Favorite Sport:* Cricket (Arnold even has his own cricket bat).

*Translator:* Only Eb Dawson, Oliver's hired hand, can translate Arnold's grunts into English.

## EB DAWSON

*Character:* In addition to his job helping Oliver run Green Acres, Eb has a second job—standing in the cornfield while Stuffy, Oliver's scarecrow, journeys to Pixley for lunch. Eb considers Oliver and Lisa his parents and calls Oliver "Dad." His hero is old-time western film star Hoot Gibson (he has a poster of him in his room in the barn) and has a pet frog named Al.

## OTHER CHARACTERS

Hank Kimball (Alvy Moore) is the totally forgetful (and irritating) state agricultural representative who may have knowledge of crops but can never correctly remember how to be helpful to farmers. Alf (Sid Melton) and Ralph Monroe (Mary Grace Canfield) are the inept brother-and-sister "handymen" Oliver hired to repair the farmhouse.

## UPDATE

The 1990 CBS TV movie *Return to Green Acres* found Oliver and Lisa returning to Green Acres after a three-year absence (having given up the farm and moved back to New York). Fred and Doris Ziffel had passed, and their farm was inherited by their niece, Daisy Ziffel (Mary Tanner). Arnold was now Daisy's responsibility, but this time Arnold could be heard in English with a voice-over by Frank Welker. Mr. Haney, while still a con artist, was seen as the owner of a hotel called Haney's House of Hospitality. Eb was now married to Flo (Lucy Lee Flippen) and the father of a teenage son named Jeb (Mark Ballou).

Eddie Albert and Eva Gabor sing the theme "Green Acres" (composed by Vic Mizzy).

# *The Green Hornet*

(ABC, 1966–1967)

*Cast:* Van Williams (Britt Reid, the Green Hornet), Bruce Lee (Kato), Wende Wagner (Lenore Case), Walter Brooke (Frank Scanlon), Lloyd Gough (Mike Axford).

*Basis:* A daring, masked crime fighter, known only as the Green Hornet and his aide, Kato, battle crime in a large metropolitan city (some sources state that it is Washington, D.C., but that is not seen on the program).

## BRITT REID

*Alias:* The Green Hornet.

*Occupation:* Editor of the *Daily Sentinel*, "America's greatest newspaper." Britt also owns the city television station DS (Daily Sentinel) TV. Above the paper's name one will see "Complete NY Stocks," "Comic Section," "Featured Writers," and "Late Sports Results."

*Prior Occupation:* Playboy. Dan Reid, Britt's father, is the publisher of the newspaper and made Britt its editor to give him a sense of responsibility. He also hired ex-cop turned reporter Mike Axford to watch over Britt's activities (Mike is unaware that Britt is the Green Hornet).

*The Change:* When Britt discovers that his great grand uncle was John Reid (alias the Lone Ranger), he decides to follow in his footsteps and battle evil to "protect the rights and lives of decent citizens." The job as editor gives him the perfect cover.

*The Disguise:* Britt dons a dark green costume (overcoat, mask, and hat) and chooses to call himself the Green Hornet (after the insect that is most deadly when aroused). He establishes a base of operations in an abandoned building and reveals his secret identity to only three people: Kato, his Asian houseboy (who also serves as the Hornet's aide and dresses in black with a black mask); Lenore "Casey" Case, his secretary; and Frank Scanlon, the district attorney (his blue sedan license plate is 762 583). There is no background information on Lenore (whom Brett calls "Miss Case" when conducting business or "Casey" when alone or with Kato and Frank). She is always stylishly dressed and can take care of herself in adverse situations (as she sometimes becomes a part of the Green Hornet's plans).

*Weapons:* As the Green Hornet, Britt has the Hornet Gun; a foldable walking stick called the Sting Ray, which can discharge sonic rays or laser beams; and the Hornet Sting (which sends a signal to the district attorney).

*The Problem:* Because the Green Hornet and Kato are considered criminal and wanted by the police, they must avenge crimes as semifugitives rather than as a law enforcement organization, always disappearing before the police arrive.

## THE CAR (THE BLACK BEAUTY)

It is a customized 1966 Chrysler Imperial Crown sedan. It features includes green glowing headlights, rockets front and rear, knockout gas in the front, and smoke in the rear for a smoke screen. It has also been rigged for silent running. The back of the building that houses the car has a billboard that reads, "Kissing Candy Mints" (on the left side; in the middle, a girl kissing a boy is depicted, and on the right side are the words "How Sweet They Are").

The elevator that gives Britt access to the Green Hornet's secret headquarters beneath Britt's home is located behind the fireplace. The Black Beauty stands on a revolving floor section. When not in use, Britt's normal street car is seen. When the Black Beauty is needed, Kato approaches a pegboard of tools. He turns the socket head of a ratchet wrench, which in turn opens a secret panel in the pegboard. He presses three buttons on a control panel. The first one clamps and secures the street car, the second one activates a revolving floor that brings the Black Beauty to the top, the third one releases the clamps and allows the car to be driven.

Bruce Lee and Van Williams. *ABC/Photofest © ABC*

*Black Beauty License Plate:* V 194.
*Britt's White Convertible License Plate:* TLH 257.

## OVERALL SERIES INFORMATION

The newspaper is housed in the Daily Sentinel Building (the paper "goes to bed" [printed] at 10:30 p.m.). Frank's telephone number is 555-6789. As a kid, Britt was a champion marble shooter. Kato sometimes uses the Hornet Shaped Dart (a throwing star) as a weapon.

# The Guns of Will Sonnett
## (ABC, 1967–1969)

*Cast:* Walter Brennan (Will Sonnett), Dack Rambo (Jeff Sonnett), Jason Evers (James Sonnett).

*Basis:* A grandfather (Will Sonnett) and his grandson, Jeff Sonnett, begin a quest to find Jeff's father, James Sonnett, a wanted gunman and killer who deserted his family 20 years earlier (1852).

### WILLIAM "WILL" SONNETT

*Trait:* Fast on the draw. Will says, "James showed promise, but he left before I could teach him half of what I know."

*Job:* Army scout stationed at Fort Leavenworth (it was said that as a boy, James would hang out at the fort trading post). Will was later stationed at Fort Kenny.

*Nickname:* Sharp Eyes (acquired from the Sioux Indian Chief Red Leaf for saving his life).

*Horse:* Marauder.

*Catchphrase:* "No brag, just fact" (when he tells people about himself and what he can do).

*Philosophy:* When facing an opponent in a gunfight, Will says, "Keep 'em waitin'; it makes 'em edgy." He also says, "They say Jim was fast. Well he ain't; I am. No brag, just fact." When lost on the trail, Will says, "Look at the sun, check the wind, and ride north till we find him [James]."

### JEFFREY "JEFF" SONNETT

*Place of Birth:* Bensfort, Wyoming.

*Year of Birth:* 1852. He is 20 years old when the series begins.

*Mother:* Name not revealed, but she died during childbirth. Jim, unable to face life without his wife, abandoned the family; Will took on the responsibility of raising Jeff as best he could.

*The Search:* It is 1872 when Jeff tells Will, "I have to go find my father." "I reckoned that's how it should be," responds Will, "so we ride, Jim's boy and me."

*The Problem:* Jim is wanted for murder, and there are a lot of people out to get him. Jim is unaware of the fact "that he is bein' sought by kin." As Will and

Jeff travel a difficult road, they learn that Jim killed only in self-defense and is actually kind and helpful to people in trouble.

*The Hope:* Each town brings Will the hope that it will be the last town they will have to visit. His faith in the Lord keeps him going: "I thought our search was over Lord; now with your help we'll start again. Please guide the path we take."

## JAMES "JIM" SONNETT

*Character:* Virtually no additional background information is given. Jim was born in 1833, and he carries a gold watch given to him by Will with the inscription "To James from His Loving Father." Like with Jeff, Will taught Jim the art of gunplay and how to fight and "to be respectful of women no matter what or where."

## THE LAST EPISODE

Will and Jeff's journey comes to an end when they find Jim and convince him to give up his life of running. With the hope of beginning new lives, the Sonnetts settle down in the town of Sampson. Will becomes the sheriff and Jim and Jeff his deputies. Had the series continued, it would have followed the Sonnetts as they attempt to maintain law and order in Sampson.

# *Hawaii Five-0*

(CBS, 1968–1980)

*Cast:* Jack Lord (Steve McGarrett), James MacArthur (Danny Williams).

*Basis:* Steve McGarrett, the head of Five-0, the special investigative branch of the Hawaii State Police, relentlessly pursues criminals in the name of justice.

### STEVEN "STEVE" McGARRETT

*Occupation:* Head of Five-0, which is housed in the Iolani Palace ("The only palace on American soil"). The palace was headquarters for Hawaii's last king and queen and was "dropped" when the real palace needed repairs and Five-0 was relocated to an unidentified building.

*Place of Birth:* San Francisco.

*Middle Name:* Aloysius. In another episode, he mentions he has the middle initial "J."

*Address:* 404 Pikoi Street in Honolulu.

*Car License Plate:* 163 958.

*Bank:* The National Bank of Oahu.

*Education:* Union High School and Annapolis Naval Academy.

*Birth Sign:* Capricorn (revealed only that he was born in the 1930s).

*Sister:* Nancy Malone as Mary Ann Whalen. She lives in California and was married to Tom (John Carter). They had a baby, Tommy, who died of cancer at six months of age.

*Military Service:* Naval intelligence officer (lieutenant commander) during World War II; stationed in Japan during the Korean War. He remained with the navy until 1961 (at which time he moved to Hawaii). He is now in the navy reserve and is recalled to active service for special missions.

*Police Career:* It appears (not made clear) that Steve became a detective with the Hawaii State Police following his military service; in 1959, he was ap-

Jack Lord. *CBS/Photofest © CBS*

pointed by the governor to head Five-0. Steve mentions that he has not taken a day off from police work since 1959. In 1968, he finally does take a vacation (to Switzerland, right before the series begins).

*Exercise:* Keeps in shape by jogging along the beach and playing tennis. He has his hair cut every Tuesday.

*Diet:* Steve claims to be a health food nut but sneaks an occasional junk food snack when he gets the urge. He is an excellent cook, and lasagna and chicken cacciatore are his favorite meals.

*Hobby:* Collecting Asian artifacts.

*Marital Status:* Single. He never married because he believes he can't be a good cop and a husband at the same time.

*Car License Plate:* 6B 891.

*Office Telephone Number:* 732-5577.

*Greatest Enemies:* Wo Fat (Khigh Dhigh), a master criminal, and Tony Aliko (Ross Martin), the syndicate boss of an underground organization called Kumu.

## OTHER CHARACTERS

Daniel "Danny" Williams is Steve's partner, whom Steve calls "Dan-O" (the phrase "Book 'em Dan-O" became a familiar part of the series). Danny was said to have been born in both Honolulu and the Midwest. He attended the University of Hawaii for one year (where he majored in philosophy) and transferred to the University of California, Berkeley, to major in police science. The phrase "Patch me through to McGarrett" also became a part of the series. Helen Hayes appeared as Danny's Aunt Clara. Tim O'Kelly played Danny in the pilot episode.

Chin Ho Kelly (Kam Fong), Duke (Herman Wedemyer), and Kono (played by Zulu) were the police officers who worked with Steve and Danny. McGarrett refers to Kono as "Big Kanaka." He had been a cop in Boston and transferred to Hawaii after his wife and child were killed. Chin Ho smoked a pipe, and Steve would jokingly call him "Fatso." Steve calls his secretary, May (Maggi Parker), "May, Love." Richard Denning played the governor, who was called by the following names: Phil, Paul Jamison, and Philip Grey. Mildred Natwick appeared as mystery writer Millicent Shand, who called him "Sonny."

*Note:* In the opening theme, Helen Torco plays the hula dancer, and Elizabeth Logue is the model seen running on the beach.

# *Hazel*
## (NBC, 1961–1965; CBS, 1965–1966)

*Cast:* Shirley Booth (Hazel Burke), Don DeFore (George Baxter),Whitney Blake (Dorothy Baxter), Bobby Buntrock (Harold Baxter), Ray Fulmer (Steve Baxter), Lynn Borden (Barbara Baxter), Julia Benjamin (Susie Baxter).

*Basis:* A busybody maid (Hazel Burke) and her efforts to care for the Baxter family (George; his wife, Dorothy; and their son, Harold; later [CBS episodes],

George's younger brother, Steve, his wife, Barbara, and their daughter, Susie).

## HAZEL BURKE

*Residence:* Hazel lives with George and his family at 123 Marshall Road in an unspecified eastern city (possibly in New Jersey, as New York and Philadelphia are mentioned as neighboring cities).

*Baxter Phone Number:* Klondike 5-8372 (later 555-8372, then 555-2679).

*Work History:* Exactly when Hazel became a maid varies. It is mentioned that George and Dorothy married in 1950 at the same time Hazel became their maid; in another episode, Hazel says she began working for George and Dorothy nine years ago, making it 1953. It is later stated that Hazel was a maid to George before he married Dorothy; this is contradicted when it is said that Hazel was a maid to Dorothy's family and she watched Dorothy grow from child to adult. This is most likely correct, as Dorothy later says she was eight years old when Hazel began working for her family. Hazel also says that when Dorothy was a little girl, she would always bake a birthday cake for her. Still, in another episode, Hazel mentions she did not begin working until she was 26 (as she had to raise her brothers and sisters; no other information given). At any rate, she considers the Baxters her family.

*Ability:* Expert cook; most famous for her fudge brownies. Never able to tell a lie (George says, "Hazel has George Washington heroics").

*Favorite Sport:* Bowling. She has an insurance policy to cover her back when she bowls.

*Awards:* Crowned champion of the 1964 Regional Bowling Association; at the age of 12, she received the Schwartz Award and $5 for saving the life of a woman choking on food in a restaurant.

*Stock:* Hazel owns 11 shares of stock in the Davidson Vacuum Cleaner Company. She also has other shares of stock (names not mentioned) based on her buying habits: purchasing one share of any stock for each company whose stock sells over 100 shares.

*Accomplishments:* Wrote a book called *Hazel's Handy Recipes* and was the television spokesperson for Aunt Nora's Instant Cake Mix. She was also voted "Maid of the Month" by *American Elegance* magazine.

*Affiliation:* President of the Ladies' Society of Domestic Engineers and head of the Sunshine Girls (a group of local neighborhood maids).

*Car:* A 1920 Model T-Ford.

*License Plate:* 306 579. She paid $25 for the car and later sold it to a collector for $1,250.

*Nicknames:* Hazel calls George "Mr. B.," Dorothy "Missy," and Harold "Sport."

*Royalty:* Hazel was related to British royalty (her great-grandmother was Countess Patricia Burke, who lived in England in 1882 and from whom she inherited six tarnished sterling silver spoons).

*Only True Love:* Gus Jenkins (Patrick McVey), whom she met in the observation tower of the Empire State Building (he was throwing paper airplanes off). He called her "Brown Eyes," and they fell in love. But he was a merchant sailor, and things just never worked out.

*Day Off:* Thursday. On Sunday, she takes time off to attend mass.

*Meals:* Hazel serves breakfast at 7:00 a.m., lunch at 12:15 p.m., and dinner at 6:00 p.m.

*Catchphrase:* Most often heard: "Everything is just peachy keen" (which she says in response to a question asked of her by George).

*Bank:* Hazel has an account at the Commerce Trust Bank; she keeps her government bonds in her footlocker.

*Relatives:* nephew, Eddie Burke (Johnny Washbrook); nephew, Walter Burke (Frank Aletter); cousin, Suzie, aka Lady Sybil (Rosemary DeCamp).

## GEORGE BAXTER

*Occupation:* Lawyer with the firm of Butterworth, Hatch, Noll and Baxter (offices located in the Arcade Building). He began practicing law in 1949.

*Education:* Dartmouth University (where he is also a member of the board of regents of the University Law School and delivers the Oliver Wendell Holmes Memorial Lectures). He is also an attorney for the Symphony Association. While in college, George earned money waiting tables.

*Car:* A convertible (license plate 49-753) and a red sedan (license plate J2R 8255, later 53-859).

*Favorite Dessert:* Chocolate fudge cake. He also enjoys Hazel's brownies and calls them "Hazel's peachy keen pecan brownies."

*Favorite Sport:* Golf.

*Problems:* A tendency to gain weight; he is constantly nagged by Hazel to stay on his diet. Telling Hazel anything associated with his work as she tries to help him with it. "It's remarkable," George says. "Two years of pre-law training, four years of law school, and 12 years of successful practice, and I still haven't learned to keep my mouth shut around Hazel."

*Biggest Client:* Harvey Griffin (Howard Smith), the owner of Griffin Enterprises.

*Affiliation:* Member of the Mayor's Advisory Committee.

*Favorite Newspaper: Daily Chronicle.*

*Presents:* For his birthday, Hazel gives George handkerchiefs (with the exception of his 1963 birthday, when Hazel gave him a sweepstakes ticket—at the same time he became a member of the antigambling committee).

*Partner:* His most frequently seen partner is Harry Noll (Lauren Gilbert), a man who believes he is irresistible to women; he married Rita Linda (Karen Steele), a famous singer who is 20 years his junior.

*Relatives:* society sister, Deidre Thompson (Cathy Lewis); Deidre's husband, Harry Thompson, a salesman for the Sawyer Computer Company (Robert P. Lieb); Nancy Thompson, Deidre's daughter (Davey Davison); cousin, Fred Baxter, later as cousin, Charlie Perkins (Fredric Downs); cousin, Grace Baxter (Linda Watkins); nephew, Kevin Burkett (Michael Callan); Kevin's wife, Helen Burkett (Margaret Bly).

## DOROTHY BAXTER

*Occupation:* Housewife, mother, and freelance interior decorator (a business name is not given).

*Maiden Name:* Dorothy Webster.

*Business Affiliation:* The I.D.S. (Interior Decorator's Society) and the local Women's Club.

*Negligee Size:* 8 (she purchases her lingerie at Blackstone's Department Store and her dresses at Montague's Boutique).

*Character:* Dorothy, unlike George, is more compassionate toward Hazel and seldom loses her temper with her (her upbringing with Hazel has taught her how to deal with the good intentions Hazel has that often backfire). She is a loving wife and mother and delights in the times that Hazel asks for her help around the house—especially cooking.

## HAROLD BAXTER

*Character:* George and Dorothy's only child. He attends an unnamed grammar school and has a dog named Smiley. His favorite breakfast is pancakes, and he calls Hazel's brownies "the good stuff." His first crush was on a girl named Zelda Warren (Vickie Cos). The infatuation was short lived when he discovered she wanted him to join her ballet class, wear tights, and be a fairy in *Sleeping Beauty*.

## STEVE AND BARBARA BAXTER

*Relationship:* George's younger brother and his wife.

*Daughter:* Suzie.

*Address:* 325 Sycamore Street (same town but unnamed).

*Occupation:* Owner of the Baxter Real Estate Company.

*Maid:* Hazel Burke. When the series switched to CBS, Hazel becomes Steve's maid when George is transferred to the Middle East (Baghdad) to handle "a big deal for Mr. Griffin." Dorothy accompanies him, and Harold is sent to live with Steve to avoid his missing a semester at school. Steve is not as tolerant as George when it comes to dealing with Hazel's antics but is often persuaded by Barbara to try to understand her intentions, not fight them.

*Hazel's Name for Steve:* Mr. Steve.

*Hazel's Activities:* Enjoys playing poker with Steve and his friends on Friday nights.

*Hazel's Moneymaking Venture:* Barbara joined with Hazel to market "Aunt Hazel's Chili Sauce" for Richie's Supermarket (it cost 15 cents to make, and a bottle sold for 98 cents).

*Note:* Unlike the NBC version of the series, very little background information is given. It is apparent by the CBS version that Hazel was not a maid in the Baxter household (as previously implied), as Steve never makes mention of the fact that Hazel was once a part of his family. Steve and Barbara were high school sweethearts who married right after their college graduation. They became parents at about the same time Steve established his office in town. Like Dorothy, Barbara is more tolerant of Hazel's good intentions (and, unlike Dorothy, becomes more a part of them). While she is a loving wife and mother, she wishes, deep down, that life was like it was before Hazel's arrival—when she cared for her family (it appears she most misses cooking). Other than attending an unnamed elementary school, there is no background information on Suzie.

### OTHER CHARACTERS

Ann Jillian has a recurring role as Steve's teenage secretary, Millie Ballard (who works after school and on Saturday). Charles Bateman and Mala Powers play Steve and Barbara's friends and neighbors Fred and Mona Williams.

## *He and She*
### (CBS, 1967–1968)

*Cast:* Paula Prentiss (Paula Hollister), Richard Benjamin (Richard Hollister), Jack Cassidy (Oscar North), Kenneth Mars (Harry Zarakardos), Hamilton Camp (Andrew Humble).

*Basis:* A young married couple (Paula and Richard) and their efforts to cope with the problems that arise from their vastly different career choices.

### PAULA AND RICHARD HOLLISTER

*Address:* 365 East 84th Street in Manhattan. The apartment in which they live is not numbered (even though the front door is seen). It appears to be a converted brownstone that Richard later buys (with a $5,000 down payment). When too many problems arise, he sells it to his friend Oscar North for $4,000.

*Richard's Job:* Cartoonist and creator of the newspaper comic strip turned television series *Jetman*. The paper for which Richard, called "Dick," works is called "The Paper" or "This Paper." Richard is seen working at home and in an office at the newspaper. It appears in some episodes that he also writes the TV scripts but in others only the comic strip.

*Paula's Job:* Employee of the Manhattan Tourist Aid Society. Not only is Paula beautiful, but she has a heart of gold and can't resist helping people in distress (this causes her work problems to become Richard's problems).

*The Meeting:* Richard and Paula met in 1962 and had their first date in the Adirondacks. Richard parked his car in a "Falling Rocks" zone, and as he attempted to kiss Paula for the first time, a rock (an upstate New York gray stone) fell and hit him on the head. Paula kept the rock as a memento of their first date. They are married five years when the series begins. When Dick and Paula go to the movies, it becomes a "His and Her" situation as Richard sees the film one way; Paula another way.

*Paula's Former Boyfriend:* Jerry Sargent (Hal Buckely), who claims that Richard stole his "Jetman" idea from his comic strip "Captain Rocket."

*Richard's Favorite Bar:* Hammond's Bar.

*Laundromat:* Paula has their clothes cleaned at the Fiore Brothers Cleaners.

## OSCAR NORTH

*Job:* The egotistical star of the TV series *Jetman* (about a superhero who battles evil, most notably his nemesis, Dr. Destructo. Jetman wears a jet-shaped helmet with two jets on the back of his vest for flying).

*Medical Condition:* Suffers from claustrophobia.

*Passion:* A connoisseur of the fine arts (he owns, for example, a then-valued at $65,000 Picasso painting).

*Dressing Room:* A large picture of Oscar North appears in his room with devotional candles on each side.

*Daily Schedule:* Oscar arrives at the TV studio at 5:30 a.m. for makeup (which takes 4½ hours to apply). *Jetman* is filmed on stage 2.

## OTHER CHARACTERS

Andrew Humble is the apartment building's not-so-handy man (he has been married 25 years and still wears the first present his wife gave him—a blue shirt). Harry Zarakardos is a fireman (with Company 26) who lives across the street from Dick and Paula. He is Greek and has placed a plank from the firehouse window to the Hollisters' window to allow him easy access to their apartment. Murray Mouse (Alan Oppenheimer) is Dick's overly frugal accountant; Norman Nugent (Harold Gould) is Dick's boss at the newspaper.

# Hey Landlord
## (NBC, 1966–1967)

*Cast:* Will Hutchins (Woody Banner), Sandy Baron (Chuck Hookstratten), Michael Constantine (Jack Ellenhorn).

*Basis:* College graduates and friends Woody and Chuck struggle to run a 10-room brownstone turned apartment house in Manhattan.

*Opening-Theme Visuals:* A tie, a pair of socks, a bathtub with a dripping pipe, and a poster of Marilyn Monroe (highlighting her lips).

## WOODROW "WOODY" BANNER

*Address:* 140 West 41st Street (a brownstone he inherited from an uncle). In the converted apartment, Woody and Chuck share a room and sleep in bunk beds: Woody on top, Chuck on the bottom.

*Place of Birth:* Ohio.

*Parents:* Lloyd and Marcy Banner.

*Sister:* Bonnie.

*Parents Occupation:* Farmers.

*Ambition:* To become a writer.

*Education:* Fillmore High School (Toledo, Ohio) and Ohio State University.

*High School Activities:* Member of the swim team and the football team (he quit when the tackling dummy broke and he substituted for it).

*Childhood Activity:* Member of the Skunk Troop (a Boy Scout–like troop).

*Favorite Book: Great Moments in Baseball* ("The one with the blonde in the bikini and a guy sneaking up on her with a baseball bat on the cover").

*Relatives:* Bonnie Banner (Sally Field); Lloyd Banner (Tom Tully); Marcy Banner (Ann Doran); uncle, Dwight (Jack Albertson).

## ELMER CHARLES "CHUCK" HOOKSTRATTEN

*Place of Birth:* New York City.

*Education:* P.S. 138 and John Quincy Adams High School (both in Manhattan) and Ohio State University (where he met Woody).

*Ambition:* To become a comedian.

*Childhood Remarks:* "I was a rotten kid." He wrote on the school walls and once tried to burn down his school (which one was not stated).

*Favorite Snack:* Hot tamales with shredded coconut.

*Relatives:* father, Leon Hookstratten (Joseph Leon); mother, Fanny Hookstratten (Naomi Stevens).

## JACK ELLENHORN
*Occupation:* Commercial photographer.
*Trait:* Easily exasperated, ulcer-ridden tenant of Woody and Chuck who feels that the antics of his landlords are tied with the aggravation of his job to see what will kill him first. As Jack says, "Why did I move into this building? They said the rent would be lower. But what about my medical bills? Who else buys pills by the gross?"
*Jack's Nickname for Chuck:* Chuckula.
*Jack's Nickname for Woody:* The Boy Landlord.
*Favorite Bar:* The Elegant Palace Bar (a three-minute walk from the apartment house).
*Favorite Model:* Gayle (played by Jayne Massey).
*Least Favorite Model:* Chuck (who was hired to do an ad for Jack's client, Sedgwick Socks).

## OTHER CHARACTERS
Ann Morgan Guilbert as Mrs. Henderson, the woman with several mischievous children who constantly "destroyed" the apartment; Pamela Rodgers as the voluptuous but slightly scatterbrained Timothy Morgan; and Mikyo Mayama as Koko Mitsui, Timothy's lovely, levelheaded roommate.

# *Hogan's Heroes*
## (CBS, 1965–1971)

*Cast:* Bob Crane (Colonel Robert Hogan), Werner Klemperer (Colonel Wilhelm Klink), John Banner (Sergeant Hans Schultz), Richard Dawson (Captain Peter Newkirk), Robert Clary (Corporal Louis LeBeau), Larry Hovis (Sergeant Andrew Carter), Ivan Dixon (Sergeant James Kinchloe), Kenneth Washington (Sergeant Richard Baker).
*Basis:* Life in a World War II German prisoner-of-war camp as seen through the antics of a diverse group of Allied captives (Hogan, Newkirk, LeBeau, Carter, Kinchloe, and Baker) as they band together to help fellow prisoners escape the German high command and secure secrets for their superiors.

## OVERALL SERIES INFORMATION
Stalag 13 is a German prisoner-of-war camp outside of Hammelburg, Germany. It is commanded by Colonel Wilhelm Klink, and Sergeant Hans Schultz assists

him. The year 1942 is established in the pilot. Colonel Hogan and his team have a secret radio receiver (disguised as a coffeepot) and a series of tunnels (except for Barracks 4) that run beneath the camp (entrances are under the guard dog house in the kennel, the tree stump in the wooded area that surrounds the camp, the lower bunk under a bed in their barracks, and under the stove in Klink's quarters). There is also a hidden microphone behind the picture of Hitler in Klink's office.

"Mama Bear" is the code name Hogan uses to contact an Allied submarine. Hogan's code names to contact London are first "Goldilocks," then "Papa Bear." For some unexplained reason, "Papa Bear" later became Hogan's personal code, while "Mama Bear" became his London contact code. Hogan also uses disguises to fool Klink and Schultz, and the tunnel under Hogan's bunk is the one most used to sneak in and out of the camp. Bruno, Hans, Heidi, and Wolfgang are the guard dogs at Stalag 13.

## ROBERT EDWARD HOGAN
*Place of Birth:* New Jersey.
*High School Honor:* Voted "Most Likely to Become a Troublemaker."
*Favorite Hangout:* Garlotti's Pizzeria.
*Military Service:* Commander of the 504th Unit of the U.S. Army Air Corps. He graduated third in his class at military school. He was captured during an air-raid mission over Hamburg.

## PETER NEWKIRK
*Place of Birth:* England.
*Occupation:* Con artist with many skills, including safecracking, picking pockets, forging, impersonations, and accents.
*Military Duty:* Royal British Air Force.
*Expertise:* An expert tailor (he designs many of the uniforms and disguises needed by Hogan). He was also given several aliases to fool Klink: London fire warden, barrister, and talent scout.

## LOUIS LEBEAU
*Place of Birth:* France.
*Occupation:* Jack-of-all-trades (skilled in everything from cooking to sewing).
*Masquerades:* "Le Smoke," a Paris fire brigade champion; "Mr. Test Tube," a famous chemist; "Yvette of Paris," a fashion designer; "Madame LeGrange," a dance studio owner; a descendant of Gypsies; and a big-game hunter.
*Weekly Assignment:* Visit Wilhelmina (Celeste Yarnell), their underground contact. LeBeau eventually fell in love with Wilhelmina, but to keep it a secret he described her as "a mean old lady" to his fellow prisoners.

*Nickname:* LeBeau is a constant annoyance to Klink and Schultz and is called "Cockroach" by them.

## ANDREW CARTER

*Place of Birth:* Muncie, Indiana.

*Bloodline:* Part Native American.

*Occupation:* Drugstore owner.

*Dream:* To become a pharmacist after the war.

*Military Service:* U.S. Army soldier (he first says he enlisted and later claims he was drafted).

*Expertise:* Explosives and archery.

*Masquerade:* Hogan passes him off as a business school graduate and interior decorator (enables him to control the distribution of supplies to the other prison camps in the area through the tunnels).

*Pilot Episode Role:* Carter is said to be a lieutenant and manages to escape from Stalag 13; he is returned as a sergeant for the series.

## JAMES KINCHLOE

*Citizenship:* U.S.

*Nickname:* Kinch (his first name was later changed to Ivan).

*Occupation:* Telephone lineman and Golden Gloves boxer.

*Expertise:* Radio and electronics (he runs the underground communications center for Hogan); able to impersonate Hitler's voice over the telephone.

## COLONEL KLINK

*Place of Birth:* Leipzig, Germany.

*Military Service:* Member of the Luftwaffe (the German air force). He received his military training in Potsdam.

*Fear:* The Gestapo (Hogan seized on this fear and was able to manipulate him and Schultz).

*Duty:* Simply performing his job as a Kommandant so he can get a promotion. He hates the war and opposes Hitler but does what he has to do because it is his job. He also feels he does not get the respect he deserves because he wears a monocle.

*Prior Occupation:* Bookkeeper (he also mentioned that he once played Peter Pan in a play).

*Nickname:* Hogan has nicknamed him "Klink the Fink" (the "Fink" standing for "Firm Impartial Nazi Kommandant"). He also gets the upper hand over Klink by telling him that he must follow the rules of the Geneva Convention.

*Revenge:* He uses sawdust for flour in the making of the prisoner's bread.

## SERGEANT SCHULTZ

*Military Service:* A member of the Luftwaffe and fearful of the Gestapo.

*Family:* It is mentioned that he has five children.

*Prior Occupation:* Toy store owner.

*Dream:* To come home alive after the conflict.

*Catchphrase:* "I know nothing, I see nothing." To avoid any confrontations (as he knows Hogan is up to no good), Schultz often looks the other way.

*Downfall:* His obsession with alcohol, women, and gambling. Food can also be included, as Hogan can easily bribe him with it.

## OTHER CHARACTERS

Fraulein Helga (Cynthia Lewis) and then Fraulein Hilda (Sigrid Valdis) are Klink's secretaries; Myrna (Nita Talbot) is the beautiful Russian spy who helped Hogan (and became fond of him). General Albert Burkhalter (Leon Askin) is Klink's stern superior who has a weakness for beautiful women; Major Wolfgang Hochstetter (Howard Caine) is devoted to Hitler's cause and intent on destroying the enemy. It is his threats to send Klink to the Russian front that keep Klink in his place.

Ivan Dixon, Bob Crane, Robert Clary, Larry Hovis, and Richard Dawson. *CBS/ Photofest © CBS*

# Honey West

## (ABC, 1965–1966)

*Cast:* Anne Francis (Honey West), John Ericson (Sam Bolt).

*Basis:* A female private detective (Honey West) and her partner, Sam Bolt, com-
bine elements of traditional sleuthing with scientific technology to solve
crimes.

## HONEY WEST

*Address:* 6033 Del Mar Vista in Los Angeles.

*Place of Birth:* California.

*Measurements:* 36-24-34.

*Hair:* Blonde.

*Eyes:* Blue.

*Distinguishing Feature:* A small mole on her lower right lip.

*Wardrobe:* Stylish (from sexy black jumpsuits to exotic fur ensembles).

*Business:* H. West and Company, a private detective business she inherited from
her late father.

*Mobile Base of Operations*: A truck disguised as "H. West TV Repairing," also
seen as "H. W. Bolt & Co. TV Service." In some episodes, the truck is displayed with the name; in others, it is a black van with no labeling.

*Surveillance Truck License Plate:* 1406 122 (later IET 974).

*Abilities:* Shrewd, uncanny, and skilled in karate (a black belt). She carries a
gun—and does use it. Honey is a master of disguises and most often goes
undercover as a society woman or wealthy playgirl.

*Faults:* Becomes upset when a case does not go well (she takes her frustrations
out at the firing range: "I come here for practice," she says, "not therapy").
She is also overconfident that she can solve a case but sometimes cannot
and lets a client down. Honey and Sam often work with the police, but
Honey cannot always promise she will go by the book. Overall, Honey, who
learned the business from her father, is not as effective as he was. She lets
cases pile up and becomes too focused on a case when it gets the best of her.
She is also a cynic and believes every case is related to a murder.

*Equipment:* In addition to her figure and the truck, Honey's earrings double as
miniature tear gas bombs when thrown and broken. Her lipstick and compact are transmitters, allowing her to contact Sam (whose eyeglasses double
as receivers). The pen that Honey gives to clients is actually a miniature
transmitter that she uses for tracking purposes. She carries a .38 revolver in
her purse and a derringer (that she conceals beneath her clothing, appropri-
ate to the outfit she is wearing).

*Apartment:* Appears luxurious, but the wall displaying various vases is the secret entrance to her lab (activated by a secret button hidden in an ornament on the right side of that wall).

*Pet Ocelot:* Bruce.

*Reputation:* While she is respected by most people for what she does and accomplishes, some criminals view her as just a "dame" and out of her league. She is often taunted by criminals ("Well, well, well. Don't you know a lady's place is in the home?"), and for being so stubborn, she does take a beating or is roughed up.

*Double:* Anne Francis also played Pandora Fox, Honey's exact look-alike, a notorious thief (in the episode "Don't Look Now, but Isn't That Me?").

*Relatives:* aunt, Meg (Irene Hervey).

## SAMUEL "SAM" BOLT

*Occupation:* Private detective and Honey's guardian. Sam worked with Honey's father and promised he would watch over her when she inherited the company.

*Address:* An apartment on North Ventura Boulevard.

*Skills:* Expert with a gun. He often becomes a part of Honey's undercover assignments by posing as a chauffeur or a playboy. Although Sam is tough with his fists, he does not always show up in time to save Honey from a beating by thugs.

*Hobby:* Collecting guns (his collection can be seen inside the truck he and Honey use and he always claims that a certain type of gun is needed for a certain type of situation). He also carries lock picks with him at all times.

*Note:* The pilot episode, "Honey West: Who Killed the Jackpot," aired on *Burke's Law.*

# *I Dream of Jeannie*
(NBC, 1965–1970)

*Cast:* Barbara Eden (Jeannie/Jeannie II), Larry Hagman (Tony Nelson), Bill
Daily (Roger Healy), Hayden Rorke (Dr. Alfred Bellows), Emmaline Henry
(Amanda Bellows).

*Basis:* An astronaut (Tony Nelson), finding and releasing a beautiful genie
(named Jeannie) from a bottle he finds on a deserted island, struggles to live
a normal life despite the problems Jeannie causes when she uses her magic
against his wishes.

## JEANNIE

*Birthday:* April 1, 64 BC, at a time when the planet Neptune was in Scorpio. In
an earlier episode, Jeannie mentions her birthday as being July 1, 21 BC.
Jeannie was born three years after her parents married.

*Place of Birth:* Baghdad for the April 1 date. Jeannie mentions Pompeii as her
birthplace with the July 1 date.

*History:* When Jeannie became of age, the Blue Djin (Michael Ansara), the most
powerful and most feared of all genies, asked for her hand in marriage.
When she refused his proposal, he turned her into a genie, placed her in a
bottle, and sentenced her to a life of loneliness for all eternity on a deserted
island in the South Pacific. She remained there for 2,000 years until Tony
found her bottle and released her.

*Sibling:* Jeannie II. No information is given regarding how Jeannie II became a
genie, although it is said that she had many masters over the centuries but
that none pleased her. She wears a green harem outfit and has been married
47 times. Her only goal is to steal Tony away from Jeannie and make him
her master.

*Home:* A purple bottle in Tony's home (when the bottle is opened, a pink smoke
emerges and materializes into Jeannie. In the black-and-white pilot episode,

it is mentioned as being a green bottle). A Jim Beam liquor decanter was used for the bottle. Depending on the quality of the print that is being watched, the bottle can also appear as red, blue, or pink.

*Weight:* 109 pounds (although, she insists, "I have never weighed over 107 pounds"), then 127 pounds.

*Blood:* Green. Her green corpuscles produce extreme envy if someone she loves betrays her.

*Wardrobe:* A two-piece, cleavage-revealing pink harem outfit.

*Hair:* Blonde.

*Powers:* Ability to grant any wish by crossing her hands over her chest and blinking her eyes. She appears and disappears in a pink smoke.

*Weakness:* Unhappiness (causes her powers to weaken); if she becomes depressed, she will vanish if not cheered up.

*Dog:* Gin Gin (who hates military uniforms and attacks people wearing them due to the palace guards beating her when she was a puppy).

*Favorite Candy:* Pip Chicks (it has a strange effect on mortals, bringing out their hidden fantasies).

*Nickname for Tony:* Jeannie originally called Tony "Master Darling"; it simply became "Master" in later episodes.

*Character:* Jeannie becomes excited if Tony asks her for a favor (as he has forbidden her to use her magic for all the trouble it gets him into). Love eventually develops between Jeannie and Tony, and they married in 1969 (she then became Jeannie Nelson).

*Inconsistency:* Due to concerns that showing a woman's navel on TV was inappropriate at the time, Barbara Eden's harem outfit supported an extra-wide waistband for "cover-up" purposes. She was, however, allowed to show ample cleavage, and in beach scenes one can see that while Barbara's navel was concealed, other girls on the beach have theirs fully exposed (including Amanda Bellows). On occasion, Jeannie's waistband did slip and shocked censors when her navel was seen. Jeannie also mentions that she cannot be photographed, but in some episodes she can be, while in others (like her wedding episode) she cannot. Jeannie first mentions that "if a mortal marries a genie, only then will she lose her powers." She later says, "Only the power of Hadji [a powerful genie leader] can take them away."

*Relatives:* mother, Fatima (Florence Sundstrom, Lurene Tuttle, and Barbara Eden); father, Mustafa (Henry Corden); uncle, Sullie (Jackie Coogan); great grandfather, Biliejk (J. Carrol Naish); uncle, Vasmir (Arthur Mallet); uncle, Asmir (Ronald Long); cousin, Hamid (Ted Cassidy).

*Note:* In the 1991 TV movie *I Still Dream of Jeannie*, Jeannie's background was changed: Jeannie is now 4,233 years old (although she claims, "I'm only 4,229").

Barbara Eden and Larry Hagman. *NBC Photofest © NBC*

She was born as a genie in Mesopotamia and attended genie school to learn her craft. She was also said to have had many masters over the centuries. Jeannie II was also seen. Like her younger sister, Jeannie II was born a genie, but because she has never had a master, she is bound to remain in Mesopotamia forever (she can leave, but for only 24 hours at a time; she must return to maintain her youth, beauty, and powers). She again seeks to steal Tony from Jeannie and make him her first master.

## ANTHONY "TONY" NELSON

*Birthday:* July 25 (year not mentioned).

*Place of Birth:* Fowlers Corners, Ohio.

*Pet as a Kid:* Tiger (a poodle).

*Education:* Fowlers Corners High School (where he had the nickname "Bunky" Nelson). After graduating from college, Tony joined the U.S. Air Force and was assigned to its astronaut training program.

*Occupation:* Astronaut, stationed at Cocoa Beach, Florida (detached from the air force to provide services for NASA).

*Military Serial Number:* 30637-A (also given as 0736-A and 10610908).

*Address:* 1030 Palm Drive (address also given as 811 Pine Street and 1137 Oak Grove Street).

*Telephone Number:* 555-7231 (also given as 343-3349).

*Weight:* 181½ pounds.

*Rank:* Captain, then major.

*Career Flights:* Tony has piloted *Apollo 14*, *Apollo 15*, *Stardust 1*, the *X-14*, *Trail Blazer*, and the *T-38* (the first fully automated plane). It was during a test flight of the *Stardust 1* that a malfunction caused NASA officials to terminate the flight and bring it down. It crash-landed on a deserted island in the South Pacific where Tony, looking for debris to make an SOS signal, found a strange-looking green bottle. After examining it, he opened it. A puff of pink smoke emerged and materialized into a genie— "not your average everyday Jeannie but a beautiful genie who could grant any wish."

*Catchphrase:* "Jeannie!" (which he says when Jeannie uses her magic and it backfires).

*Relatives:* mother (June Jocelyn and Spring Byington); father (Hal Taggart); cousin, Arvel (Gabriel Dell); great great great great grandmother, Lady Diane Nelson, flashback sequence (Elaine Devery).

## OTHER CHARACTERS

Roger Healy is Tony's best friend (first a captain, then a major), who is the only other person aware that Jeannie is a genie. He is a swinging bachelor and lives in Apartment 217 (also seen as Apartment 213); an address is not given. He attended Horace Mann Elementary and High School. Due to Roger's contact with Jeannie, he contracted the Persian flu and became the only known case in 2,000 years. Dr. Alfred Bellows is the base psychiatrist who, after meeting Tony, has set two goals for himself: to prove to someone else that something strange is going on (as he is always alone when he becomes a victim of Jeannie's misguided magic) and to figure out what it is. He is an opera buff and is married to Amanda, a woman who becomes Jeannie's friend (and suspicious of both Jeannie and Tony for the strange things she witnesses). He and Amanda live at 310 Orange Drive.

# I Spy
(NBC, 1965–1968)

*Cast:* Robert Culp (Kelly Robinson), Bill Cosby (Alexander Scott).
*Basis:* Espionage agents Kelly Robinson and Alexander Scott travel the world seeking to stop enemies of the United States (Cold War agents and industrial spies) from carrying out their dastardly plans of destruction.

## KELLY ROBINSON
*Occupation:* Spy for the U.S. government. Although it is assumed he and Scott work for the Pentagon in Washington, D.C., it is never actually stated. Through dialogue, Kelly and Scott mention their superiors as "our people," "our superiors," or "Washington."
*Cover:* Tennis pro. Kelly calls himself a "tennis bum" and has won Davis Cup trophies (but he doesn't always win; he lost, for example, five sets at Forest Hills). When asked why he chose tennis, he responds, "It's better than digging ditches."
*Nickname:* Called "Kel" by Scott.
*Place of Birth:* Ohio.
*Education:* Princeton University (where he studied law and played on two Davis Cup tennis teams).
*Abilities:* Skilled in karate (but still manages to take a beating from the enemy).
*Hobbies:* Fishing, golfing, and duck hunting.
*Bad Habit:* Repeating what the person he is talking to says; smokes (too many cigarettes) and drinks.
*Favorite Foods:* Steamed clams (Scott continually warns him that he must curtail his culinary pursuits, "or you'll look like a lox on the court").
*Problem:* Kelly considers himself a ladies' man, but a romance can last only as long as an assignment lasts.

## ALEXANDER SCOTT
*Occupation:* Spy.
*Cover:* Kelly's trainer/masseur.
*Nickname:* Scotty (as called by Kelly).

*Place of Birth:* Philadelphia.

*Education:* Allentown High School (Scott contemplated becoming the school's basketball coach at the time).

*Abilities:* Skilled in karate and blessed with the instincts of an alley cat. He has training as a chemist and is an expert in explosives (he can, for example, make a bomb out of almost anything).

*Fault:* He will shoot to kill (or shoot first and ask questions later). He also has a tendency to argue with Kelly over everything, especially how an assignment should be handled.

*Note:* The 1994 TV movie update *I Spy Returns* reveals that Kelly is now a senior intelligence official and heads the SSA (Special Services Agency) of the government, and Scotty has become a college professor. It also introduces Nicole Scott (Salli Richardson) as Scotty's daughter and Bennett Robinson (George Newbern) as Kelly's son, the next generation of agents; the project however, failed to sell.

# *The Invaders*
## (ABC, 1967–1968)

*Cast:* Roy Thinnes (David Vincent).

*Basis:* David Vincent, a man returning from a business trip, witnesses the landing of a UFO but is unable to convince anyone of it happening. Determined to prove that what he saw happened, Vincent begins a lone journey to gather the facts and expose an alien invasion.

## DAVID VINCENT

*Address:* 36 Heming Drive, Santa Barbara, California.

*Education:* Santa Barbara State College.

*Occupation:* Architect.

*Car License Plate:* 812 249.

*Business:* Partners with Alan Landers (James Daly) in the firm of Landers and Vincent. Landers, the senior partner, began the firm 30 years ago.

*Business Address:* 3006 Willow Street, Santa Barbara, California.

*Business Telephone Number:* 555-5235.

## THE NIGHTMARE

*The Time:* 4:20 a.m.

*The Place:* Outside of a closed diner (Bud's Diner) on a deserted road off Highway 166.

*David's Condition:* Tired. He has been driving nonstop for 20 hours (returning from a business trip).

*The First Evidence:* A strange noise followed by a bright light as a spacecraft from another galaxy lands in a field.

*The Problem:* Although David reports the sighting, he is disbelieved after an investigation turns up nothing and he is targeted as a man who had gone too long without sleep and imagined what he saw.

*The Solution:* After investigating on his own, Vincent uncovers evidence that aliens from another planet are planning an invasion (to take over the Earth, as their planet is dying). He must now risk his life to "convince a disbelieving world that the nightmare has already begun." David resigns from his job and now travels around the country taking menial jobs to survive.

*The Help:* The Believers, a group of people who have seen what Vincent has, have banded together to stop the aliens. Kent Smith as Edgar Scoville is the only Believer with a recurring role. Carol Lynley (as Elyse Reynolds) and Anthony Eisley (as Bob Talman) are two of the Believers group.

## THE ALIENS

*Planet:* Never revealed.

*Plan:* To assume human form and assimilate into human society.

*Flaw:* "Some of them have mutated hands: a crooked fourth finger." They have no pulse or heartbeat and exist without blood.

*Alien Form:* An actual physical appearance is never seen. It is shown that the Invaders cannot sustain their human form without recharging in glass-like tube regeneration chambers (they become unstable). Failure to rejuvenate in time causes aliens to disintegrate in a glowing light (all that remains is an ash-like substance). It is also suggested that in their natural form, the aliens are horrifying and indistinguishable. They reproduce by passing electricity through seawater.

*Spaceships:* Cup-and-saucer shaped with a large center light and two smaller lights (to each side of the center).

*Weapons:* Captured humans are subject to hypnotic interrogation, and by using a metal disk (made of a substance unknown on Earth), they can take over and become that human. That metal disk, when placed on the back of a human's neck, can also cause death through a heart attack or cerebral hemorrhage.

*The Warning:* "You can't stop it [the invasion], it is going to happen. Don't fight us" (what the aliens tell David). As the show's narrator tells us, "David will fight, for they must be stopped, they must be exposed, If David Vincent doesn't do it, who will?"

# Iron Horse
## (ABC, 1966–1968)

*Cast:* Dale Robertson (Ben Calhoun), Gary Collins (Dave Tarrant), Bob Rando (Barnabas Rogers), Roger Torrey (Nils Torvald), Ellen McRae (Julie Parsons).

*Basis:* An enterprising gentleman gambler (Ben Calhoun), stuck with a near-bankrupt railroad as his winnings in a poker game, attempts to make the line profitable during the 1870s.

### BENJAMIN P. CALHOUN

*Occupation:* Owner of the Buffalo Pass, Scalplock, and Defiance Railroad (BPS&D). He is not only penniless but deeply in debt.

*Winning Card Hand:* With four queens and a 2 of spades, Ben won the railroad.

*Place of Birth:* Virginia.

*Military Service:* 9th Virginia Army of the Confederacy during the Civil War (also said to be the 9th Virginia Calvary); he later says the 79th Pennsylvania Volunteers during the Civil War.

*Belief:* That the future is the railroad and that once his line is built and connects with the Union Pacific Railroad, it will open up the 16 million acres of land to settlers and make him rich. Ben is laying track beginning in Wyoming and heading west to California to hook up tracks with the Union Pacific Railroad.

*Image:* People say Ben is arrogant; he says, "I'm lucky" (but he's also a con artist, a schemer, and a cheat—he will do what it takes to get what he wants).

*Operations:* Ben begins his takeover by adding a luxurious sleeping coach (the La Bonne Chance) as part of his train. It is preceded by a passenger/mail/baggage car and a coal car.

*Engine Number:* 3.

*Horse:* Hannibal.

### OTHER CHARACTERS

Dave is Ben's construction engineer (they have to lay track through each town as they head west to California), Barnabas is Ben's assistant, Nils is Ben's logger (acquires the wood for the track ties), and Julie is the freight line operator. Ulysses is Barnaby's raccoon.

# It Takes a Thief
## (ABC, 1968–1970)

*Cast:* Robert Wagner (Alexander Munday), Malachi Throne (Noah Bain).

*Basis:* Sophisticated cat burglar Alexander Munday performs daring missions for the U.S. government in exchange for his release from prison.

**ALEXANDER "AL" MUNDAY**

*Occupation:* Master con artist and thief.

*Personality:* Suave, sophisticated, and charming. He is also a ladies' man.

*Mistake:* Careless and caught red-handed in 1962 during a jewel heist.

*Sentence:* 10 years at the San Jobal Prison.

*Prison ID:* Number 131245.

*Reprieve:* A U.S. government pardon to steal for them ("I am by far the best thief they ever talked into working for them").

*Superior:* Noah Bain of the SIA was assigned as Munday's "parole officer" (oversees his missions).

*Frequent Cover:* International playboy.

*Assignments:* Highly dangerous feats of thievery to acquire articles or information the government requires.

*Expertise:* Master pickpocket, escape artist, and explosives expert and skilled at posing as someone else. Al can recognize style in a thief and claims, "I can spot a pickpocket in the middle of St. Petersburg Square on Easter Sunday."

*Inspiration:* His father, Alistair Munday (Fred Astaire), a retired master thief who was called "The Panther."

*Home:* A fashionably furnished (by the government) TV-monitored mansion on Washington Square in Washington, D.C. (SIA headquarters). It appears the government can't always trust Al, and he needs to be watched all the time.

*Job Summation:* "I'm a simple thief, and killing plays no part in my book of rules."

*Note:* Wally Powers (Edward Binns) replaced Noah in final-season episodes; Charlotte Brown, nicknamed "Chuck" (Susan Saint James), is the pretty but kooky thief who complicates Al's assignments when she appears at the scene of one of Al's assignments.

# *It's about Time*
(CBS, 1966–1967)

*Cast:* Frank Aletter (Captain Mac MacKenzie), Jack Mullaney (Lieutenant Hector Canfield), Imogene Coca (Shad), Joe E. Ross (Gronk), Mary Grace (Mlor), Pat Cardi (Breer), Cliff Norton (Cave Boss), Mike Mazurki (Clon).

*Note:* Imogene Coca's correct character name is Shad, *not* Shag (or Shadd or Shagg). Shag does appear in the opening theme, and she is called this in the pilot episode but at no other time. When the producers learned that "Shag" was a British slang vulgarism, they changed the name; due to the cost involved in redoing the theme, it was left in as "Shag" in the original format; it was changed for the revised format theme (but in that revised theme, the title is seen as *Its about Time* and not the correct *It's about Time*).

*Original Format:* During the flight of a U.S. spaceship, two astronauts (Mac and Hec) break the time barrier and find themselves in the prehistoric age where they must not only survive the dangers that exist but also find a way to repair their ship and return home.

*Revised Format:* Mac and Hec manage to repair their ship and with a cave family as passengers (Gronk, Shad, Mlor, and Breer) return to the twentieth century. As the cave family attempts to live in a modern world, Mac and Hec struggle to keep their presence a secret, fearing they will become the concern of scientists and placed in confinement.

## THE SPACE SHIP

*NASA Space Capsule:* The *Scorpion*. It was launched from Cape Kennedy.
*Identification Number:* E-X-1.
*Speed:* 60,000 miles a second when it broke the time barrier.
*Capsule Color:* Appears as both silver and blue.
*Construction:* It took 184 men (50 of whom were scientists) 39 months to build.
*Sustained Damage:* Damaged condenser points (later said to be the filament of the solenoid transistor block, which controls liftoff).
*Repairs:* Mac first says they need crystal and carbon to repair the damage; he later says only copper and finally aluminum (which is also needed to repair the ship's intake valves).

## THE ASTRONAUTS MAC AND HEC

*Salary:* $12.50 an hour (flight pay).
*Place of Birth:* Mac in Los Angeles, Hec in Columbus, Ohio (he later mentions Riverview, Ohio). Hec (sometimes called Hector) was born in 1939 and mentioned he was a Boy Scout as a child.
*Residence:* A cave that they both share. Mac and Hec first believed they were on another planet until they spotted a dinosaur (a tyrannosaurus rex) and saved a cave boy (Breer) from falling off a cliff. They estimate they are in the year 1,000,000 BC.
*Cover:* To present themselves as friendly to the cave people, Mac and Hec pretend to be strangers from the "Other Side of the Hill." They were originally thought to be evil spirits (by their astronaut dress).
*Ritual:* To be accepted as part of the cave people, Mac and Hec had to present the Cave Boss with a dinosaur tooth.

## THE CAVE PEOPLE

*Tribe:* The Village.

*God:* The Fire God (Volcano).

*Enemies:* The Painted Ones.

*Cave Family Befriended by Mac and Hec:* Gronk and Shad (parents) and their children Mlor (teenage girl) and Breer (boy).

*Shad and Gronk:* Shad, the intelligent one, calls the dim-witted Gronk "Gronkie" and is known for her Cookarooku soup (made from the eggs of the Cookarooku bird); Gronk's favorite meal is rib of dinosaur.

*Mlor and Breer:* Mlor is a beautiful blonde and dresses in skins that Shad believes are a bit too revealing and wishes she would dress more conservatively. While Mlor believes she is a good cook, Hec calls her meals "yuck," which Mlor believes is a compliment. Each year, "when leaf on tree turn red," the Village selects one girl to become a sacrifice for a dinosaur so the creatures will not attack their village. Mlor received the "honor" (by selecting the long stick and "winning") but was saved by Hec and Mac. Her favorite beverage is milk from coconut. Crek, Shad's mother, claims that "Mlor hair [blonde] shine bright like moon on water buffalo mane." Mlor is also the village's most proficient weaver (can turn vines into ropes). Breer is in the process of becoming a "man" (must perform certain customs to achieve his status). Breer, like Mlor, is seen only when needed in first-format episodes (and their absence is never explained).

*Village Leader:* Boss. He is also the village's witch doctor and rules by his "Sacred Necklace" and "Sacred Club."

*Boss's Assistant:* Clon, a dim-wit who obeys orders (Hec calls him the "Simple Simon of the cave people").

*Relatives:* Crek, Shad's mother (Imogene Coca); Mrs. Boss, also called Wife of Boss (Kathleen Freeman); Blob, Boss's daughter (Mary Farnow); Brak, Boss's son, also called Brak, Son of Boss (Edson Stroll). Not seen were Shad's father ("He was lost in jungle and never came home") and Gronk's mother ("She live on other side of tar pits").

## REVISED FORMAT

Although Mac and Hec find copper in the Dinosaur Cave, it is apparently not enough to make repairs. When Gronk realizes what minerals Mac and Hec need, he takes a diamond from the eye of his tribal idol. Mac is able to repair the condenser points (as the diamond contains the crystal and carbon they need), and he reverses the flight information from their last trip and programs it into the computer. However, when the Cave Boss discovers what Gronk has done, he believes Gronk and his family are evil spirits and orders them killed. When Mac and Hec learn what has happened, they shelter the cave family aboard the capsule and blast off. The *Scorpion* again breaks the time barrier, this time returning the astronauts (after five months) and their passengers to twentieth-century Los Angeles (the capsule lands on the front lawn of a house for sale about 50 miles outside of Los Angeles; surprisingly, the air force is not too concerned about retrieving the capsule, as it just remains there, or about rescuing Mac and Hec, as they are the ones who have to call the air force to tell them they have landed).

*The Cover-Up:* Fearing the cave family will be taken into custody if NASA discovers them, Mac and Hec hide them out in their three-room apartment (Apartment 909; the cave family sleeps in the bedroom, Mac and Hec on chairs in the living room). They tell Mr. Tyler (Alan DeWitt), the building superintendent, that their roommates, the Gronk family, are from a small country called Nordania and need time to adjust to life in America. Their hope is to prevent anyone from discovering who the cave family really are (even though the Gronk family still wear their cave clothing; Mac tried to get them to wear modern clothes but, as Gronk said, "Like old clothes better"). The cave family believes that Los Angeles is the "Other Side of the Hill."

*Reaction:* The cave family found their new world strange, and their efforts to fit in became very confusing for them. The radio was "box with sound," cars were "strange animal," and rocking chairs were "alive chair." The first "monster" the cave family encountered was a Volkswagen driven by an elderly lady (Gronk "killed the beast" with his club).

*Recording Artists:* When Rick Stewart (Jack Albertson) hears the cave family singing a song ("Dinosaur Stew"), he signs them up for a deal with Big Beat Records; the cave family (as the Cave Family Swingers) then perform the song on the TV program *The Fred Gulliver Show.* In this episode, "Cave Family Swingers," Hec mentions that his favorite recording artists are Morris the Missionary and Dick the Dentist and His Four Cavities.

# *The Jetsons*
(ABC, 1962–1963)

*Voice Cast:* George O'Hanlon (George Jetson), Penny Singleton (Jane Jetson), Janet Waldo (Judy Jetson), Daws Butler (Elroy Jetson), Don Messick (Astro).

*Basis:* Life in the twenty-first century as seen through the experiences of the animated Jetson family: parents George and Jane and their children Judy and Elroy.

## GEORGE JETSON

*Age:* Said to be in his mid-30s.
*Address:* The Sky Pad Apartments.
*Telephone Number:* Venus-1234.
*Hair Color:* Red.
*Occupation:* Engineer at Spacely Space Sprockets. The company produces 3 million sprockets a day. In the opening theme, when George is seen driving his space car, it transforms into a briefcase when he lands.
*Boss:* Cosmo G. Spacely (voice of Mel Blanc).
*Military Service:* U.S. Space Guards Division of the army. Stationed at Camp Nebula; George is now in the army reserves.
*Favorite Actress:* Gina Lolajupiter (a takeoff of actress Gina Lollobrigida).
*Favorite TV Show:* "Dr. Ken Stacey" (a takeoff of the series *Ben Casey*).
*Favorite Newscast: The Stuntley-Hinkley Report* (a parody of NBC's *The Huntley-Brinkley Report* newscast).

## JANE JETSON

*Age:* 33.
*Occupation:* Housewife.
*Measurements:* 36-26-36.

*Dress Size:* 8.

*Hair Color:* Orange.

*Favorite Department Store:* Satellite City.

*Favorite Beauty Parlor:* The Constellation Beauty Salon.

*Award:* Jane won the title "Miss Western Hemisphere" in the Miss Solar System Beauty Pageant.

*Favorite Song:* "Saturn Doll" (based on "Satin Doll") by Count Spacey and His Orchestra (a takeoff of Count Basie and His Orchestra). While dating, she and George danced to the song.

## JUDY JETSON

*Age:* 15.

*Measurements:* 32-22-32.

*Hair Color:* White.

*Education:* Orbit High School.

*Car:* A jalopy with the license plate 738.

*Diary:* Judy has a talking diary (voice of Selma Diamond) that she calls "DiDi."

*Career Ambition:* To become a musical recording artist (a pop star).

## ELROY JETSON

*Age:* Said to be both six and a half and eight years old.

*Hair Color:* Blonde.

*Education:* The Little Dipper School (where he is a member of the Little Dipper League baseball team).

*Pet Dog:* Astro.

*Favorite TV Show: Spies in Space.*

## OTHER CHARACTERS

Rosie (voice of Jean Vander Pyl) is the Jetson family robotic maid. She is a model XB-500 Service Robot, and the family acquired her from U-Rent-a-Maid. Cosmo Spacely and his wife Stella live at 175 Snerdville Drive. Cosmo's competition is Cogswell Cogs, a company owned by Mr. Cogswell (voice of Daws Butler). Henry Orbit (voice of Howard Morris) is the janitor at the Sky Pad Apartments.

# *The Joey Bishop Show*
## (NBC, 1961–1964; CBS, 1964–1965)

*Original Cast* (1961–1962): Joey Bishop (Joey Barnes), Marlo Thomas (Stella Barnes), Madge Blake (Mrs. Barnes), Warren Berlinger (Larry Barnes), Joe Flynn (Frank Grafton), Virginia Vincent (Betty Grafton).

*Revised Cast* (1962–1965): Joey Bishop (Joey Barnes), Abby Dalton (Ellie Barnes), Guy Marks (Freddie), Corbett Monica (Larry Corbett), Joe Besser (J. J. Jillson), Mary Treen (Hilda Hinkelmeyer).

*Original Basis* (1961–1962): The home and working life of Joey Barnes, a public relations man.

*Revised Basis* (1962–1965): Events in the life of Joey Barnes, a former nightclub comedian turned host of a television talk and variety series.

## JOSEPH "JOEY" BARNES (1961–1962)

*Occupation:* Public relations agent for Wellington, Willoughby, and Jones (originally called the J. P. Willoughby Company). The sign on Joey's front desk reads "Keep Smiling."

*Address:* A home on Wilshire Boulevard.

*Telephone Number:* 257-7734.

*Marital Status:* Single (although he is the sole support of his family, his widowed mother, and siblings Stella and Larry).

*Catchphrase:* "Son of a gun."

*Military Service:* Army sergeant (with the 82nd Airborne Division, Able Company, during World War II).

*Affiliation:* As a child, he was a Boy Scout (won a merit badge).

*Sister:* Stella. She is studying to become an actress.

*Brother:* Larry. He is studying to become a doctor and is attending medical school. He has a "used skeleton" called Mr. Bones that he paid $60 for and it has become their "skeleton in the closet."

*Mother:* Mrs. Barnes (a first name is not given). Joey gives her $300 a month to run the house, and she looks to be in her 60s but claims she is 55 and is actually 57.

*Brother-in-Law:* Frank Grafton (married Joey's older sister, Betty). Frank is lazy and impresses people by telling them he doesn't need a job. He is an "idea man" and feels his ship has not yet come in (he can't find a job that fits his weird talents). He often sponges off Joey and did hold jobs (like potato peeler salesman, used car salesman, and process server) but quit because they were just not right for him.

Frank and Betty live in an apartment (236), and his favorite pastime is entering contests (as an example, he entered the Aunt Martha Bird Seed Contest and won a year's supply of birdseed [he had to borrow money from Joey to buy the birds] and actually won $10,000 in the Sweetheart Biscuit Contest with this slogan: "When it comes to biscuits, let's not be wishy-washy; be sure they're Sweetheart Biscuits because they're never squishy-squashy").

*Girlfriend:* Nancy Hadley played Barbara Simpson, who is also Joey's secretary.

*Note:* The original pilot, "Everything Happens to Me," aired as a segment of *The Danny Thomas Show* on March 27, 1961. Here Joey Bishop played Joey Mason, a Hollywood press agent. Billy Gilbert and Madge Blake played his parents, "Pop" and "Mom" Mason.

## JOSEPH "JOEY" BARNES (1962–1965)

*Place of Birth:* South Philadelphia (where he grew up on Tenth Street).

*Occupation:* Host of the 60-minute talk and variety television series *The Joey Barnes Show* (airs weeknights from 11:00 p.m. to midnight on NBC; Sundays at 9:30 p.m. on CBS opposite NBC's *Bonanza*).

*Prior Occupation:* Nightclub comedian who gave up the circuit in 1960 (at which time *The Joey Barnes Show* premiered).

*The Show:* On NBC, it was mentioned that the show was broadcast from Studio 5-H at 30 Rockefeller Plaza (NBC's Manhattan headquarters). On CBS, all references to NBC were deleted. No reason is given why NBC canceled Joey's show. After three weeks of unemployment, Joey receives a phone call from CBS offering him a job at the network. The first thing Joey did was to take down the painting of the NBC Peacock (the network's logo) he had on his living room wall and replace it with a painting of the CBS logo—the CBS Eye. In real life, NBC felt the show was not supplying the ratings they wanted and canceled it. CBS picked up the series because it was a cheap investment (especially since it was in black and white). The program began in black and white (1961–1962), switched to color (1962–1964), and returned to black and white (1964–1965).

*Awards:* The TV Critics Association placed Joey's show in 12th position in the comedy category just ahead of *The Bullwinkle Show* cartoon series.

*Wife:* Eleanor, called "Ellie."

*Son:* Joey Barnes Jr. (played by Matthew David Smith). He was born at Mid-Town Hospital in Manhattan in 1963.

*Address:* The Carlton Arms Apartments, Apartment 711 (New York–based episodes; the last season is set in Los Angeles, although the apartment looks the same).

*Joey's Catchphrase:* "Son of a Gun."

*First Skit Joey Performed on His Show:* His impression of a midget sneezing.

*Lucky Charm:* His shirt cuff links.

*Bad Habits:* Showing up late for appointments and making jokes about everything.

## ELEANOR "ELLIE" BARNES

*Place of Birth:* Texas.

*Occupation:* Housewife and mother.

*Prior Occupation:* Librarian. In a later episode, Joey mentions that Ellie was a model when they were dating.

*Song:* Ellie wrote the song "The One I Love Most," which Joey thought was the worst song ever written, but singer Bobby Rydell thought differently and recorded it. Here is a sampling: "I love Gracie, she reads me Dick Tracy. . . . I love Jewel, she lets me beat her at pool, but the one I love most is my mother."

*Nickname:* Texas (as called by Joey).

*Hobby:* Putting complex puzzles together.

*TV Debut:* Ellie, Joey, and four-month-old Joey Jr. appeared on a special edition of Joey's show called "An Evening with the Barnes Family."

*Favorite Eatery:* Max's Delicatessen.

## OTHER CHARACTERS

J. J. Jillson is the building's overweight, henpecked superintendent. He is married to the overbearing and never seen (only heard) Tantalia (voice of Maxine Semon). Tantalia watches the 11:00 news for laughs and is always yelling at Jillson. The one word Jillson wishes he could pronounce is *aluminum* ("I'd give anything to say that word right"). Jillson is always called "Jillson" or "Mr. Jillson." In the 1963 episode "Jillson and the Cinnamon Buns," Joey challenged Jillson to lose five pounds, and when he did, Jillson appeared as a guest on Joey's show; it is here that Joey introduces him as "J. J. Jillson." Larry Corbett is Joey's business manager and writer (Joey's filing system for Larry's jokes is crumbling them and then tossing the paper into the wastebasket). Joey and Larry met in 1953, when Larry was a struggling writer. Before his role as Larry, Corbett Monica played Johnny Edwards, a comedian at the Purple Pussycat Club. Freddie is Joey's agent and friend since childhood. Hilda is Joey's maid, who also doubles as the baby's nurse.

# Land of the Giants
### (ABC, 1968–1970)

*Cast:* Gary Conway (Steve Burton), Don Marshall (Dan Erickson), Heather Young (Betty Hamilton), Deanna Lund (Valerie Scott), Don Matheson (Mark Wilson), Kurt Kasznar (Alexander Fitzhugh), Stefan Arngrim (Barry Lockridge).

*Basis:* A futuristic spaceship on a routine flight from New York to London is engulfed in a strange atmospheric disturbance and propelled into a world of giant-appearing humans. The struggles of its crew and passengers to survive in their new world and find a means to reverse the time warp and return to their own world are depicted.

## OVERALL SERIES INFORMATION

*The Time:* June 12, 1983 (the date of series creator Irwin Allen's birthday).

*The Ship:* The *Spinthrift*, Suborbital Flight 612. In the original concept it is Flight 703 of a ship called the *Shamrock*.

*Crew:* Captain Steve Burton, copilot Dan Erickson, and stewardess Betty Hamilton.

*Passengers:* Valerie Scott, Mark Wilson, Alexander Fitzhugh, and Barry Lockridge.

*The Disaster:* Without warning, the *Spinthrift* loses all communication with the London control tower when it is propelled into a large glowing green cloud. The ship is 500 miles above the Earth and 17 minutes from London. Burton, unable to contact the control tower, spots what he believes are airport lights and lands the craft. Although a thick fog makes visibility zero, Steve and Dan venture outside the ship to investigate. Suddenly, an enormous car passes over them. They next hear footsteps and rush back to the *Spinthrift*. As Steve attempts to take off, a giant boy (the footsteps they heard) picks up the ship. Steve accelerates and manages to escape the giant's grip, but at 5,000 feet they are still passing buildings. With the reserve power nearly exhausted, Steve manages to land the ship in a dense forest, which becomes their temporary home.

## THE CREW

*Steve Burton:* Age 26 and a three-year veteran of futuristic transports. He is single and has no immediate plans of marrying.

*Dan Erickson:* 25 years of age, an ex–decathlon star; Steve's copilot since 1978. He is also single.

*Betty Hamilton:* 22 years old and unsure she has made the right career choice (as she becomes nervous during flights). She is single and, as the series progressed, became more sure of herself and a help to Steve and Dan in keeping their passengers safe. In the original concept, the character was named Diane Hamilton.

## THE PASSENGERS

*Valerie Scott:* A beautiful but rich and spoiled socialite and heiress. In the original concept, the character was named Joan Templeton, a genetics professor (possessing DSc, MD, and PhD degrees). Her destination was the International Scientific Meeting at the Royal Academy of Medicine.

*Mark Wilson:* 34 years of age, an engineer and wealthy business tycoon traveling to London to close a $50 million business deal. In the original concept, Mark was an ex–construction boss, ex–wildcatter, and self-made millionaire.

*Alexander Fitzhugh:* A master thief who is fleeing authorities and carrying a briefcase with $1 million in cash. In the original concept, the character was named Peter Linglehopper (alias "The Loop" and "The Hop"), a master con artist who is posing as a navy commander (and carrying a stolen $1 million).

*Barry Lockridge:* Age 11, an orphan being sent to London to live with relatives he has never seen. He has a dog named Clipper.

## THE GIANTS

The planet is never named. It is depicted as a world parallel to Earth, as everything is just bigger (even the Chrysler cars used in scenes). But it is referred to as the "Land of Giants" by the crew and passengers. As the earthlings become known, they are branded the "Little People" (they are only about six inches tall), and a reward has been offered for their capture; death is the penalty for assisting them. The giant Kobic (Kevin Hagen) is the police-like inspector seeking to capture them.

# *Lost in Space*
## (CBS, 1965–1968)

*Cast:* Guy Williams (John Robinson), June Lockhart (Maureen Robinson), Marta Kristen (Judy Robinson), Angela Cartwright (Penny Robinson), Mark Goddard (Donald West), Jonathan Harris (Zachary Smith), Bob May (Robot), Dick Tufeld (Robot's voice).

*Basis:* A pioneering Earth family, the Robinsons, attempt to survive the unknown dangers of unexplored space when their craft malfunctions and they become lost in space.

## OVERALL SERIES INFORMATION

It is the year 1997, and one family, the Robinsons (parents John and Maureen, and their children Judy, Penny, and Will), who possess the unique balance of scientific achievement, emotional stability, and pioneer resourcefulness, have been chosen from 2 million volunteers to explore the planet Alpha Centauri in the hope it will support life to reduce overcrowding on Earth. To make the mission possible, the *Jupiter II* is constructed. All is progressing well until an enemy agent (Dr. Zachary Smith) attempts to sabotage the ship but accidentally traps himself aboard. The *Jupiter II* is thrown off course (due to Smith's extra weight) and strands them in outer space with no way to return home.

## *JUPITER II* STATISTICS

*Cost:* $30 million. When scientists became concerned with overpopulation in the year 1967, construction on the *Jupiter II* began; it was completed in 1997 and launched on October 16, 1997. It is under the command of the Alpha Control Center.

*Original Ship:* The *Gemini XII* (in the original unaired pilot; changed to avoid confusion with the actual U.S. Gemini space project).

*Height:* Two stories.

*Freezing Tubes:* Six (preserves humans for long-duration flights, such as for the Robinsons, whose mission was estimated to take 98 years).

*Lower Deck:* Houses the pulsating atomic motors "that will propel the ship to new worlds." Also contained here are the family's living quarters, staterooms, and galleys.

*Upper Level:* The guidance control system (linked to the lower level via an electronic elevator).

*Space Pod:* The *Chariot* (allows for short-distance flights).

*First Planet Landing:* Preplanis (where the Robinson's established a temporary home during the first season). They require carbon tetrachloride for food purification.

## THE ROBINSON FAMILY

Very little background information is given.

*John Robinson:* A professor of astrophysics at the University of Stellar Dynamics.

*Maureen Robinson:* A biochemist with the New Mexico College of Space Medicine; the first woman in history to pass the International Space Administration's grueling physical and emotional screenings for intergalactic flight.

*Judith "Judy" Robinson:* Age 19 and said to have "heroically postponed all hopes for a career in the musical comedy field"; D-12 is her room on the ship. Judy was crowned "Miss Galaxy" when she was chosen to compete in an outer space beauty pageant.

*Penelope "Penny" Robinson:* Age 11. With an IQ of 147, she is a specialist in zoology. She had an invisible friend she discovered in a grotto who she called Mr.

Seated: Billy Mumy and Angela Cartwright; standing: Mark Goddard, Marta Kristen, June Lockhart, and Guy Williams. *CBS/Photofest © CBS*

Nobody and a pet Bloop (chimpanzee with llama ears) she named Debbie. As a child, she had a pet cat named Princess.

*William "Will" Robinson:* Age nine. A graduate of the Campbell Canyon School of Science at his current age; held the highest average in the school's history. He is an expert in the field of electronics. He plays the guitar (the only song he knows is "Greensleeves").

## OTHER CHARACTERS
Major Donald West, the ship's pilot, is a geologist and world-famous radio astronomer. He is a graduate student from the Center for Radio Astronomy. He "rocketed the scientific world with his theory of other planets' fitness for human habitation." He was also an officer in the U.S. Space Corps. Colonel Zachary Smith is an enemy agent for an unnamed world power. He operates under the code name Aeolus 14 Umbre. He attended Oxford University and was champion for three years in the school's chess club. He enjoys peanut butter and salami sandwiches before bed and is most often responsible for a setback. He is literally a coward and greedy and devoted to money (he turned the *Jupiter II*, for example, into a hotel he called the "Happy Acres Hotel" to accommodate [and fleece] visiting aliens). He calls Will "William," and to get out of doing work, he uses "my delicate back" as an excuse. Henry Jones played Jeremiah Smith, Zachary's cousin. Robot is an environmental control unit (called Robot) whose key function is to perform the final analysis of the physical environment of the new planet. Although Robot has no official name, it calls itself Robot Model B-9 (in the episode "The Ghost Planet") and "I Am a Robot of the Class M-3" (in the episode "The Colonists"); it continues to say, "Programmed to provide information to all *Jupiter II* personnel."

Colonel Smith sees Robot as a slave and calls him various names, such as "Bucket of Bolts," "Potbellied Pumpkin," "Disreputable Thunderhead," and "Tin Plated Tattletale." His favorite name for him is "Booby." Robot most often obeys Smith but does object at times: "A robot does not live by programming alone. Some culture is required to keep my tapes in balance. My computer tapes are not programmed for day and night work. I need eight hours rest like other robots."

Robot defends itself with electrical discharges and is most attached to Will Robinson ("Danger Will Robinson" is often heard when Robot senses troubling situations).

Sue England is heard as various female computer voices; Dawson Palmer plays various aliens; Virina Marcus is Athena, the Green Alien Lady; Dee Hartford is Nancy Pi Squared, the Space Beauty; and Fritz Feld is Mr. Zumdish, the space entrepreneur. He was originally the keeper of the Intergalactic Department Store, the owner of a tourist business called Outermost Fundish, Ltd. ("Let Fun Be Your Guide"), and, finally, owner of the Zumdish Insurance Company. Leonard J. Stone appeared as Farnum the Great.

*Note:* An animated pilot film called *Lost in Space* aired on ABC in 1973 that found the *Jupiter II* operating as a space shuttle and battling strange creatures on other planets. Craig Robinson (voice of Michael Bell) was the ship's pilot. Jonathan Harris voiced Professor Smith, Sherry Alberoni was Dodi Carmichael, and Vincent Van Patten was Linc Robinson.

# Love on a Rooftop
## (ABC, 1966–1967)

*Cast:* Judy Carne (Julie Willis), Peter Deuel (Dave Willis), Rich Little (Stan Parker), Barbara Babcock (Carol Parker), Herbert Voland (Fred Hammond), Edith Atwater (Phyllis Hammond).

*Basis:* A poor apprentice construction worker (Dave) and the daughter (Julie) of a rich car salesman (Fred) attempt to enjoy their life as newlyweds, surviving on what little money Dave earns despite Fred's endless efforts to provide a better life for Julie (as he believes Dave will never be able to support her).

## JULIE WILLIS
*Maiden Name:* Julie Hammond.
*Age:* 22.
*Parents:* Fred and Phyllis Hammond.
*Place of Birth:* San Francisco.
*Address* (before marriage): 3654 Algonquin Place.
*Address* (after marriage): 1400 McDougal Street (a rooftop apartment in San Francisco above the Loomis Gift Shop. Numbers do not appear on any apartment doors). There is a ladder that leads from their apartment to the roof. Julie considers the roof to be a patio; Dave considers it a roof ("Honey, where I come from, anything with TV antennas and pigeons is a roof").
*Ambition:* Artist (she is currently taking art classes).
*Trait:* Emotional and sensitive. She gives human characteristics to inanimate objects (a bed, she says, should be a member of the family, and when the telephone rings, "it cries to be picked up when nobody does").
*Wedding Gift from Fred:* A window for their apartment (prior to this, Judy had painted a window on a wall to represent one).

## DAVID "DAVE" WILLIS
*Age:* 24. Orphaned as a child.
*Occupation:* Apprentice architect with the firm of Bennington and Associates.
*Salary:* $85.37 a week.
*Trait:* Completely independent.

*First Meeting:* Dave, perched atop a construction girder, dropped his lunch, a sandwich that landed in the open handbag of Julie as she walked by. He chased his lunch and met Julie, and it was a love at first sight.

*That Sandwich:* First said to be liverwurst on rye, later said to be liverwurst on pumpernickel.

*Favorite Dinner:* Beef stroganoff.

*Spare Key:* Dave and Julie hide their spare key in the lamp next to their apartment door.

*Prior Girlfriend:* Barbara Ames (played by Gayle Hunnicutt), an airline stewardess.

## FRED AND PHYLLIS HAMMOND

Fred, Julie's father, was in Europe on business when Julie married Dave and says, when first meeting Dave, "If I had been here, I would have stopped this marriage." (Dave responded with, "Nice to meet you too, Mr. Hammond.")

There is virtually no information on the couple. It is learned that when Fred and Phyllis first married, they lived in an apartment "smaller than a pillbox." "I didn't know the difference then; I thought everybody lived that way." While Julie relinquished her life of luxury, Fred had set his goal to convince Dave to accept his help.

## STAN AND CAROL PARKER

Julie and Dave's downstairs neighbors who are struggling to live on a small income Stan earns as an inventor (or, as Carol says, "a freelance genius"). Stan is hoping to invent something that everyone needs; the problem is, "I can't figure out what that is because it is so obvious." Stan often says that "I amaze myself" with his crazy ideas (like the "Stan Instant Alert System"—a cowbell attached to a door to announce that someone has entered their home—and "L.I.L.L.Y.— Let's Lose Leap Year. "When I'm through," Stan says, "February will have 30 days just like every other month." He figured out how to do this with the "Parker Time Clock," a clock that gains two minutes and 43 seconds a day, 365 days a year, and uses up February 29. "Everyone will have to have my clock"). Of all the weird ideas Stan had, "Drive a Drunk" is not that strange—"Someone gets drunk at a party, and they call me to drive them home."

# The Man from U.N.C.L.E.
### (NBC, 1964–1968)

*Cast:* Robert Vaughn (Napoleon Solo), David McCallum (Illya Kuryakin), Leo G. Carroll (Alexander Waverly).

*Basis:* Napoleon Solo and Illya Kuryakin, agents for U.N.C.L.E. (United Network Command for Law Enforcement), battle the evils of THRUSH, an organization bent on world domination. Alexander Waverly is their superior.

## OVERALL SERIES INFORMATION

*U.N.C.L.E. Headquarters:* Based in Manhattan with the Del Floria Taylor Shop in Manhattan on Second Avenue and 40th Street as its front.

*U.N.C.L.E. Sections:* 1. Policy and Operations. 2. Operations and Enforcement. 3. Enforcement and Intelligence. 4. Intelligence and Communications. 5. Communications and Security. 6. Security and Personnel. 7. Propaganda and Finance. 8. Camouflage and Deception.

## NAPOLEON SOLO

*Place of Birth:* Kansas City, Kansas (another episode claims he was born in Montreal, Canada, where his father owned a hotel and his mother was an actress).

*Military Career:* Served with the army during the Korean War.

*Address:* The Alexandria Hotel at 221 Fifth Avenue in Manhattan.

*Favorite Dinner:* Appears to be steak, although he also enjoys Danish food and chicken soup.

*Abilities:* Napoleon can fly a helicopter and ride a motorcycle and is knowledgeable in several languages (Italian, French, and Russian). He is not a man of action. He would rather use his considerable charm to talk his way out of a situation than use physical force (although he is well versed in the martial arts; he is also an expert swordsman).

*Car:* (Metallic Blue Piranha) License Plate: U.N.C.L.E.

*Ambition:* Longs for a wife and family.

*Character:* Napoleon is called the "Top U.N.C.L.E. Agent in America." He is a suave and sophisticated ladies' man and an expert at chess, and he prefers a well-chilled martini (although he also orders one with two onions). Napoleon carries a flask and takes his coffee with cream and no sugar. He is a college graduate and often quotes from the Bible, Shakespeare, and poems.

## ILLYA KURYAKIN

*Place of Birth:* Russia, but speaks with what appears to be a British accent.

*Education:* He first attended the University of Georgia in Ibilisi (where he learned gymnastics), then the Sorbonne in France (postgraduate work), and finally England's Cambridge University (where he acquired a degree in mechanics). He graduated from the U.N.C.L.E. Survival School in 1956.

*Military Career:* Service with the Russian navy.

*Abilities:* Knowledgeable in many fields and well versed in the martial arts. He is also an expert marksman and archer.

David McCallum, Leo G. Carroll, and Robert Vaughn. *NBC/Photofest © NBC*

*Specialty:* While not much of a drinker (prefers only wine or beer), he is a gourmet eater, not a cook. He likes his coffee black and prefers cats to dogs.
*Astrological Sign:* Scorpio.
*Fault:* Prone to catching colds (due to his allergies).
*Badge Number:* 2.
*Weapon:* A Magnum 35, a refined version of the Magnum 44. He communicates with headquarters with his pen, which is set to Channel D.

*Note:* In the TV movie update, *The Man from U.N.C.L.E.: The 15 Years Later Affair*, it is learned that Illya quit U.N.C.L.E. to open his own fashion boutique called Vanya. Although it appeared that Alexander Waverly had been grooming Napoleon to take his place, the update discloses that Napoleon had quit the organization in 1968 to begin his own computer company.

See also *The Girl from U.N.C.L.E.*

# *Mannix*

(CBS, 1967–1975)

*Cast:* Mike Connors (Joe Mannix), Gail Fisher (Peggy Fair).
*Basis:* The cases of investigator Joe Mannix, first as an employee of Intertect, then as an independent private detective.

## JOSEPH "JOE" MANNIX

*Heritage:* The son of Armenian parents (who operated a vineyard in California).
*Place of Birth:* Summer Grove, California (most likely in the early 1930s).
*Height:* 6 feet, 1½ inches tall.
*Weight:* 180 pounds.
*Eyes:* Brown.
*Hair:* Dark brown.
*Blood Type:* AB+.
*Languages:* English, French, and fluent Armenian.
*Address:* First lived at 2742 Canyon Road, then at 17 Pasco Verdes, in Los Angeles.
*Telephone Number:* 555-6644.
*Education:* Western California University (Class of 1955). He acquired his private investigator's license (no. 13007) a year later.
*Occupation:* Private detective, first with Intertect, a computerized investigative firm run by Lew Wickersham (Joseph Campanella). A year later (1968), Mannix resigns and opens his own detective agency.
*Intertect Phone Number:* KL5-2271.

*Military Service:* Air force lieutenant (fighter pilot) during the Korean War.

*Abilities:* Possesses a black belt in karate; can fly airplanes and helicopters.

*Hobbies:* Sailing, golf, and swimming.

*Guns:* Mannix carries a .38 snub-nose Smith and Wesson (but he also uses a Beretta 9 mm, a Colt .45 ACP, and a Walther PPK).

*Favorite Drink:* Irish (usually on the rocks).

*Cars:* Mannix first drove a customized Oldsmobile Toronado (license plate UQW 477). He later drove a Dodge Dart (plate NMO 918), a Barracuda (plate 700 AKN), and a Cuda (plate 714 AQU).

*Car Phone Numbers:* KL5 277, KG6 2114, and AG6 2114.

## MARGARET "PEGGY" FAIR

*Occupation:* Secretary (girl Friday) to Joe Mannix.

*Place of Birth:* Los Angeles.

*Phone Number:* KL-5 6175.

*Marital Status:* Widow (her late husband, Marcus Fair, was a police officer killed in the line of duty in 1968; they had been married since 1961).

*Son:* Toby (played by Mark Stewart).

*Ability:* While proficient as a secretary, Peggy occasionally goes undercover to help Joe on assignments and uses her contact at the division of motor vehicles for license plate background checks.

*Relaxation:* Watching Humphrey Bogart movies and listening to music (mostly pop, jazz, and blues).

*Affiliation:* Secretary for the local branch of the Boy Scouts (Toby is a scout).

*Favorite Food:* Soul food.

*Wardrobe:* While always smartly dressed, Peggy is fond of short skirts.

*Note:* Peggy's role was originally intended for Nichelle Nichols (Lieutenant Uhura on *Star Trek*), but commitments to the series forced her to relinquish the part.

# *McHale's Navy*

## (ABC, 1962–1966)

*Cast:* Ernest Borgnine (Lieutenant Commander Quinton McHale), Tim Conway (Ensign Charles Parker), Joe Flynn (Captain Wallace B. Binghamton), Bob Hastings (Lieutenant Elroy Carpenter), Carl Ballantine (Lester Gruber), Gary Vinson (George "Christy" Christopher), Gavin MacLeod (Joseph "Happy" Haines), Bobby Wright (Willy Moss), Billy Sands (Harrison "Tinker" Bell), Edson Stroll (Virgil Edwards), Yoshio Yoda (Fugi Kobiaji).

*Basis:* World War II comedy about a torpedo boat commander (Quinton McHale), his crew, and their efforts to enjoy the war (having turned their South Pacific island base into the "Las Vegas of the Pacific") despite a stubborn captain (Binghamton) who sees McHale and his crew as a bunch of cutthroats and seeks a way to rid his island of them.

## QUINTON McHALE

*Place of Birth:* Michigan.

*Ancestry:* Italian (his mother and father were from Italy). Ernest Borgnine also played his Italian cousin, Giuseppe.

*Rank:* U.S. Navy lieutenant commander.

*Commission:* In charge of Squad 19 and PT boat 73.

*Base:* Taratupa, an island in the South Pacific. McHale and his crew actually have their own segment of the island they call "McHale's Island."

*Prior Occupation:* Tramp steamer captain.

*Trait:* Somewhat unmilitary and becomes military only when he has no other choice. He has considerable knowledge of the various islands and natives. He can speak Japanese and some of the local native languages.

*Off-Duty Dress:* Hawaiian-style clothing.

*Term of "Endearment" for His Crew:* "Goofballs."

*Nickname:* His crew calls him "Skip" (short for "Skipper").

*Love Interest:* Although Quinton showed no romantic interest in her, Navy Nurse Molly Turner (Jane Dulo), a New Jersey–born woman, was forever trying to change his way of thinking. Joyce Jameson played Kate O'Hara, a former friend (and possibly former love interest) who tried to rekindle what she had with McHale (but to no avail); Jean Willes played Maggie Monahan, the owner of a gambling house on New Caledonia (near Taratupa) who was also an apparent love interest from the past who also failed to rekindle that light.

*Catchphrase:* Since the antics of his crew always upset him, McHale is often heard saying, "Knock it off you eight-balls." He also says, "Well-a, well-a, well-a" when he is stumped for what to say.

## CHARLES PARKER

*Rank:* U.S. Navy ensign.

*Place of Birth:* Chagrin Falls, Ohio.

*Middle Name:* Beaumont.

*Trait:* Klutzy and a bit dim-witted (thus, he doesn't get the respect a person of his rank deserves). He is also a bit naive and easily taken advantage of.

*Fault:* He has a big mouth and never knows when to keep it shut to avoid exposing a scheme by McHale (at these times, it can be seen that McHale stomps on Parker's foot or knocks him in the knee with his leg to stop him from going any further).

*Nickname:* Chuck (by McHale) and Mister Parker by the crew.

*Year of Birth:* Based on dialogue, he was born first in 1920, then in 1916.

*Prior Job:* Employed by the Chagrin Falls *Gazette* (his exact job at the newspaper is not made clear).

*Disbelief:* Parker believes he is all navy but doesn't realize that without the help of McHale and the crew, he could not survive as an officer. He is also fond of reciting naval regulations, although no one pays attention to him.

*Other Roles:* In addition to playing his uncle, Admiral Parker (whom Charles called "Uncle Admiral"), Tim Conway also played British admiral Clivedon Sommers, British general Smythe-Pelly, and Admiral Chester Beatty.

*Love Interest:* Although shy (but having a girlfriend back home—Mary, played by Kathleen Gately), Parker did attract the attention of several women: Yvette Gerard (played by Claudine Longet), the French girl from an island close to Taratupa; Lieutenant Nancy Culpepper (Sheila James); Lieutenant Melba Benson (Ann Elder); and Sandra Collins (Maura McGiveney), a by-the-books ensign.

## WALLACE B. "WALLY" BINGHAMTON

*Rank:* U.S. Navy captain (actually a navy reservist).

*Place of Birth:* Youngstown, Ohio.

*Year of Birth:* 1902.

*Middle Name:* Burton.

*Nickname:* Called "Old Lead Bottom" by McHale's crew. The term resulted from a bullet wound Binghamton received to the derriere.

*Prior Occupation:* Commodore of the Long Island Yacht Club and the editor of a yachting magazine.

*Wife:* Mrs. Binghamton (played by Ann Doran; first name not revealed). He calls her "Pumpkin"; she calls him "Teddy Bear." It is mentioned that she lives in San Diego.

*Trait:* Easily angered, cantankerous, and actually a coward. He is virtually blind without his eyeglasses.

*Dream:* To become an admiral (but his goofy antics, especially in front of higher personnel, prevent that from happening).

*Goal:* "Get the Goods" (as he says) on McHale and "His Band of Pirates" (as he calls McHale's crew).

*Only Pleasure:* Throwing darts at a picture of McHale.

*Catchphrase:* While Binghamton does say a lot, he is most often associated with "I could just scream" (over McHale's antics) and "What in the name of the blue

Pacific." He responds to McHale's "Well-a . . ." with "Wha', wha', wha', What?" When McHale gets the best of him, he responds with "Why me?"

## McHALE'S CREW

Christy is the radioman, Tinker Bell is the engineer and machinist mate, Virgil is the gunner's mate, Happy is a seaman, Gruber is a quartermaster, and Fuji is a Japanese prisoner of war (actually a deserter from the Imperial Japanese Army captured by McHale [and hidden from Binghamton] who serves as McHale's houseboy). In one episode ("A Letter for Fuji") he is called Fujiwara Takeo.

Christy is the only married crew member (he wed Lieutenant Gloria Winters [Cindy Robbins] in the episode "Operation Wedding Party"). When they had a baby girl, she was named after McHale and his crew: Quintina (for McHale) Charlene (for Parker) Leslie (for Gruber) Wilhelmina (for Moss) Harriet (for Virgil) Virginia Hetty (for Happy) and Fujiana (for Fuji). Gloria now resides in San Diego. Willy Moss was born in Tennessee and operates the crew's still. Gruber is a former used car salesman from Brooklyn, New York, who is also an expert con man and amateur magician. Fuji's catchphrases are "Oy vey" and "Mama Mia" in Italy-based (final-season episodes). He calls McHale "Skippa-san."

## OTHER CHARACTERS

Lieutenant Elroy Carpenter is Binghamton's aide, a man who tries to be all military but in reality is a klutz. Urulu (Jacques Aubichon) is the native chief and witch doctor who is as conniving as McHale and his crew (and seeks ways to swindle money out of the navy). Big Frenchie (George Kennedy) is an old friend of McHale's, a French smuggler, and con artist. Roy Roberts played Admiral Rogers (Binghamton's superior; his first name is given as John and Bruce), and Herbert Lytton was Admiral Roscoe G. Reynolds.

## FINAL-SEASON EPISODES

McHale, his crew, Binghamton, and Carpenter are transferred to the Italian theater of war (supposedly sometime in 1944). The coastal town of Voltafiore (said to be in southern Italy) becomes their new home, but the format is the same: Binghamton trying to expose McHale and his crew for the criminals he believes they are. Here Binghamton is the military governor, and Mayor Mario Luggatto (Jay Novello) becomes the new Urulu—a moneymaking schemer. Fuji, who hid away on the PT boat while traveling to Italy, finds refuge in Voltafiore when McHale and his crew stumble on an abandoned wine cellar (which, in essence, becomes the new "McHale's Island"). Simon Scott was General Bronson, Binghamton's superior.

*Note:* During the first-season theme song, only McHale is seen on the PT boat; for the remainder of the series, Parker and Binghamton also appear. All of McHale's crew were either first- or second-class petty officers, except for Happy, who was classified only as a seaman. The original concept, titled *Seven against the Sea*, aired as a segment of *Alcoa Premiere* in 1962 and was a strict military show, not a comedy, and depicted McHale and his crew's efforts to foil the Japanese, who have a strong presence in the South Pacific. Ernest Borgnine played Quinton McHale; Ron Foster was his superior, Lieutenant Durham; and Gary Vinson (Christy Christopher), William Bramley (Boatswain Gallagher), and John Wright (Willy Moss) were his crew.

# *Mister Ed*

## (Syndicated, 1960–1961; CBS, 1961–1966)

*Cast:* Alan Young (Wilbur Post), Connie Hines (Carol Post), Allan "Rocky" Lane (voice of Mister Ed).

*Basis:* Architect Wilbur Post's efforts to cope with the antics of Mister Ed, a mischievous horse that speaks only to him.

### WILBUR POST

*Wife:* Carol.

*Address:* 17230 Valley Spring Lane in Los Angeles (also given as 1720 Valley Road, 17340 Valley Boulevard, 14730 Valley Boulevard, 17230 Valley Stream Road, and 17290 Valley Spring Lane). In scenes where the front of the house is seen, the number 17230 is displayed. Wilbur conducts his business from the barn, which doubles as the home to Mister Ed. The house was purchased from Golden Acres Real Estate.

*Home Telephone Number:* State 1781 (also given as State 1120).

*Business Telephone Number:* Poplar 9-1769 (also given as Poplar 1769).

*Place of Birth:* Connecticut (later lived in Los Angeles when his parents moved to California).

*Occupation:* Freelance architect (although in early promotional material, Wilbur was said to be a lawyer).

*Nickname as a Child:* Wee Bee (because he couldn't say "Wilbur").

*Education:* Mulholland High School (algebra was his favorite subject) and UCLA (where he majored in architecture).

*Military Career:* He joined the air force after college (he made 50 parachute jumps, and Donald Duck was his squad's mascot). Wilbur claims he acquired the ability to jump from his time as a child when he would walk along the tops of fences.

*Car:* He drives a two-door Studebaker (plate FIM 921; also seen as IJM 921) and later a sedan (license plate RJY 908).

*Astrological Sign:* Taurus (born in May).

*Last Season Job:* In addition to his architectural work, Wilbur and Mister Ed work as spies for the Secret Intelligence Agency.

*Club Affiliation:* A member of the Lawndale Men's Club.

*Character:* Mister Ed's antics cause Wilbur to become the fall guy, as he appears unstable to most people, and looked upon as a fool by others as he tries to hide the fact that he has a talking horse. Carol is unaware of Mister Ed's ability to talk and does not know what to believe half the time as Wilbur tries to explain his unusual actions.

*Relatives:* father, Angus Post (Alan Young); aunt, Martha, who had a pet parrot named Tootsie (Eleanor Audley).

## CAROL POST

*Maiden Name:* Carol Carlyle (also given as Carol Higgins). She and Wilbur are newlyweds when the series begins and just moving into their first home.

*Place of Birth:* California.

*Education:* Hollywood High School.

*Measurements:* 36-22-36.

*Occupation:* Housewife. Before marrying, Carol was a professional dancer, then an instructor at Miss Irene's Dance Studio in Hollywood.

*Weight:* Claims to be 108 pounds, but she is actually eight pounds heavier and sometimes goes to drastic measures to keep her shapely figure.

*Hobbies:* Playing tennis (Wilbur enjoys seeing how sexy she looks in her tennis shorts) and maintaining her vegetable garden.

*Affiliations:* A member of the neighborhood Women's Club and the Civics Club.

*Abilities:* Excellent cook and housekeeper.

*Greatest Fear:* The times her father comes to visit. Her father often experiences Wilbur's strange behavior, and he believes Wilbur is a "kook." While Wilbur's explanations often satisfy Carol, they fall on deaf ears when it comes to Carol's father (who threatens to take Carol back home with him).

*Carol's Thoughts:* "You really don't know a man until you marry him. I did, and I still don't" (referring to all the crazy things she witnesses through Wilbur). But no matter how much mischief Wilbur gets into (thanks to Mister Ed), Carol assures him that she will stand by him (Mister Ed assures Wilbur that if Carol should ever leave him, he will clean and keep house for him).

*Wilbur's Description of Carol:* "You are an orchid in the Garden of Love."

*Relatives:* father, Mr. Carlyle (Barry Kelly).

## MISTER ED

*Type of Horse:* Palomino. He became Wilbur's property when the prior home owner left him behind. Wilbur most often calls him "Ed."

*Birthday:* May 1952 (although in another episode, Ed mentions he was born on February 28).

*Astrological Sign:* Taurus.

*Ancestry:* Dates back to Plymouth Rock and the year 1620 ("A bad year for the Pilgrims," he says). It was at this time that a horse saved the Pilgrims' lives by getting corn seed from the Indians. The horse, called "Brave Horse," made a harvest possible, and thus the Thanksgiving tradition was born.

*Place of Birth:* Happy Time Stables.

*Address:* The barn attached to Wilbur's home.

*Parents:* Mister Ed's father was sold to a retired sailor (who had an anchor tattooed on the horse's left flank. He then sold the horse to a traveling circus, where he now works). Mister Ed's mother still resides at the stables where she was born.

*Weight:* Mister Ed weighed 68 pounds at birth (another episode mentions 98 pounds, and he was an incubator baby).

*Infatuation:* Fillies (Mister Ed considers himself the "Playboy Horse of Los Angeles").

*Inherited Family Curse:* A fear of heights (begun when his grandfather was chasing a filly and fell off a cliff).

*Idiosyncrasies:* Superstitious ("Why do you think I walk around in horseshoes?").

*Horseshoe Size:* 9½.

*Dream:* As a young horse, Ed dreamed of joining a circus.

*Accomplishments:* Believes he can do anything a human can do (including driving a car, playing baseball, attending college, and becoming a doctor).

*Song:* Ed wrote and sang "Pretty Little Filly."

*Book:* Ed wrote the book *Love and the Single Horse.*

*Abilities:* Ed can cook, sew, read (with the aid of glasses), and dial the telephone (using a carrot to rotate the dial). He also enjoys solving crossword puzzles.

*Favorite Baseball Team:* Los Angeles Dodgers.

*Favorite TV Shows:* Doctor programs.

*Most Enjoys:* Wilbur reading him a fairy tale at bedtime, and carrots (but eating too many carrots causes him to get a hangover).

*Marital Status:* Single (he never married because he never met a filly worthy of sharing his feed bag).

*Social Security Number:* 054-22-5487, which he applied for under the name Edward Post to provide for his old age (when he created a drink called a Wilburini—a combination of apple and carrot juice strained through day-old hay). He also became the first horse to collect an unemployment check when the drink failed.

*Job:* Tally Ho Stables (where people could ride him for a fee).

*Organization:* A crusader for animal rights (he began the Society for the Prevention of Horseback Riding).

*Shortwave Radio Call Letters:* NAG (when Mister Ed feels he needs to talk to other humans, he uses a shortwave radio).

*Bad Habits:* Crying when he doesn't get something, eating crab apples from the neighbor's tree, and not keeping his stable clean (Wilbur usually takes his TV-viewing privileges away until he does what he is told).

*Expertise:* Excellent chess player.

*Favorite Hangout:* Sunnybrook Stables ("Because the horses there really swing"; he has a 9:00 p.m. curfew).

*Favorite Word:* "Filly" (he considers it "the prettiest word in the English language").

*Friends:* Princess, Domino, Joy Boy, Flossie, and Frenchie are the horses Ed visits at the Tally Ho Stables.

*Affliction:* Charlie People ("Horses get Charlie People; people get Charlie Horses").

*Catchphrase:* "Oooh, Wilbur!"

*First Words to Wilbur:* "It's been a long time since I was a pony." Mister Ed talks only to Wilbur because he is the first human he likes well enough to talk to.

## OTHER CHARACTERS

Larry Keating and Edna Skinner played the Posts' original neighbors, Roger and Kay Addison (both of whom were retired, although Roger occasionally ventured into business projects). They lived at 7138 Valley Spring Road, and DLO-2599 was their telephone number. They have been married for 19 years, and Roger, who is tight with money, was a member of the Sigma Nu Delta fraternity in college. They were replaced by Leon Ames and Florence MacMichael as Gordon and Winnie Kirkwood. Gordon was a colonel in the air force, and Wilbur served under him.

*Note:* The project was originally titled *The Wonderful World of Wilbur Pope* and featured Scott McKay as Wilbur Pope (the owner of Mister Ed) and Sandra White as Wilbur's wife, Carlotta Pope.

# Mod Squad

(ABC, 1968–1973)

*Cast:* Michael Cole (Pete Cochran), Peggy Lipton (Julie Barnes), Clarence Williams III (Linc Hayes), Tige Andrews (Captain Adam Greer), Simon Scott (Chief Barney Metcalf).

*Basis:* Three troubled youths (Pete, Julie, and Linc), arrested on minor charges, are recruited by Chief Adam Greer of the Los Angeles Police Department to form the Mod Squad, youthful-looking police officers who can infiltrate the places regular cops cannot ("They can get into a thousand places that we can't. Who is going to suspect kids?").

## PETER "PETE" COCHRAN

*Character:* Pete is from a wealthy family and lived in a 14-room, five-bathroom Beverly Hills mansion. He simply met the wrong kind of people and was kicked out by his parents for being anti everything. Pete had rejected all the efforts his parents made to help him and was arrested for taking a joy ride in a stolen car. Pete is too impatient during assignments and too anxious to make things happen.

*Car:* A 1950 Mercury station wagon, license plate 188-458. The car, commonly called a "Woodie," was destroyed in a second-season episode when it was driven off a cliff.

*Relatives:* mother (Anita Louise); cousin, Karen (Diana Ewing); Karen's mother, Virginia (Nina Foch); Karen's father, Arthur Westphal (Arthur Franz).

*Ex-Fiancée:* Sassy Alexander (played by Brenda Scott); Dennis Patrick plays her father.

*Miscellaneous:* In the 1979 TV movie update, *Return of the Mod Squad*, Pete moved home to Beverly Hills to take over his late father's business.

## JULIE BARNES

*Character:* Julie comes from a broken family. After her father had deserted the family, Julie lived with her mother in San Francisco. But when Julie discovered her mother was a prostitute, she ran away and lived on the streets. She was arrested in Los Angeles for having no visible means of support. Julie couldn't handle her mother's life of one-night stands and just "split." She has lost track of her mother and does not know where she is or if she is still alive. Julie is restless during assignments and sometimes plunges headfirst into situations without thinking first. Like Pete and Linc, Julie breaks all the rules to get the job done.

*Address:* 1643 Woods Drive, Apartment 3.

*Car License Plate:* 936 AQ1.

*Miscellaneous:* In the 1979 TV movie update, *Return of the Mod Squad*, Julie finally found happiness, married Dan Bennett (Roy Thinnes), and moved to a ranch in northern California, where she lives with her husband and daughter.

## LINCOLN "LINC" HAYES

*Character:* Linc was born and raised in the Watts section of Los Angeles. He lived in a three-room apartment with 13 people and grew up bitter and disillusioned. He believed in the black cause, but during the Watts riots, he started a fire and was arrested for arson. He has now come to respect people of all races, and color doesn't matter when arresting criminals although, he does say, "I hate to fink on a soul brother." Linc is the calm one and usually brings focus to the group.

*Miscellaneous:* The 1979 TV movie update, *Return of the Mod Squad*, finds that Linc had moved to New York City, completed his college education, and acquired a job as a schoolteacher (he is also the father of an adopted son named Jason, played by Todd Bridges). He, Julie, and Pete are reunited to stop an unknown assassin from killing their former captain, Adam Grier.

## THE SQUAD

Pete, Julie, and Linc were headed for nowhere, and Adam gave them a chance to change the course of their lives. They are not permitted to carry guns, and they rely on their street smarts to accomplish their goals.

The squad was designed for Linc, Julie, and Pete to melt in, not stand out. Adam believes this is possible, although his superior, Chief Barney Metcalf, believes they are just kids on probation. Adam becomes upset when the squad is arrested as part of a bust and feels their attitudes will expose their undercover operations.

Clarence Williams III, Peggy Lipton, and Michael Cole. *ABC/Photofest © ABC*

# The Monkees
(NBC, 1966–1968)

*Cast:* Davy Jones, Peter Tork, Micky Dolenz, Mike Nesmith (as themselves).

*Basis:* An up-and-coming but always down-on-their-luck rock group, the Monkees (Davy, Peter, Micky, and Mike) seek fame and fortune in the music world.

## OVERALL SERIES INFORMATION

*Address:* 1334 Beachwood Street in the town of Centerville (apparently in California); their address is also given as 1438 Beachwood Street in Los Angeles.

*Car:* The Monkeemobile, a 1966 GTO (with room for six, a parachute, and an eight-track stereo system).

*License Plate:* NPH 623 (also seen as PER 540).

*Band's First Job:* A "Sweet 16" party at the Riviera Country Club (they sang "I Wanna Be Free" and were paid $150).

*Instruments:* Tambourine (Davy), drums (Micky), keyboard (Peter), and guitar (Mike).

*Award:* Chosen "Typical Young Americans" by *Sheik* magazine.

*Film Role:* Extras (for $30 a day) for the beach movie *I Married a Teenager from Out-of-Town.*

*Recorded Songs:* Although a variety of Monkees songs can be heard, only three are mentioned: "Daydream Believer," "I'm a Believer," and "The Last Train to Clarksville."

*Home Answering Service:* The incompetent Urgent Answering Service.

*Signs Posted in Their Home:* "Denver Chamber of Commerce," "Money Is the Root of All Evil," "Bus Stop," and "No Smoking in Street Clothes."

*House Resident:* Mr. Schneider (a life-size dummy).

*Note:* In the opening theme, over the song "Hey, Hey We're the Monkees," Peter's name is seen four times—once as his own credit and once for each of the other three Monkees.

## CHARACTERS

Very little background information is given.

*Davy Jones:* Born in England and the most sensible member of the group. He is most often the one who keeps the group together when situations become trying.

*Micky Dolenz:* Born in Burbank, California. As a kid, his mother called him "Goo Goo Eyes." In one episode, Micky mentions that he hasn't attended the circus since he was a kid (referring to his role on *Circus Boy*, where he was billed as Mickey Braddock). In one episode, Micky played his evil double, a killer named Baby Face Morales, "The Most Wanted Man in America."

*Peter Tork:* Born in Connecticut and is quite shy around girls. He was first enrolled in a private school, but when he complained that he didn't like it, his mother placed him in public school. Peter is quite emotional (cries at virtually everything, including card tricks), gets the hiccups during auditions for producers, has hay fever, and is prone to seasickness.

*Mike Nesmith:* Born in Texas and was an Eagle Scout as a kid. He collects fortune cookies and has a dog that only he can see.

# The Mothers-in-Law
## (NBC, 1967–1969)

*Cast:* Eve Arden (Eve Hubbard); Kaye Ballard (Kaye Buell); Herbert Rudley (Herb Hubbard); Roger C. Carmel, then Richard Deacon (Roger Buell); Deborah Walley (Suzie Hubbard); Jerry Fogel (Jerry Hubbard).

*Basis:* A young engaged (then married) couple (Suzy and Jerry) struggle to live a life on their own without the continuous interference of their mothers-in-law (Eve and Kaye), who feel their children cannot survive without their help.

## SUZIE HUBBARD AND JERRY BUELL
*Suzie's Parents:* Eve and Herb Hubbard.
*Suzie's Address:* 1805 Ridgeway Drive in Los Angeles.
*Jerry's Parents:* Eve and Roger Buell.
*Jerry's Address:* 1803 Ridgeway Drive.
*Age for Both:* 18.
*School for Both:* UCLA.

*Note:* Suzy and Jerry become the parents of twins they name Hildegard and Joseph after Eve's middle name (Hildegard) and Kaye's middle name (Josephine).

## EVE AND HERB HUBBARD
Herb works as an attorney, and Eve was a secretary. Eve and Kaye were neighbors and became pregnant at the same time. Thus, Suzie and Jerry grew up together and eventually fell in love. Eve and Kaye's meddling forced Suzie and Jerry to elope, and they set up housekeeping in Eve and Herb's converted garage. Eve wrote poetry in college and was the scenic designer for its drama club. She prides herself on being able to impersonate actress Marlene Dietrich. Her (and Kaye's) favorite TV show is *Brave New Day.*

## KAYE AND ROGER BUELL

Before moving next door to Eve and Herb, Kaye and Roger lived in Encino, California. Kaye was a singer (performed as Angelina DeVina, "The Little Girl with the Big Voice," for the Ozzie Snick Orchestra and a group called Harvey Banks and His Ten Tellers). Her maiden name is Belotta, and she can also play the flute. Kaye can also impersonate Bette Davis, and she sings "La Dona Mobalay" when she irons clothes.

Roger began his career as a radio writer in the 1940s (for such shows as *The First Nighter*, *The Lone Ranger*, and *Miss Primrose of Feathertop Hill*). He now writes for television.

*Note:* In the unaired pilot film (produced for CBS), Kay Cole played the role of Suzie Hubbard.

# *Mr. Terrific*
## (CBS, 1966–1967)

*Cast:* Stephen Strimpell (Stanley Beemish), Dick Gautier (Hal Waters), John McGiver (Barton J. Reed).

*Basis:* Stanley Beemish, the only man capable of taking a special power pill without becoming ill, transforms into Mr. Terrific, a not-so-daring superhero, to battle crime.

## STANLEY BEEMISH

*Birthday:* July 17, 1939.

*Birth Weight:* 4 pounds, 3 ounces.

*Occupation:* Co-owner of Hal and Stanley's Service Station.

*Company Slogan:* "Capital Gas in the Nation's Capital."

*Business Address:* Northwest and Wyoming streets in Washington, D.C.

*Home Address:* Apartment 2-A (which he shares with Hal); an address is not given.

*Favorite Eatery:* The Hungry Nose.

*Favorite Food:* Peanut butter and jelly sandwiches.

*Secret Job:* Agent (Mr. Terrific) for the Bureau of Special Projects.

*Special Projects Telephone Number:* National 8-0397.

*Power Source:* A pill invented by Dr. Reynolds (Ned Glass). It gives animals great strength "but made the strongest of men quite ill."

*Abilities:* Incredible strength, impervious to bullets, and the ability to fly (by flapping the wings on his costume). He also wears goggles to conceal his true identity.

*The Pill:* For each assignment, Stanley receives a box with three pills: one base pill that gives Stanley the strength of 1,000 men for one hour and two booster pills. The pills cost $10,000 each, and Stanley can take only three such pills per day. The pills are specially candy coated so that Stanley will take them (even then, by the expressions on Stanley's face, they appear to be foul tasting).

*Disadvantage:* Stanley is trouble prone and has a difficult time attempting to master the powers he has (not only do the pills wear off at crucial moments, but Stanley is prone to difficult landings and crashing into things).

## OTHER CHARACTERS

Barton J. Reed is Stanley's superior. He will always say "A-C-T-I-O-N" (spelling out the word) and sounds the Purple Alert to summon Stanley. Paul Smith played Reed's assistant, Harvey Trent (who didn't have the faith Reed had in Stanley); Ellen Corby played Hal's meddling mother, Mrs. Waters. Hal is a playboy and was kept in the dark as to Stanley's secret alias (although Stanley would hide his costume in a locker at the gas station, Hal never discovered it). Hal's introduction to women is "Hi. I'm Hal, gas station attendant, snappy dresser and lady killer."

*Note:* In the original unaired pilot, *Mr. Terrific*, Alan Young played Stanley Beemish as a shoe salesman for Mr. Feeney (Edward Andrews). Here Stanley was recruited by the Office of Special Assignments. Jesse White played Stanley's superior; Sheila Wells was Stanley's girlfriend, Gloria Dickinson.

# *The Munsters*
## (CBS, 1964–1966)

*Cast:* Fred Gwynne (Herman Munster); Yvonne DeCarlo (Lily Munster); Al Lewis (Grandpa); Beverley Owen, then Pat Priest (Marilyn Munster); Butch Patrick (Eddie Munster).

*Basis:* A family who resemble movie monsters of the 1930s and 1940s seek to live a normal life—believing they are normal and everyone else is weird.

## OVERALL SERIES INFORMATION

*Address:* 1313 Mockingbird Lane in the town of Mockingbird Heights. In some episodes, Herman claims that he owns the house; in others, he says he has to "scare up the rent each month." The spooky-looking residence has nine rooms and one dungeon.

*Pets:* Spot, a fire-breathing dragon that Grandpa found while digging in the backyard and that now lives under the staircase in the living room (he eats Doggie's Din Din pet food); an unnamed Raven that utters Edgar Alan Poe's famous line, "Nevermore"; and Kitty Kat (a cat with the roar of a lion).

*Recognition: Event Magazine* named the Munsters the "Typical American Family."

## HERMAN MUNSTER

*Creator:* Dr. Frankenstein (who assembled him from body parts at the Heidelberg School of Medicine in Germany ["I was in three jars for six years"]). Electricity brought the assembled Herman to life in 1814.

*Wife:* Lily.

*Son:* Eddie.

*Height:* 7 feet, 3 inches tall.

*Weight:* "Three spins on the bathroom scale."

*Skin Color:* Green (resembles Frankenstein's monster from the 1931 film *Frankenstein*).

*Hair:* Long on the sides and flat on the top.

*Birthmark:* A lightning-like bolt on his forehead. He has bolts on each side of his neck for conducting electricity (which brought him to life).

*Ears:* Two (but mismatched; as Lily says, "Only the family can tell").

*Forehead:* Overhangs (to keep the water out of his eyes when he showers).

*Jaw:* Called a "lantern jaw."

*Blood Pressure:* Minus 3.

*Body Temperature:* 62.8.

*Heartbeat:* None.

*Pulse:* 15.

*Musical Ability:* Can play the organ.

*Occupation:* Gravedigger at the Gateman, Goodbury, and Graves Funeral Parlor. According to Lily, "Herman always arrives home from work at 5:13 p.m. sharp."

*Employer:* Mr. Gateman (John Carradine).

*Temporary Jobs:* Rodeo bronco buster, private detective (Agent 702 for the Kempner Detective Agency), wrestler (as the Masked Marvel), assistant at Tom Fong's Chinese-American Laundry, and welder (through the Cleaver Employment Agency) at the Crosby Shipyards (he wore badge ID 13).

*Talent:* Poet of sorts (submits his morbid verses to the *Mortician's Monthly* magazine; his first poem was "Going Out to Pasteur"). He also carries his "Goodie Book" with him at all times in his inside jacket pocket (a small black diary-like pad wherein he writes down things not to do to avoid getting into trouble).

*Favorite Singer:* Doris Day.

*Favorite Fairy Tale:* Goldilocks and the Three Bears.

*Favorite TV Show: My Three Sons.*

*Favorite Food:* Cream of vulture soup.

*Favorite Magazine: Shocking Detective.*

*Cars:* The Munster Mobile (customized from a roadster and a hearse that Lily purchased from Diamond Jim's Used Cars and presented to Herman as a birthday present; license plate HAJ 302). The family also had the Drac-u-La, a coffin on wheels built by Grandpa (with the plate "Born: 1367. Died?" It represents Grandpa's birth year).

*Ham Radio Call Letters:* W6XRL4.

*Catchphrase:* "Darn, darn, darn."

*Recording:* Herman became a recording star with a pop variation on the song "Dry Bones."

*World War II Army Service:* Four years, with his initial service at Fort Benning (he was then sent overseas).

*Most Embarrassing Day:* Accidentally walking onto the set of the TV show *Queen for a Day* and almost being crowned "Queen for a Day."

*Hates Most:* Dancing (he claims to have "two left feet," which, Grandpa claims, is "what happens when you're put together in the dark").

*Affiliations:* A member of the Indian Guides.

*Likeness:* The totem pole for the Owagi Indians in Buffalo Valley (in Arizona) has the carved image of their god, Wanatoba—an exact likeness of Herman.

*Relatives:* Charlie Munster, twin, con-artist brother, and prototype, Johan (Fred Gwynne).

*Note:* In the 1988 series update, *The Munsters Today*, Herman (John Schuck) was "born" in Dr. Frankenstein's lab in Transylvania over 300 years ago. His teeth squeak when he gets thirsty; his eyes are brown, blue, and undetermined; and the neck bolts (for the electricity that supplied life) itch when he gets an idea. He possesses the Golden Shovel Award for best gravedigger, and eating refried armadillo bladders gives him nightmares. Weasel burgers are his favorite snack, rack of lamb is his favorite dinner, and "legs" Benedict are his favorite breakfast. *Married with Children* is his favorite TV show, and he is a member of the Christina Applegate Fan Club (Kelly Bundy on the show).

## LILY MUNSTER

*Spouse:* Herman Munster. Lily met Herman in the early 1860s, and they married in 1865. They honeymooned on Devil's Island and were forced to leave Transylvania when angry villagers drove them out of town with torches and threatened to burn them at the stake.

*Maiden Name:* Lily Dracula.
*Father:* The infamous Count Dracula (now called "Grandpa").
*Son:* Eddie.
*Heritage:* A hauntingly beautiful vampire.
*Year of Birth:* 1664.
*Age:* 304 (in another episode, Lily mentions she is 137 years old, making her birth year 1827).
*Place of Birth:* Transylvania.
*Wardrobe:* A cleavage-revealing dress made from coffin lining (which Herman acquires from his job).
*Favorite Jewelry:* A bat necklace.
*Favorite Perfume:* Chanel No. 13.
*Favorite Charity:* Bundles for Transylvania.
*Specialties:* A proficient housekeeper (who ensures that their home is always gloomy) and an excellent cook. Meals prepared by Lily include filet of dragon, eggs (gloomy side up), chopped lizard livers and curried lizard casserole, and cream of buzzard and cream of iguana soups. Salads include salamander with centipede dressing and cactus salad. Cold rhinoceros appears to be the family's favorite sandwich. The family also has their own vulture coop in the backyard for fresh vulture eggs. Meals are always topped off with devil's food cake.
*Favorite Food:* Bat milk yogurt.
*Series Jobs:* Palm reader at the Golden Earrings Tea Room; fashion model for Laszlo Brastoff, Couturier; welder at the Crosby Shipyards (badge ID 7); and Madame Lily's Beauty Salon (which she operated with Marilyn). Lily also applied for the following jobs but did not acquire them: secretary, bus driver for the City Transportation Company, and nurse at the Senior Citizen's Sanitarium.
*Occupation before Marriage:* Nurse's aide to Florence Nightingale.
*Checking Account:* Lily and Herman have a joint account at the Mockingbird Heights National Bank.
*Nickname for Herman:* Poopsie.
*Relatives:* uncle, Gilbert, the Creature from the Black Lagoon (Richard Hale); Lester Dracula, brother, a werewolf (Irwin Charone).

*Note:* In the 1988 syndicated update, *The Munsters Today*, Lily (Lee Meriwether) is now 324 years old (born in 1654) and married Herman 299 years ago (in 1689). Before she wed, Lily worked as a singer at Club Dead in Transylvania. She was crowned "Miss Transylvania of 1655" (which would have made her one year old) and won the Silver Shroud Award for fashion design. Her normal body temperature is 25.8 degrees, and "Transylvania the Beautiful" is her favorite song. Lily, called "Lilikins" by Herman, gives birth within 24 hours of becoming pregnant (a tradition with vampires in her family). Lily claims that she first met Herman when he was walking along the moors in Transylvania and saw her stretched out on the ground. They looked at each other, and it was love at first sight.

## GRANDPA

*Real Name:* Count Vladimir Dracula. For reasons that are not explained, he is also called "Grandpa Munster."

*Daughter:* Lily.

*Son-in-Law:* Herman Munster.

*Occupation:* Mad scientist. Before moving to America, he operated a blood bank, worked as a guillotine janitor, performed as a magician, and owned a fang-sharpening business.

*Place of Birth:* Transylvania.

*Year of Birth:* 1586 (in another episode, it is seen as 1367).

*Age:* As Lily calls him, a "378-year-old mad scientist."

*Marital Status:* Currently single. He has been married 167 times (his wife Katja gave birth to Lily in 1664; she left him when she became tired of ironing capes and cleaning dungeons).

*Education:* A graduate of the University of Transylvania (where he majored in philosophy).

*Affiliation:* A member of the A.V.A. (American Vampire Association).

*Pet Bat:* Igor ("a mouse with wings who joined the Transylvanian Air Force").

*Possessions:* The only known set of blueprints for Herman's creation; a book that contains a variety of centuries-old recipes (from curing headaches to curing the bubonic plague); his proudest item, a transistorized divining rod (which tends to pick up reruns of *My Little Margie*); and a crystal ball (which he uses to contact people).

*Dream:* To be back in the old country, where, when the moon was full, he could roam free as a wolf (strangely, not as a bat).

*Favorite TV Show: My Three Sons.*

*Favorite Chair:* The electric chair in the living room.

*Favorite Newspaper:* The *Transylvania Gazette.*

*Favorite Food:* Bird's nest stew.

*Favorite Drink:* Bloody Mary.

*Temporary Job:* Magician at the Domino Club in Mockingbird Heights.

*Note:* In the 1988 series update, *The Munsters Today*, Grandpa (Howard Morton) attended the University of Transylvania and was a member of the Sigma Alpha Aorta fraternity. After college, he and Genghis Khan opened the first blood bank in town. He and his wife Katja met at the Joan of Arc roast, and the first home they purchased when they came to America was the Bates Motel (made famous in the Alfred Hitchcock film *Psycho*). They later sold it to "a nice young fellow and his mother," referring to Norman Bates. Katja, however, was not Grandpa's first love; it was a woman named Shirley Ziebnik (he also claims Joan of Arc had a crush on him and wrote him love letters exclaiming, "Vlad, you enflame me"). Igor is his pet lab bat, Stanley his lab rat, and Leonard, the skeleton he befriended in college. His computer is named Sam.

## MARILYN MUNSTER

*Character:* The young and beautiful (to viewers) but unattractive, outcast member of the Munsters. Marilyn's looks make her the black sheep of the family, and her history is somewhat sketchy. She calls Herman her uncle and Lily her aunt, but they are not sure whose side of the family produced "such a hideous creature." She is said to be from Herman's side of the family, then Lily's side. In the episode "All Star Munster," Herman pinpoints Marilyn as "Lily's sister's kid"—although no other mention is ever made of Lily's having a sister. Exactly how Marilyn came to live with the family or who her parents are (normal or monster) is not revealed (only that she has been living with the family since she was a baby).

*Age:* 21.

*Hair Color:* Blonde.

*Eyes:* Blue.

*Education:* Studying art at State University.

*Bedroom:* Bright and cheery and rather unpleasant to the rest of the family.

*Regret:* Not being like the rest of the family and feeling "I'm so ugly that I will never attract a man" (she fails to realize that when new boyfriends see Herman, it is he who scares them off, not Marilyn).

*Note:* Hilary Van Dyke plays Marilyn in the 1988 series update, *The Munsters Today.* Marilyn is younger (17 years old) and is a student at Mockingbird Heights High School. She is somewhat boy-crazy but feels her small breasts (not Herman) are the reason why no boy wants her (she feels "being a 36D" will solve all her problems). Here Marilyn was also studying art but yearned to be an actress (then a magazine writer-editor). She has a porcelain bunny collection and won the Bronx Cheer Pom Pom Award as a member of the school's cheerleading squad. She also appeared in the school's production of *To Kill a Mockingbird.*

## EDDIE MUNSTER

*Full Name:* Edward Wolfgang Munster.

*Parents:* Herman and Lily Munster.

*Heritage:* Werewolf. He is green like Herman but has fangs and pointy ears.

*Age:* Eight.

*Education:* Mockingbird Heights Grammar School (where he won an award for his composition "My Parents: An Average American Family," printed in the reddest ink his teacher has ever seen—blood).

*School Activity:* Member of the track team.

*Wardrobe:* A Little Lord Fauntleroy suit.

*Musical Ability:* None (although he attempted to play the trumpet).

*Bad Habit:* Biting his nails—not those on his fingers but those found in hardware stores.

*Doll:* Woof Woof (a werewolf).

*Pet Snake:* Elmer (who lives under the garbage pail in the backyard).

*Favorite TV Show: Zombo* (a kiddie show hosted by the zombie-like Zombo [played by Louis Nye]).

*Mechanical Brother:* Boris, a robot made by Grandpa (Rory Stevens).

*Note:* In the series update, *The Munsters Today,* Jason Marsden portrayed Eddie as a teenager and attending Mockingbird Heights High School. He has a pet Tasmanian devil named Irving and has dreams of becoming a rock video producer. He is a member of the Dukes Little League team and buys his clothes at Kiddie Casuals.

## ORIGINAL PILOT
Filmed in color with Joan Marshall playing Herman's wife, Phoebe, and Happy Derman as Eddie.

## UPDATES
*Munster Go Home* is a failed 1966 color pilot that was released theatrically and wherein Debbie Watson played Marilyn. In *The Munsters Revenge*, a 1981 NBC TV movie, Jo McDonnell played Marilyn with K. C. Martel as Eddie. The cast was completely revised for the 1995 Fox TV movie *Here Come the Munsters*: Edward Herrmann (Herman Munster), Veronica Hamel (Lily Munster), Robert Morse (Grandpa), Christine Taylor (Marilyn), and Matthew Botuchis (Eddie Munster). Marilyn is given the last name of Hyde, and the program explores how the Munster family came to America (forced to leave their home in Transylvania by angry villagers).

*Mockingbird Lane* is a 2012 unsold pilot that changes history a bit. Here Grandpa (called "Sam Dracula") built Herman for Lily, as he could not find a man good enough for her. Marilyn is said to be Lily's niece; Eddie is a full-fledged werewolf. Cast: Jerry O'Connell (Herman Munster), Portia de Rossi (Lily Munster), Charity Wakefield (Marilyn Munster), Eddie Izzard (Grandpa), and Mason Cook (Eddie).

# *My Favorite Martian*
## (CBS, 1963–1966)

*Cast:* Ray Walston (Uncle Martin), Bill Bixby (Tim O'Hara), Pamela Britton (Lorelei Brown), Alan Hewitt (Detective Bill Brennan).

*Basis:* A Martian (Uncle Martin), stranded on the primitive planet Earth, struggles to adjust to a new life style while seeking a way to repair his damaged space ship and return home.

## UNCLE MARTIN

*Real Name:* Exigius 12½.

*Place of Birth:* The planet Mars.

*Age:* Martin mentions in 1963 that his parents are celebrating their golden wedding anniversary (500 years on Mars) and that he is 450 years old. Later, however, he says, "I'm 1,000 years ahead of Earth" and that "on Mars people just reaching 1,000 are still teenagers" (his physical appearance, however, does make him appear older than a teenager but younger than a senior citizen).

*Pulse:* 218 (normal for a Martian).

*Normal Temperature:* 131 degrees.

*First Visit to Earth:* During the reign of Montezuma (the Aztec period).

*Earth Residence:* Lives with his "nephew" Tim O'Hara at 21 Elm Street (Tim rents an apartment above a garage in a home owned by Lorelei Brown). The address is also given as 347 Palm Court and 1436 Greenhill Road.

*Cover:* A relative from Ireland who has come to stay with his nephew.

*Space Suit Color:* Silver (same as his spaceship). The smog causes rust-like spots on the ship.

*Spaceship Mileage:* As Martin says, "Hardly broken in with only 385 million miles on it."

*Dog Tags:* The Martian identity disk.

*Qualities:* Superior intelligence, the ability to disappear (by raising the antenna on the back of his head), levitation (by his right index finger), communicating with animals, reading minds, projecting his dreams, and replaying historical events he has witnessed (both visual and audio through the silicon wafers in his brain). He also has a Television Audio System that allows him to sense things (what he says Earthlings foolishly call the "sixth sense").

*Antenna Abilities:* When Martin's antenna is raised (like rabbit ears on the back of an analog TV set), he can pick up AM and FM radio signals and short-wave and police call frequencies (he uses his nose as a tuner). He can also pick up TV signals (projected through his eyes), but he must be in the dark to do so.

*Faults:* Living on Earth has presented a number of problems for Uncle Martin: he fears thunderstorms (if he is struck by lightning, it can short-circuit him, causing Popsy, uncontrollable appearing and disappearing); eating peppers causes his antenna to remain visible; Earth perfume fragrances, such as those contained in "Homme Fatale," can immobilize him; and a common Earth cold can cause his powers to malfunction. Earth gravity prematurely ages him; mosquito bites can cause the next person to be bitten by that mosquito to absorb Martian traits (the condition is called SymSymSymapatheticus). Eating foods with polyunsaturated ingredients causes Uncle Martin to dream in 3-D, allowing anyone to see his dreams (he normally dreams in 2-D). Once every 300 years, Sneeze-a-Phobia occurs, causing Uncle Martin to become temporarily forgetful every time he sneezes. If Uncle Martin develops a short circuit in his telesensory transmitters, what he sees is broadcast like a TV signal for the world to see. The Martian disease Virus M (commonly called Fluosis) is common among Martians, but if an Earthling catches it (like Tim), it causes stripes across the face and drastic changes in body temperature; it can be cured only with bio carnie delirium.

*Belief:* Humans lack intelligence. He is also puzzled by human emotion.

*Main Devices:* The CCTBS (Cathode Ray Centrifugal Time Break-a-Scope), a time machine; EWS (Early Warning System), which allows him to experience human emotions; and the Ultrasonic Microcosmic Molecular Separator, which breaks down objects to their individual molecules.

*Information "Man":* George, the dog Tim is caring for while his boss, Mr. Burns, is away, which supplies Uncle Martin with information about what is happening in and around the neighborhood.

*Most Needed:* Silbolt, an alloy composed of silicone and cobalt (not yet invented on Earth) to repair his spaceship.

*Job:* Feeling he needed to help Tim with expenses, Martin took a job as a night watchman in a warehouse on Avenue C.

*Toy:* Martin's antenna started a craze when his raised antenna were spotted by a young boy, and a resulting toy, "Be a Martian Antenna," was produced.

*Relatives:* mother, fantasy sequence (Madge Blake); Andromeda (called Andy) and nephew, who visited him in one episode (Wayne Stam).

## TIM O'HARA

*Occupation:* Newspaper reporter for the Los Angeles *Sun* (it is also called the *Daily Sun*).

*Education:* UCLA (where theater arts was one of his majors).

*Inspiration:* His high school teacher, Miss Pringle, who inspired him to become a newspaper reporter.

*Relationship to Uncle Martin:* His nephew. It was Tim who witnessed the Martian's spacecraft (cruising at 9,000 miles per hour) veering to avoid colliding with a U.S. Air Force test plane, the X-15 (traveling at 4,332 miles per hour). The Martian's ship crash-landed, and Tim came to his rescue, allowing the now stranded alien (whom he named Uncle Martin) to stay at his home and hide the spaceship in Mrs. Brown's garage.

*Convertible Car License Plate:* JF1 561.

*Awake Time:* 8:00 a.m. Tim has three alarm clocks set to ring within seconds of each other.

*Second Job:* Tim and Uncle Martin work on occasion for Top Secret, a government organization that battles the evils of CRUSH.

*Relatives:* Uncle Seamus O'Hara (Sean McClory), Uncle Ralph O'Hara (Bruce Glover), Aunt Martha O'Hara (Suzanne Taylor), Uncle Clarence O'Hara (Allan Melvin), Cousin Harvey O'Hara (Paul Smith).

## LORELEI BROWN

*Occupation:* Appears to be a housewife and landlord (an exact job is never mentioned). Various episodes portray her as having other sources of income: selling Christmas cards, giving bridge (card) lessons, studying real estate, learning how to become a private detective, and selling beauty creams.

*Maiden Name:* Lorelei Wanamaker.

*Marital Status:* Widow. She is very pretty but is what one would call "slightly dizzy" (like a dizzy blonde).

*Daughters:* Angela Brown (played by Ann Marshall) and Annabell Brown (Ina Victor). In the unaired pilot episode, Lorelei had only one daughter, Annabell (played by Ina Victor), who was Tim's romantic interest.

*Organization:* Lorelei is a member of the Women's Club.

*Famous For:* Her fudge brownies.

*Abilities:* Can play the violin and piano.

*Quirks:* Plays the stock market with a Ouiji board.

*Pet Cat:* Mr. McPhee.

*Favorite Charity:* Overseas Relief.

*Relatives:* Alvin Wanamaker, brother (Gavin MacLeod); Dulcy, sister (Yvonne White); Leroy Wanamaker, brother (Bill Idelson); Paula Clayfield, niece (Marlo Thomas).

*Boyfriend:* Originally a romantic link existed between Martin and Lorelei until Martin felt threatened by Bill Brennan, a detective with the Los Angeles Police Department who took a liking to Lorelei. He is called "Bulldog Brennan" (and the "Human Bulldog") and suspects there is something not right with Martin (whose antennae quiver when Brennan is near). Bill majored in criminal psychology at Duke University, and his mobile car code to police headquarters is 343. He later says he attended Yale University and studied pathology.

# *My Living Doll*
## (CBS, 1964–1965)

*Cast:* Bob Cummings (Bob MacDonald), Julie Newmar (Rhoda), Jack Mullaney (Peter Robinson), Doris Dowling (Irene Adams).

*Basis:* A playboy psychiatrist (Bob MacDonald) attempts to humanize a beautiful robot (Rhoda) as part of the U.S. Air Force's plans to incorporate robots for its space program.

## RHODA

*Air Force Identification:* Subproject AF 709 (which is to be integrated with the Project Orion space program). She was created at the SRC (Space Research Center) by Dr. Carl Miller (Henry Beckman).

*Characteristic:* Rhoda is a technically advanced robot that can duplicate any aspect of a human and is the first such creation for a highly complex experiment in outer space. She doesn't eat or drink, "but I can compute." Rhoda mentions that "once you are familiar with my design details and circuit diagrams, my equipment is not difficult to assemble."

*Cover Name:* Rhoda Miller (a patient of Bob's that requires special treatment due to her shyness). She lives with Bob and his widowed sister Irene (whom Bob asked to move in with him and act as a chaperone until her creator, Carl Miller, returns from a business meeting in Pakistan. Carl completed her assembly two weeks before leaving the country but kept her a secret, as she was not yet perfected).

*Measurements:* 37-26-36.

*Height:* 5 feet, 10 inches tall. Rhoda can remain vertical and stand due to the gyroscopic controls built into her system.

*Hair:* Blonde.

*Body:* Constructed from low-modulus polyethylene plastic, miniature computers, "and assorted components." Her body is similar to one-piece die casting, but "I am hand molded." Her thought processes have been programmed to eliminate human emotion to prevent conflict within her system. Rhoda is also right handed and does not wear makeup (her coloring is cosmetically mixed into her facial skin and will never fade).

*Body Temperature:* A constant 98.6 degrees. Her cosmetic plastic skin (which has the same characteristics as human skin) gets its warmth from the infrared rays of the atmosphere (which are picked up by her microscopic sensors), and thus she is immune to cold.

*On and Off Emergency Switch:* Under her right elbow.

*Emergency Control Buttons:* The four small birthmarks on her back. The one farthest to the right turns off her power, the square one activates her computer memory, the round one reactivates her motion (turns her back on), and the triangular one controls her hearing, vision, and speech.

*Power:* Rhoda's eyes absorb power from light and the sun (which charge her solar batteries). Covering her eyes causes her to shut down (although her computers are still active; she is, however, unable to take commands).

*Nighttime Activity:* Rhoda rests her transistors and associated components as well as shutting down her solar batteries.

*Memory Bank:* 90 million items of information (she first says 50 million) and can call up any piece of that information in less than one second.

*Response to Something She Doesn't Understand:* "That does not compute."

*Abilities:* Plays the piano; able to emulate any human action once she sees it. She has Time Based Generators built into her system that are synchronized with the Naval Observatory (thus, she can give accurate time). Rhoda was also entered in the Chamber of Commerce Beauty Pageant (by Bob's sister; she was Contestant #6 but lost due to a system malfunction when playing the piano). She can also compute common denominators of six fractions in less than one second.

*Fault:* Hearing anything (like *Alice in Wonderland*) written by Lewis Carroll. Carroll used precise mathematical patterns in his writings, and these patterns will set up a conflict with the mathematical patterns programmed into Rhoda and cause confusion (which develops in her as vertigo). She has to be reprogrammed to prevent it from happening again. Rhoda has not been programmed for romance, and encountering anything dealing with it causes confusion in her circuits, as she does not know how to compute it.

*Carl's Names for Rhoda:* It, 709, and Robot (he doesn't see her as a beautiful woman, just a robot).

*Job:* Bob's secretary (types 240 words per minute). Bob originally programmed Rhoda to help Irene maintain the apartment.

*Note:* In the opening theme, Rhoda first appeared in a sexy baby doll nightgown, then in an evening gown when the nightgown was considered too provocative. The program was originally titled *Living Doll*, and Rhoda was identified only as 709 (no "AF" before it).

## DR. ROBERT "BOB" MacDONALD

*Address:* 1170 Maple Drive, Apartment 9-C, in Los Angeles (where he lives with his widowed sister, Irene Adams). Their ZIP code is 80046. Irene sometimes calls Bob "Sigmund" (after Sigmund Freud for the way he deals with Rhoda); Bob considers Irene a gossip—"What goes into her ears comes out of her mouth."

*Occupation:* Psychiatrist with the Cory Psychiatric Clinic in Los Angeles (where he is also chairman of the Fund Raising Committee). He also has office 15 at the SRC (Space Research Center), where he works as a psychiatric consultant (as seen on his office door). Bob is also the author of a book called *How Not to Be Dominated by Females.*

*First Meeting:* Rhoda, wearing a sheet as a dress, had wandered out of Carl's lab and found her way into Bob's office. Naturally, Bob thought she was a real girl until Carl explained otherwise. When Bob first brought the robot to his apartment, he called her "Miss 709." When he realized he needed a name for her, he called her "Rhoda" (named after his Aunt Rhoda) and made her Carl's niece (thus making Carl her uncle).

*First Impression:* Bob called her "Incredible. You're a fabulous arrangement of complicated electronic equipment."

*Biggest Fear:* That someone will discover that Rhoda is not human.

*Plan:* To make Rhoda the perfect woman.

*Favorite Eatery:* The Galaxy Club.

*Car License Plate:* JFB 453.

*Affiliation:* Bob is chairman of the Citizen's Road Committee (for traffic safety).

*Note:* When Bob Cummings left the series after 21 episodes, his character was said to be on assignment in Pakistan. Bob's friend, coworker, and neighbor, the slightly confused physicist Peter Robinson (who had a crush on Rhoda), became Rhoda's guardian. Peter drives a sports car with the license plate HAE 471, and although he thinks he is a ladies' man, Bob says, "He has yet to convince any women of that."

# *My Mother the Car*
## (NBC, 1965–1966)

*Cast:* Jerry Van Dyke (Dave Crabtree), Maggie Pierce (Barbara Crabtree), Cindy Eilbacher (Cindy Crabtree), Randy Whipple (Randy Crabtree), Avery Schreiber (Captain Bernard Manzini).

*Basis:* A married man (Dave Crabtree) must protect his mother (who has been reincarnated as a 1928 Porter) from a family who prefer a station wagon and an antique car collector (Captain Bernard Manzini) who seeks to acquire (by any means possible) the Porter for his collection.

## MOTHER
*Name:* Gladys Crabtree.
*Maiden Name:* Gladys Brown.

*Date of Passing:* August 23, 1949.

*Reincarnation:* A car because Mother loved automobiles and figured this was the best way she could come back and help guide Dave's life ("You need help, son").

*Cost:* Dave found Mother as a "fixer-upper" in a used car lot and paid $200 for her.

*First Words Spoken By Mother:* "Hello Davey." Mother speaks through the car radio (a light blinks as she speaks). She sees through the car's headlights.

*Overhaul:* Dave had Mother repaired at Doc Bensen's Auto Clinic and painted at A. Schreib's Auto Painting.

*Auto Supplies:* Dave shops at Bill and Norm's Auto Store.

*License Plate:* PZR 317.

*Car Colors:* Candy apple red body with a white roof and a gold trim radiator with three tan leather straps encircling the hood. The wheels have bright chrome-plated spokes; the headlights are covered with protective cowls. The interior is all black leather; a wicker basket is on the rear of the car.

*Distinguishing Feature:* An arrow darts through the nameplate ("Porter") on the radiator grill.

*Emergency Money:* Dave keeps $2 under the seat for gas money.

*Number of Cylinders:* Four.

*Brakes:* Mother has Stops on a Dime Brakes (for which she did a TV commercial produced by the Video Advertising Agency).

*Carburetor:* Stromley-Gaxton (which contains 16 nuts, 14 screws, and three bolts).

*Fan Belt:* Size 39-24-84B.

*Car Chrome Polish:* Brite-O-Chrome.

*Car Wax:* Shino-O Wax.

*Top Speed:* 12 miles per hour. Later mentioned as eight, then nine, miles per hour.

*Favorite TV Show: Jalopy Derby* (which Mother watches on a $30 used TV that Dave purchased for her).

*Favorite Movie Actor:* Sonny Tufts.

*Fault:* Antifreeze causes Mother to get drunk; bumping her fender causes amnesia.

*Enjoyment:* A cup of tea (Dave places a tea bag down Mother's radiator cap).

*Nickname for David:* Davey.

*Routine:* Dave places Mother in the garage each night after watching the 11:00 news (to protect her from the dew) and places a blanket over her radiator (so she won't catch cold). He then stays with her for five minutes before returning to the house. Saturday afternoons are a special time for Dave, as he polishes Mother until her paint is bright and shiny.

## DAVID AND BARBARA CRABTREE

*David's Occupation:* Lawyer.

*Nicknames:* Dave and Davey.

*David's Birth Sign:* Sagittarius.

*David's Salary:* $5,000 a year (Dave's father was also a lawyer).

*David's Musical Ability:* Plays the banjo.

*David's Strange Ability:* To trip over his shoelaces when he wears loafers or slip-ons (which have no shoelaces).

*David's Favorite Dinner:* Pot roast (he also says dessert is his favorite part of dinner).

*David's Enjoyment:* Smoking a pipe and reading the newspaper on the blue and white hammock in the backyard.

*Barbara's Nicknames:* Barb and Barbs.

*Barbara's Birth Sign:* Cancer (later mentioned as being a Moon Child, born under the sign of the Crab).

*Barbara's Maiden Name:* Barbara Natwick.

*Children:* Cindy and Randy. Cindy is taking ballet lessons; Randy can play the violin. Their one major fault is always missing the school bus (thus, Dave and Mother have to drive them to school). In the unaired pilot, Harry Moses played Dave and Barbara's son as Harry.

*Family Dog:* Moon.

*Address:* 485 Maple Street.

*Phone Number:* Madison 6-4699.

*Dave and Barbara's Favorite TV Show: Stump the Experts* (a quiz program).

*Relatives:* Barbara's mother, called Mother Natwick (Paula Winslow). She mentions, in a strange twist on mothers-in-law, that she actually likes Dave.

## CHARACTER OVERVIEW

Both Dave and Barbara were born in Danville, Ohio, and were high school sweethearts (and, according to Dave, both were also cheerleaders together). After they graduated from Danville High School in 1953, they continued to see each other and married four years later when Dave completed law school. In another episode, Dave mentions that he married Barbara, whom he calls a "child bride," while they both were in school (not stated whether high school or college). Barbara laments that they could not take a honeymoon because Dave had to return to school for midterm exams. It is not mentioned when Dave attended law school, but according to Barbara, after graduation Dave had to find a job, and Barbara could not begin a career, as she became pregnant with Cindy, then Randy. Barbara is depicted as good wife, mother, and housekeeper, and she uses Blue Bird Brand Soap Powder (as seen on the box) for the laundry.

Captain Bernard Manzini is seen driving a number of different antique cars but believes that acquiring the Porter will be the crown jewel in his collection. He owns Manzini Enterprises and is very wealthy (although he offers to buy Mother from Dave only for a starting price of $500 and increasing to $4,000, but mostly $1,500). While Manzini becomes a bit irrational when Dave refuses to sell Mother, he retaliates by calling Dave numerous variations of his last name (e.g., Crabwell, Crabcake, Cranberry, Crabmaster, Crabpuff, and Crabgrass); Dave always responds by correcting his name, and Manzini counters with "Whatever." Brun DeSota appeared as Manzini's uncle, Louie.

# My Three Sons
### (ABC, 1960–1965; CBS, 1965–1972)

*Cast:* Fred MacMurray (Steven Douglas), Tim Considine (Mike Douglas), Don Grady (Robbie Douglas), Stanley Livingston (Chip Douglas), William Frawley (Bub), William Demarest (Uncle Charlie), Barry Livingston (Ernie Douglas), Beverly Garland (Barbara Harper), Dawn Lyn (Dodie Harper), Tina Cole (Katie Miller), Ronne Troup (Polly Williams), Meredith MacRae (Sally Ann Morrison).

*Basis:* A widower (Steve Douglas) attempts to raise his three sons (Mike, Robbie, and Chip) with the help of his father-in-law, Bub, then Bub's brother, Uncle Charlie.

## STEVEN "STEVE" DOUGLAS
*Height:* 6 feet, 3 inches tall.

*Birth Sign:* Virgo.

*Address:* 837 Mill Street in the town of Bryant Park (ABC episodes; CBS episodes are set in North Hollywood, California, but an address is not given).

*Phone Number:* Larson 0-6719.

*Car License Plate:* JXN 127 (later JIN 627). When Chevrolet sponsored the program, Steve first drove a 1961 Impala station wagon; he is later seen in various blue Pontiac Bonneville station wagons. When Ford Lincoln became the sponsor (1970–1972), Steve drove a Mercury Marquis station wagon.

*Family Pet Dog:* Tramp (Steve paid $3 for him).

*Occupation:* Aeronautical engineer (structural design) for Universal Research and Development Company.

*Prior Occupation:* Test pilot.

*Education:* Graduate of Midwest University (Class of 1938). In that graduating class, there was only one female student, Heather Marlowe (played by Frances Rafferty).

*Relaxation:* Wearing his cardigan sweater and smoking a pipe.

*Late Wife:* Louise. Steve married Louise O'Casey (age 19) when he was 21 years old; she died 12 years later on the night before Chip's first birthday. He has been a widower for six years when the series begins. Her cooking specialty was Spanish rice and prunes.

*Current Wife:* Barbara Harper, a schoolteacher.

*Barbara's Daughter:* Dorothy, called "Dodie."

*Dodie's Favorite Doll:* Myrtle.

*Note:* Barbara was Ernie's substitute teacher when she and Steve met in 1969. Her late husband was named Larry and, like Steve, smoked a pipe. Dodie was less than three years old when Larry passed; the family had a dog named King. Steve and Barbara were married in a chapel with just the family present (Robbie was the best man). Reverend Glassel (Maurice Manson) performed the ceremony. Dodie is in the first grade when introduced.

*Relatives of Barbara:* Mrs. Vincent, mother (Eleanor Audley); father-in-law, "Grandpa" Harper, a professor of Oriental philosophy (Lew Ayres).

*Flashbacks:* George Spicer played Steve as a college student; David Macklin, Steve as a high school student; and Tom Skerritt, Steve when he proposed to Louise. Vera Stough played Steve's fiancée, then wife, Louise.

*Relatives of Steve:* Fergus McBain Douglas, Scottish cousin (Fred MacMurray); Aunt Harriet, sister (Joan Tewksbury); Selana "Selly" Bailey, mother's cousin (Mary Jackson).

*Note:* Fergus was a Scottish laird (lord) and during his visit with Steve fell in love with and married Teri Dowling (Anne Francis), a waitress at the Blueberry Bowling Alley. Alan Caillou voiced Fergus.

## MICHAEL "MIKE" FRANCIS DOUGLAS

*Age:* 18 (Steve's eldest son).

*Education:* Bryant Park High School (a senior when the series begins; a member of the track team) and State College (where he is a member of the Sigma Gamma Chi fraternity).

*Wife:* Sally Ann Morrison, whom he met in 1963 (they married in the fall of 1965 when the series switched networks). He yearned to attend Stanford but didn't have the grades.

*Prior Girlfriend:* Jean Pearson (Cynthia Pepper).

*Occupation:* It is said that Mike joined the air force reserves (1965) and then began his career as a psychology professor in an unnamed locale (it is also said that Mike is "an assistant psychology instructor back East" in California episodes).

*Note:* Bub gave Sally a wedding shower on the occasion of his 50th wedding anniversary. When Mike was born, Steve bought a pipe and reading glasses to appear studious.

*Relatives of Sally:* Thomas Morrison, father, an archaeologist (Sebastian Cabot); Helen Morrison, mother (Doris Singleton); aunt, Alice (Ezelle Poule).

*Relatives of Jean:* father, Henry Pearson (Robert P. Lieb); mother, Florence Pearson (Florence MacMichael).

## ROBERT "ROBBIE" DOUGLAS

*Age:* 14 (the middle child; June was mentioned as his birth month).

*Education:* Webster Elementary School and Bryant Park High (where he was a member of the school band and played trumpet). The college Robbie attended in California is not named.

*After-School Hangout:* Freddy's, a hamburger joint.

*Occupation:* Structural engineer.

*As a Kid:* A member of the Chieftains Club.

*Temporary Job:* Singer-guitarist at the Coffee House.

*Song:* Wrote and sang the song "Ugga Bugga."

*Car:* A 1954 Pontiac Star Chief convertible, called the "Old Coffee Grinder" by his friends.

*Wife:* Kathleen "Katie" Miller. He met Katie in 1967 and became the father of triplets two years later: Charley, Steve Jr., and Robbie II (Michael, Joseph, and Daniel Todd). When Robbie and Katie move out of his family home (season 10), they take up residence one and a half blocks away. In California episodes, Robbie joins the army reserves. Chip was Robbie's best man at his wedding (replaced Clark [Gil Rogers], who became ill with a 104-degree temperature); Chip was an usher. Gracie (Kay Cole), Judy (Barbara Boles), and Kay (Jane Zachary) were Katie's bridesmaids. When Don Grady left the series during the final season, his absence was explained as his being transferred to Peru to complete a bridge project.

*Relatives of Katie:* Lorraine Miller, mother, lives in St. Louis, her husband is deceased (Joan Thompkins); Grandma Collins (Kathryn Givney); Cousin Elson, lives in Glendale, California (Mason Curry); Aunt Annie (Barbara Collentine); Cousin Grace (Dorothy Love); Aunt Cecile, mother's sister, lives in Boston (Marsha Hunt).

## RICHARD "CHIP" DOUGLAS

*Age:* Seven (Steve's youngest son).

*Education:* Webster Elementary School (also called the Buchanan Elementary School). When the series switched locales, additional school names were not given.

*Affiliation:* As a kid, Chip was a member of the Moose Patrol Scout troop.

*Nicknames:* Although "Chip" is most often heard, Steve sometimes calls him "Chipper." In the second grade, when a girl named Doreen Peters devel-

Seated: Stanley and Barry Livingston; standing: Fred MacMurray, Don Grady, and William Demarest. *CBS/Photofest © CBS*

oped a crush on Chip, he was called "Hot Lips Douglas" by his classmates (Chip felt girls were "icky" and called her "Goof Eyes").

*Wife:* Polly Williams. Chip and Polly loved each other, but her father was opposed to their marriage, causing Chip and Polly to elope (they honeymooned in Mexico, where they stayed at the Concha Azul Hotel—the same honeymoon site as his father and stepmother, Barbara).

*Relatives of Polly:* father, Tom Williams (Norman Alden); Margaret Williams, mother (Doris Singleton).

## ERNEST "ERNIE" STANLEY THOMPSON

*Character:* Steve's adopted son. Chip and Ernie were friends (1963) and attended the Buchanan Elementary School (Ernie originally attended the Suzie B. Dorsey Elementary School). When Ernie's parents are killed (how is not stated), he is sent to live with foster parents, the Thompsons, then to the King's County Children's Home. When the Thompsons move to Japan, Steve takes an interest in his case and later adopts him. At this time, Ernie had a dog named Wilson. Ernie can play the clarinet and guitar.

*Relatives:* foster mother, Mrs. Thompson (Barbara Collentine and Barbara Perry); foster father, Mr. Thompson (Richard Jury).

## MICHAEL FRANCIS ALOYSIUS O'CASEY

*Character:* Steve's father-in-law (Steve's first wife, Louise, was his daughter). He received the nickname "Bub" from Mike (when Mike was an infant, he tried to say "Grandpa," but it came out as "Bub"). However, in another episode, it is mentioned that when Chip tried to say the name, it came out "Bub." Bub was a member of the Brotherhood of the Cavaliers and left the series in 1964 to help his Aunt Kate celebrate her 104th birthday (Steve did not exactly tell the truth to his sons and said that Bub went to Ireland to visit his mother). To temporarily fill the void left by Bub's absence, Steve hired Fedocia Barrett (Reta Shaw) as a temporary housekeeper until Bub's return. Bub claims his eyes are "cornflower blue."

Prior to moving in with Steve, Bub was the manager of the Royal Theater in Evansberg, Ohio; his favorite part of the daily newspaper is the funnies. He cleans, cooks, looks after the kids, and is the nearest thing to a lady around the house (in some episodes, he calls himself the "lady of the house"). In a flashback sequence, Bee Peters played Bub's wife, Mary O'Casey.

## CHARLES "CHARLIE" O'CASEY

*Character:* Bub's brother. Like Bub, he was born in Sandusky, Ohio, and became a part of the series when he came to Bryant Park to visit his brother. Charlie is a former merchant marine and was en route to the Caribbean when Steve invited him to stay with the family for a few days. This upset Fedocia, who refused to cook for another male Douglas and quit. Charlie, who comes to be called "Uncle Charlie," stays to help Steve care for his sons.

## THE TOWN OF BRYANT PARK

Founded by Seth Bryant, an itinerant pots-and-pans salesman who established the town after his wagon broke down and forced him to stay.

# My World . . . and Welcome to It
## (NBC, 1969–1970)

*Cast:* William Windom (John Monroe), Joan Hotchkis (Ellen Monroe), Lisa Gerritsen (Lydia Monroe). Susan Gordon played Lydia in the pilot.

*Basis:* A cartoonist (John Monroe) retreats to the world he creates through his cartoons to become a hero and escape reality. The series is based on the work of James Thurber.

## JOHN MONROE

*Occupation:* Cartoonist for *Manhattanite* magazine. The magazine is housed in the Manhattanite Building in Manhattan, and the Metropolitan Paper Company supplies the publication's paper.

*Dislikes:* John hates his office (which is next to the freight elevator) and that his boss, Hamilton Greeley (Harold J. Stone), constantly complains that his cartoons "speak with their mouths closed."

*Wife:* Ellen.

*Daughter:* Lydia.

*Address:* 130 Post Road in Westport, Connecticut.

*Family Pets:* Dogs Christabel (who loves raspberries and asparagus) and Irving.

*Ambition:* To write a book ("Wanting to do a book is important; what it is about comes later").

*Fear:* Life and women. "The trouble with women is that when you get to know them and trust them, you realize that you can never get to know them and you can't trust them." Life is uncomfortable for John, and retreating to his secret world of cartoons provides him with tolerance, and he is viewed as irresistible to women and a tower of strength in the eyes of men. He is also suspicious of smart children and hostile animals.

## ELLEN AND LYDIA MONROE

*Character:* Ellen is totally dedicated to John and worries that he is much too critical of the world that surrounds him. Lydia is 10 years old and attends Compton Elementary School. She is pretty and bright and carries a flower-decorated lunchbox to school. She wears a retainer at night for her teeth and yearns to attend Yale University ("I better start getting all 'A's' now"). John believes he is raising "a girl with the IQ of a 55-year-old CPA." Ellen believes Lydia is a sensitive child.

*Relatives:* John's mother, Mrs. Monroe (Betty Kean); John's sister, Katie Monroe (Carole Cook).

# *National Velvet*

(NBC, 1960–1962)

*Cast:* Lori Martin (Velvet Brown), Arthur Space (Herbert Brown), Ann Doran (Martha Brown), Carole Wells (Edwina Brown), Joey Scott (Donald Brown), James McCallion (Mi Taylor).

*Basis:* A young girl (Velvet Brown) and her experiences with her horse (King) as she trains him for competition in the Grand National Steeplechase. Based on the Elizabeth Taylor feature film of the same title.

## VELVET BROWN

*Parents:* Herbert and Martha Brown.

*Sister:* Edwina Brown.

*Brother:* Donald Brown.

*Age:* 12 (when the series begins).

*Year and Place of Birth:* 1948 in Birch City.

*Residence:* A midwestern community called the Valley (located on the outskirts of Birch City; Flintwood and Cornwall are neighboring towns).

*Family Business:* The owners of the Brown Dairy Farm.

*Education:* Valley Elementary School.

*Associations:* The Pioneers Club (young children who explore nature).

*Horse:* King, a chestnut steed (won by her father in a raffle).

*Name Origin:* "You hold your head so high," Velvet says, "and you look so proud, I'm going to call you King." Mi Taylor, her horse trainer and ranch hand, suggests Blaze King (which becomes the horse's official name). Before being auctioned off by Homer Ede (Tim Graham), Velvet's neighbor, King's colt, Prince was born. Mr. Ede had previously put King out for stud. Nora Marlowe played Tim's wife, Aggie Ede.

*Velvet's Most Difficult Task:* Breaking King to a saddle.

*Restriction:* Velvet is not allowed to ride King bareback or after dark.

*King's First Championship:* The Junior Hurdle at the Valley Hunt Club, where King jumped six hurdles in a figure-eight track.

*King's Race Time:* Can run a mile in 1 minute, 44 seconds.

*Dream:* While she yearns to enter King in the Grand National, King is too young (not yet four), and the question of acquiring the funds to ship King to England (mentioned as "a lot of money") is a problem.

## EDWINA BROWN

*Age:* 16.

*Place and Year of Birth:* Birch City in August 1944.

*Nickname:* Winna.

*Education:* Valley High (where she is a sophomore).

*Association:* Member of the Teen Club.

*Hobby:* Breeding canaries (which she does in the bedroom she shares with Velvet).

*Favorite Magazine: The Canary Breeders Journal.* Although the canaries are seen, Edwina never calls one by name.

*Curfew:* 9:00 p.m.

*Restriction:* She cannot date on school nights.

*Make-Out Site:* Honeymoon Lane.

*Lucky Charm:* A nameless doll she has had since she was a little girl.

*Boyfriends:* Carl Crow played her boyfriend, Theodore P. Wilson, an anthropology major at State College (his father is the high school principal); Michael Vandever was Carl Evans, her occasional boyfriend.

## DONALD HERBERT BROWN JR.

*Age:* 6.

*Education:* Valley Elementary School.

*Hobby:* Collecting bugs (he has a small collection that he keeps in a jar and wears around his neck on a string).

*Faults:* Fibs and blames his sisters for something he did.

*Association:* A member of the Pioneers Club.

*Favorite Dessert:* Blueberry pie.

*Pet Canary:* Africa.

## MICHAEL "MI" PATRICK TAYLOR

*Position:* Ranch foreman (he has been with the Brown family for seven years).

*Prior Occupation:* Steeplechase rider in England. He was thrown from a horse during a race and injured his leg; he now walks with a limp.

*Place of Birth:* Ireland.

*First Horse Mi Rode:* Calico King (he received an English five-pound note as his fee).

*Favorite Pastime:* Playing checkers with Velvet.

*Favorite Words:* Using his grandmother's "words of wisdom" to get a point across (e.g., "As me wise grandmother used to say, the wise man laughs at himself and the fool laughs at everything else").

*Note:* There is virtually no information on Velvet's parents. The family sells milk in Flintwood at the Winters Dairies; Herbert's Dodge pickup truck license plate is E 35 947. Herbert reads *Dairyman* magazine, and Martha's maiden name is Harwell. Edgar Buchanan appeared as Martha's father, called "Grandpa Harwell."

# The Patty Duke Show
## (ABC, 1963–1966)

*Cast:* Patty Duke (Patty Lane/Cathy Lane/Betsy Lane), William Schallert (Martin Lane), Jean Byron (Natalie Lane), Paul O'Keefe (Ross Lane), Eddie Applegate (Richard Harrison). Rita McLaughlin plays Patty when Patty Duke is Cathy and Cathy when Patty Duke is Patty.

*Basis:* Incidents in the lives of a typical American teenage girl (Patty Lane) and her sophisticated identical-looking cousin (Cathy Lane).

## OVERALL SERIES INFORMATION
*Family Pet:* Tiger (dog).

*Address:* 8 Remsen Drive in Brooklyn Heights, New York (also given as 5 Remsen Drive; in final-season episodes, 450 is seen as the house number; it is at this time that the series switched filming locations from New York to Los Angeles).

*Telephone Number:* 624-0198.

*House History:* The Lanes live in Prescott Manor, a historic home built in 1720 by Adam Prescott, whose son Jonathan served under General George Washington. Jane, Adam's daughter, offered the house to General Howe and charmed him in order to give Washington and his troops time to rest and regroup during the American Revolution.

## PATRICIA "PATTY" LANE
*Age:* 16.

*Birthday:* December 1947.

*Birth Sign:* Sagittarius.

*Father:* Martin Lane.

*Mother:* Natalie Lane.

*Brother:* Ross Lane.

*Nickname for Her Father:* Poppo. She sometimes calls her mother "Mommo."

*Education:* Brooklyn Heights High School (Patty is a sophomore when the series begins). The school colors are red and gold.

*School Grades:* C.

*School Activities:* Editor of the school newspaper, the *Bugle* (where she was also the advice columnist "Simon Says"); president of the Brooklyn Heights High debate team; captain of the cheerleading team; and mascot for the girls' basketball team.

*After-School Hangout:* The Shake Shop (later called Leslie's Ice Cream Parlor). Patty and her friends also frequent the Platter, a record store, and the dance club Ga-Ga-a-Go-Go.

*Career Goal:* "A practical nurse or an astronaut."

*Jobs:* Hospital candy striper; waitress at the Pink Percolator, a coffeehouse that served 75 flavors of coffee; model for an ad campaign called "Stay in School"; Gypsy-like "seer," offering advice to her friends; temporary secretary to her father at the New York *Chronicle*; selling Jet Set Reducing Belts (over the phone); and waitress at the Shake Shop (at $15 a week).

*Author:* Patty wrote the book *I Was a Teenage Teenager* ("A story about love, war, poverty and cooking recipes").

*Publisher:* Frye Publishing (a vanity press); 100 copies were printed.

*Dress Size:* 5.

*Hair Color:* Brunette.

*Favorite Ice Cream:* Chocolate coconut thrill.

*Allergies:* Allergic to gardenia perfume and horsehair.

*First Date:* A boy named Herman Brinckerhoff.

*Stock:* Patty owns five shares of stock in the McGregor Electric Company (a birthday present from her father).

*Schemes:* To make money, Patty attempted the Doctor's Baby Sitting Service and Patty Lane, Inc. (wherein she sold stock in herself offering 200 shares at $1 a share); see Cathy Lane for Patty and Cathy's joint ventures.

*Talent:* Singing (Patty sang the songs "Tell Me Mama," "Henry VIII," and "Funny Little Butterflies" on the program); she also attempted to play the tuba and can tap dance.

*Catchphrase:* "Cu-koo."

*Boyfriend:* Richard Harrison. He and Patty have been dating for five years. Richard attends the same school as Patty and worked as the manager of the Pink Percolator. His father, Jonathan Harris (played by David Doyle), was first mentioned as being a bank manager, then a construction engineer. Patty, however, is very fickle. Whenever she sees a cute boy, she acts like Richard doesn't exist. Richard is also a member of the school's football team. Amzie Strickland played Richard's mother.

*Nemesis:* Sue Ellen Turner (played by Kitty Sullivan), the girl who sought to steal Richard away from Patty. Sue Ellen's father was president of the First Mortgage and Trust Company.

*Resentment:* Patty mentions that she sometimes resents Cathy for her brilliance ("She comes off like Albert Einstein," especially when Cathy will not help Patty with her homework; she feels Patty should do it by herself).

## CATHERINE "CATHY" MARGARET ROLLIN LANE

*Age:* 16.

*Birthday:* December 1947.

*Birth Sign:* Sagittarius.

*Relationship:* Patty's first cousin (Martin's twin brother Kenneth's daughter).

*Hair Color:* Brunette.

*Father:* Kenneth Lane (a widower).

*Kenneth's Occupation:* Foreign correspondent for the *New York Chronicle*. It was Kenneth's idea to send Cathy to live with Martin until Cathy could finish her education without being constantly uprooted due to the nature of his job.

*Kenneth's Nickname for Cathy:* Kit Kat.

*Prior Residence:* Glasgow, Scotland.

*Education:* Mrs. Tuttle's of Mountain Briar (where she was the debating champion), Brooklyn Heights High School (where she is a member of the Literary Club).

*School Grades:* A.

*Musical Ability:* Composes music and plays the piano and violin and can also sing arias. She composed the music for a poem called "Where Love Has Gone" (which she also sang and accompanied herself on the piano).

*Languages:* Cathy can speak English, French, Italian, and Spanish.

*Dress Size:* 5.

*Hobbies:* Reading, listening to classical music, and knitting.

*Job:* Deejay (playing classical music) on the Brooklyn Heights radio station BHBH.

*Schemes with Patty:* Catnip dresses (Cathy designed a dress with a cat that sold for $9.95, while Patty turned the idea into the World Wide Dress Company); Mother Patty's Preserves (an apricot jam, bottled in jars from the Fleming Bottle Company, that Cathy based on a recipe she found in a book by England's Charles II. The company slogan: "The Jam of Kings—King of the Jams").

*Quirk:* Cannot tell a lie (she has a built-in lie detector, and if she attempts to fib, she develops the hiccups).

*Resentment:* Cathy mentions that she is often jealous of Patty because she is so popular with boys.

## BETSY LANE

*Relationship:* Patty's distant cousin. Although Betsy (real name not given) is identical to Patty and Cathy in appearance, her father does not resemble Patty (or Cathy's) father.

*Place of Birth:* Atlanta, Georgia. She is residing with the Lanes in Brooklyn Heights during her school vacation (although it appears that school for Patty and Cathy is still in session).

*Age:* 16.

*Hair Color:* Blonde.

*Parents:* Gaylord and Cissy Lane (Martin mentions that Gaylord is "one of the distant Lane cousins").

*Makeup:* While Patty wears little makeup and Cathy just a touch, Betsy is more prone to accentuating her facial features with makeup.

*Favorite Doll:* Sara Jane (which acts as her security blanket).

*Dream:* To become part of a real family. Betsy's parents are working to build their business (only called "The Store") and have little time to devote to Betsy. During vacations from boarding school, they "ship her off" to relatives so they can continue to focus on their business.

*Patty's "Nickname" for Betsy:* A Confederate Cleopatra (for the way she makes boys swoon over her). Betsy also has trouble remembering boys' names (in Brooklyn Heights, she calls them "northern boys" and finds them "sweet and friendly").

*Dislike:* Betsy hates cowboy movies.

*Relatives:* Gaylord Lane (George Gaynes) and Cissy Lane (Frances Heflin), parents.

## MARTIN LANE

*Occupation:* Managing editor of the *New York Chronicle*. The *New York Record* is its competition.

*Birth Sign:* Virgo.

*IQ:* 135.

*Education:* While a name was not given, he was captain of his college football team.

*Prior Jobs:* Only mentioned that as a kid, Martin worked in a drugstore, and he worked his way through college playing the piano. While working for the *Chronicle*, Martin was also the temporary editor of the *Oklahoma City Post*.

*Family Ancestors:* Lieutenant Noah Lane, the first Union officer captured at Bull Run, and Joshua Lane, who established the first general store in Vermont.

*Relatives:* Kenneth Lane, brother, and Jed Lane, uncle (William Schallert); aunt, Pauline (Ilka Chase). Unseen relatives were Aunt Martha and Uncle Ben; Aunt Kay (who sends Martin a basket of peaches every year from the farm); Martin's niece, Ann; and his cousins, Clarence and Fran.

*Note:* Mark Miller played Martin in the original unaired pilot.

## NATALIE LANE
*Occupation:* Housewife and mother.
*Prior Job:* Secretary.
*Education:* No school was mentioned for Natalie, but it was made clear that Martin, who is older than Natalie, married Natalie when she was 17 years old (presumably right after she graduated from high school; it is mentioned in another episode that they were high school sweethearts). They honeymooned at Lake George in upper New York State. They are married 20 years when the series begins.
*Wedding Date:* Only "the 14th" was given.
*Birth Sign:* Pisces.
*Pastime:* Crocheting.
*Hobby:* Raising roses.

## ROSS LANE
*Birth Sign:* Taurus.
*Education:* P.S. 8 Elementary School.
*Allowance:* 50 cents a week.
*First Girlfriend:* Nikki Lee Blake (played by Susan Melvin).
*Favorite Ice Cream Flavor:* Strawberry.
*Favorite Game:* Chess.
*Sport:* Pitcher on the Brooklyn Heights Little League team.

*Note:* Charles Herbert played Ross in the original unaired pilot.

## UPDATE
In the CBS 1999 TV movie, *The Patty Duke Show—Still Rockin' in Brooklyn Heights*, Patty, now the principal of Brooklyn Heights High School, had married Richard, but they divorced after 27 years of marriage; Cathy was a widow and living in Scotland; Ross was a musician; and Martin and Natalie had retired and moved to Florida.

In the unaired pilot version (reedited to form the last first-season episode, "Cousins"), Patty and Cathy have different hairstyles and also have separate rooms (in the series, they share a bedroom). The Lanes live in San Francisco, where Martin is editor of the *San Francisco Express*.

# Pete and Gladys
## (CBS, 1960–1962)

*Cast:* Harry Morgan (Pete Porter), Cara Williams (Gladys Porter).

*Basis:* "When strange things are looking to happen, somebody gives them Gladys's address" can best sum up a program about a levelheaded husband (Pete) and his efforts to put up with the antics of his scatterbrained wife (Gladys).

## PETER "PETE" PORTER

*Wife:* Gladys.

*Address:* 726 Elm Street in Westwood, California.

*Telephone Number:* Granite 5-5055.

*Occupation:* Salesman for the Springer, Slocum, and Klever Insurance Company in Los Angeles.

*Military Service:* Clerk at a PX during World War II (although he brags to Gladys that he was a hero for single-handedly capturing a Japanese patrol).

*Hobby:* Restoring old cars (something thrust on him when Gladys felt he needed a hobby). His first project: a 1924 Hupmobile roadster (license plate JFH 647) that Gladys purchased for $20.

*Annual Gathering:* Each year, Pete attends the Veterans Convention.

*Relatives:* uncle, Paul Barton, who gave him his first pair of roller skates and believes "Gladys is an idiot" (Gale Gordon).

## GLADYS PORTER

*Maiden Name:* Gladys Hooper.

*Husband:* Pete Porter.

*Occupation:* Housewife.

*Prior Job:* Secretary. Gladys and Pete worked at the same insurance company and married in 1951 (in the small town of Colbyville; C. A. Cavanaugh [Will Wright] performed the ceremony).

*Trait:* Forgetful and clumsy.

*Favorite Eatery:* Petroni's Italian Restaurant (the song "Santa Lucia" can be heard in the background when they attend).

*Favorite TV Show: Life Can Be a Problem* (mythical).

*Clubs:* Entertainment chairman of the Junior Matron's League of the Children's Hospital and the Westwood Bowling League (she bowls with a Sindler bowling ball).

*TV Appearance:* Gladys was a contestant on "Lucky Lady," a *Queen for a Day* type of program wherein contestants tell sad stories to win prizes. Here, Gladys, who possessed the winning audience ticket (24931), won a stuffed penguin and was told never to come back for her made-up story about Pete dying from an unknown disease. She had hoped to win a trailer and summer vacation.

*Hobby:* Entering slogan contests (e.g., Kitty Kat Snacks and Fine Line Spark Plugs).

*Relatives:* father, Henry Hooper (Ernest Truex); nephew, Bruce (Bill Hinnant); cousin, Helen Franklin (Sue Randall); cousin, Violet (Muriel Landers). Unseen were aunt, Wilma, and cousin, Warren. Gladys's father is most always called "Pop" in episodes, but in the closing theme he is credited as "Pops."

## OTHER CHARACTERS
Verna Felton is Gladys's friend, Hilda Crocker, and Shirley Mitchell and Peter Leeds are the Porters' neighbors, Janet and George Colton. The program is a spin-off from *December Bride*, wherein the character of Gladys was spoken about but never seen.

# *Petticoat Junction*
## (CBS, 1963–1970)

*Cast:* Bea Benaderet (Kate Bradley); Edgar Buchanan (Joe Carson); Jeannine Riley, then Gunilla Hutton, then Meredith MacRae (Billie Jo Bradley); Pat Woodell, then Lori Saunders (Bobbie Jo Bradley); Linda Kaye Henning (Betty Jo Bradley); Frank Cady (Sam Drucker); Smiley Burnette (Charley Pratt); Rufe Davis (Floyd Smoot); Mike Minor (Steve Elliott).

*Basis:* A widow (Kate Bradley) with three beautiful daughters (Billie Jo, Bobbie Jo, and Betty Jo) attempts to run a small-town rural hotel with the help of her uncle, Joe Carson.

## KATHERINE "KATE" BRADLEY
*Marital Status:* Widow.
*Children:* Billie Jo Bradley, Bobbie Jo Bradley, and Betty Jo Bradley.
*Late Husband:* Bill.

*Business:* Owner of the Hotel Shady Rest (as seen on the building; it is called the Shady Rest or the Shady Rest Hotel in dialogue). There is a pay phone in the lobby, but it is not operational (just there to give the hotel class, as Uncle Joe says).

*Residence:* Kate and her daughters reside at the hotel, which is located in the town of Hooterville (an elevation of 1,427 feet; a community of 72 farms). The hotel is 25 miles from the town.

*Yearly Tradition:* The Jamboree (a night of singing and dancing held at the Shady Rest).

*Hotel Bird:* Phoebe (a mynah bird that appears to live in the nonoperational elevator cage that is next to the front-lobby staircase).

*Hotel Dog:* The family dog is simply called "Boy" or "Dog" (although in one episode, he is called "Higgins"). The dog became a part of the family when he, apparently a stray, followed Betty Jo home from school.

*Hotel Rates:* $2.50 a day (the hotel was built by Kate's grandfather).

*Part-Time Job:* Advice columnist (as "Dear Minerva") for the town newspaper, the *Hooterville World Guardian.*

*Ability:* Cooking. She is famous for her fruit pies and, most notably, "bachelor's butter."

*Vanity Cream:* Kate believes that as she grows older, she needs to "wash those wrinkles away" and uses Scab and Wrinkle Youth Beauty Cream.

*Note:* In 1968, when Bea Benaderet became ill, Rosemary DeCamp appeared as Aunt Helen before June Lockhart joined the cast as Dr. Janet Craig and became the show's mother figure (as she set up practice from the Shady Rest). Shortly after, following Bea's passing, Uncle Joe became the hotel owner instead of its manager.

## JOSEPH "JOE" CARSON

*Relationship:* Said to be both Kate's brother and her uncle (Joe does mention in some episodes that Kate is his niece).

*Job:* General manager of the Shady Rest Hotel. He calls himself an "idea man," as he constantly needs to think of ways to raise money and keep the hotel operating. According to Uncle Joe, the hotel never has more than three guests at a time. His most ambitious but also his most disappointing moneymaking scheme was selling spray-on cologne for women (Lady Violet) and men (Lord Violet).

*Favorite Pastime:* Relaxing (napping) in the rocking chair on the front porch of the hotel (although he claims he isn't napping, "I'm thinking").

*Hobby:* Playing checkers and hanging out at Sam Drucker's General Store.

*Affiliation:* Captain of the Hooterville Volunteer Fire Department, head of the Hooterville Barbershop Quartet (with Sam Drucker, Floyd Smoot, and farmer Newt Kiley), and member of the Royal Order of Camels Lodge.

*Belief:* Uncle Joe believes the hotel is haunted by the ghost of Chester W. Farnsworth, a guest who stayed at the hotel 50 years ago.

*Work:* Virtually nothing, as he fakes an attack of lumbago when he is asked to do something.

*Best Friend:* A wooden Indian, named Geronimo (Kate claims that it is Joe's best friend), that is part of the hotel's decor.

## BILLIE JO BRADLEY

*Full Name:* Wilhelmina Josephine Bradley (Kate's eldest daughter).

*Education:* Hooterville High School, then Pixley Secretarial School.

*Ambition:* To become a Hollywood actress. Her father had set aside $500 for Billie Jo to become a doctor, but Billie Jo found she could not follow that course, as she faints at the sight of blood.

*Attribute:* Stunning blonde who is a bit ditzy at times (when Jeannine Riley played the role). When Gunilla Hutton, then Meredith MacRae, portrayed Billie Jo, the character was not as boy crazy as the original Billie Jo. She also changed her career ambition from actress to wanting to become a singer.

*Lingerie:* Billie Jo orders her lingerie from the Hollywood Lingerie Company. While what she wears is not seen, Kate refuses to let her order anything in black.

*Nicknames:* Boys referred to the original Billie Jo as a "blonde bombshell"; Bobbie Jo called her the "Tuesday Weld of Hooterville" (referring to the sexy 1960s actress who is perhaps best known for her role as Thalia Menninger on *Dobie Gillis*).

*Job:* Season 3 episodes feature Billie Jo as the secretary to world-famous writer Oliver Fenton, the author of such books as *Dr. Love*, *Fall on a Spring Afternoon*, and *The Carpet Sweepers*. Billie Jo also sang in a Pixley nightclub under the name "Monique." In the last episode, Billie Jo is seen preparing to open a child day care center.

*Note:* Sharon Tate was originally cast as Billie Jo but backed out at the last minute on the advice of her agent.

## BOBBIE JO BRADLEY

*Full Name:* Roberta Josephine Bradley (Kate's second-born daughter).

*Education:* Hooterville High School (where she was a member of the Omicron Epsilon Pi sorority house).

*Image:* People see Bobbie Jo as a "walking encyclopedia."

*Trait:* The intellectual Bradley sister. She prefers to read books rather than date boys (although this often changes when she sees a cute boy and books are suddenly not that important).

*Ability:* Like her sisters, Bobbie Jo could sing (Uncle Joe organized her, Billie Jo, and Betty Jo into a singing group he called the "Lady Bugs").

*Hotel Job:* At dinnertime, Bobbie Jo is responsible for clearing the table (Betty Jo sets the table, Kate washes the dishes, and Billie Jo dries them).

## BETTY JO BRADLEY

*Full Name:* Elizabeth Josephine Bradley (Kate's youngest daughter).

*Education:* Hooterville High School.

*Trait:* Tomboy. Also handy at "fixing things and plumbing."

*Volunteer Job:* Relief engineer on the Hooterville *Cannonball*.

*Sports:* Played shortstop on the Hooterville Hawks baseball team (the Pixley Pirates were their opponents). She was also her class leader in gymnastics, ice hockey, and basketball.

*As a Kid:* Betty Jo had a bug collection and enjoyed catching frogs.

*Boyfriend:* Steve Elliott. A crop duster she married on June 7, 1967 (according to the date on the marriage license). They honeymooned in Hawaii and later moved into their own cottage (which was in need of extensive repairs) that Betty Jo found "off the beaten path" (deep in the woods). They had originally planned to rent an apartment in Pixley, and Betty Jo and Steve later become the parents of a daughter they named Kathy Jo Elliott (played by twins Elaine and Danielle Hubbel). Steve first saw Betty Jo when he flew his plane over the *Cannonball*'s water tower and saw her and her sisters in their swimsuits (as the girls used the tower to cool off on hot summer days).

*Steve's Later Job:* Steve becomes partners with Uncle Joe when they form the Carson-Elliott Crop Dusting Company.

*Job:* When finances became tight, Betty Jo opened her own day care center at the Shady Rest (since there was no operating telephone at the Shady Rest, she purchased a post office box [46] at Sam Drucker's for responses).

*Relatives:* Steve's mother and father, first names not given (Hugh Beaumont and Ann Doran); Steve's uncle, George (Don Ameche).

## OTHER CHARACTERS

Sam Drucker is the owner of the general store (called Sam Drucker's and seen as Sam Drucker's General Store). He is also the postmaster, editor of the town newspaper, justice of the peace, and virtually anything else Hooterville requires. Charley Pratt (engineer) and Floyd Smoot (conductor) operate the *Cannonball Express*. Three toots of the *Cannonball*'s whistle alert the valley's children that it is time for school.

The title refers to the *Cannonball*'s watering tank stop at the Shady Rest Hotel where the Bradley sisters swim on hot days and their petticoats can be seen hanging over the top rim. In the opening and closing theme, when the girls are seen in the water tank, the order is Billie Jo, Bobbie Jo, and Betty Jo. Beginning with the third season, the order is Betty Jo, Bobbie Jo, and Billie Jo.

## THE HOOTERVILLE *CANNONBALL*

An 1890s 4-6-0 steam engine owned by the C. & F.W. Railroad (the 4-6-0 refers to the engine's wheel arrangement: four lead wheels, six driving wheels, and no trailing truck). Charles Lane appeared in early episodes as Homer Bedlow, the railroad vice president who sought numerous ways to take the *Cannonball* out of service in hopes of becoming a company big shot; he was always foiled, however, by Kate. The engine carried the number "3" in black-and-white episodes and the number "8" in color episodes. The engine carries a coal car and a combination mail/baggage/coach car (which has the number "5" on its sides).

# *Pistols and Petticoats*

## (CBS, 1966–1967)

*Cast:* Ann Sheridan (Henrietta Hanks), Douglas V. Fowley (Andrew Hanks), Ruth McDevitt (Effie Hanks), Carole Wells (Lucy Hanks), Gary Vinson (Harold Sikes).

*Basis:* In a wild-and-woolly town called Wretched, Colorado (1871), the peace-loving Hanks family (Henrietta, Lucy, Grandma, and Grandpa) assist the inept town sheriff, Harold Sikes, in maintaining law and order.

## HENRIETTA HANKS

*Marital Status:* Widow.

*Parents:* Andrew and Effie (called Grandpa and Grandma). See note below.

*Nickname:* Hank (although she is totally feminine and never dresses like a "cowboy").

*Ability:* Sharpshooter ("Could fire a gun with one hand milking a goat and hit a coyote on the run"). She never lets her guard down no matter how many handsome "city slickers" try to take advantage of her simply because she is a woman.

*Residence:* The Hanks Ranch (located two miles outside the town of Wretched).

*Mail Delivery:* Because of their distance from the town, mail is sometimes delivered by Indian arrow (Bald Eagle perches himself on a hill next to the Hanks farm and simply uses his bow and arrow to deliver the mail).

*Shopping:* When in town, Henrietta shops at the Paris Department Store.

*Henrietta's Law:* Assuring citizens that drinking at the town saloon (Al's Tankard Saloon) will not occur before its scheduled opening time of 1:00 p.m.

*Curse:* Henrietta, like her parents, is literally helpless when they are struck by the "Grip" (a cold) and become vulnerable to outlaws. Lucy appears to be immune as she takes care of them.

*Wake-Up Time:* Very early in the morning (6:00 a.m.).

## LUCILLE "LUCY" HANKS

*Relationship:* Henrietta's beautiful and alluring daughter.

*Goal:* Marrying the elusive town sheriff, Harold Sikes.

*Ability:* Although Lucy rarely uses a gun, she is an expert shot and conceals one in the lacy garter she wears on her right leg. Lucy, however, tends to faint when a gun is pointed at her.

*Talent:* Plays the piano.

*Wardrobe:* Always elegantly dressed but sometimes wears dresses that are too revealing in the eyes of her mother. Henrietta describes Lucy as "dainty, sweet, feminine, warm, and loving."

*Education:* Miss Scoengrams School for Young Ladies.

*Note:* Chris Noel played Lucy in the unaired pilot.

## ANDREW "GRANDPA" HANKS

*Relationship:* Henrietta's father.

*Military Service:* Union army private.

*Weapon:* Never without his former army rifle.

*Disability:* Virtually blind without his eyeglasses.

*Pet Wolf:* Bowzer.

*Mule:* Molly.

*Retreat:* Each year, Andrew "takes to the hills" to get away from it all while the lady folk use this time to clean the house. Andrew claims that the scouring powder gives him hay fever, and thus he avoids cleaning.

*Enjoyment:* Looking at pictures through his stereo-optician viewer.

*Trait:* Grandma claims that Andrew is mean when he is awoken from his sleep.

## EFFIE "GRANDMA" HANKS

*Relationship:* Henrietta's mother.

*Trait:* Sweet-looking elderly lady "who was best at shootin' buttons off a rustler's vest."

*Ability:* Sharpshooter (handgun or rifle).

*Name for Henrietta:* Most often calls Henrietta "Daughter."

*Problem:* Effie is still plagued by her former beau (before she met Andrew), Orville Snipe (Charlie Ruggles), who writes her once every five years to see if Andrew "kicked the bucket" so that he can marry her. It has been 40 years, and Orville has not given up hope.

## HAROLD SIKES

*Position:* Town sheriff.

*Trait:* Clumsy and inept. He cannot shoot straight or draw fast (as his gun always gets stuck in his holster).

*Belief:* He can overpower outlaws by starring at them. Although he believes it is his badge that Indians and outlaws fear, it is actually the Hanks family that secretly maintains the peace.

*Instituted Laws:* Wretched Beautiful (an antilittering law where violators are fined 50 cents), a Wanted Board (displays the wanted posters of outlaws), the Hitching Law (horses must be properly tied to hitching posts), and the Sunday Law (prohibits shooting guns).

*Supporter:* Lucy. She is the only one who has faith in Harold's abilities but can't convince her family that "Harold can rescue people in distress and things like that." Grandma tells her, "That's woman's work."

*Name for Lucy:* Miss Lucy.

*Grandma's Name for Harold:* Harold, Dear.

*Tradition:* Harold and Lucy share a vanilla malt when she comes to town.

*Relatives:* cousin, Fred Kent (Kent McWhirter).

*Note:* Joel D. McCrea played the sheriff (as Sheriff Eric) in the unaired pilot.

## OTHER CHARACTERS

Bernard Courtney (Robert Lowery) is the land baron seeking to obtain the Hanks' ranch, Jed Timmins (Stanley Adams) is the crooked lawyer, Eagle Shadow (Lon Chaney Jr.) is the chief of the Kiowa Indians, Great Bear (Jay Silverheels) is the chief of the Atona Indians, and Gil Lamb plays the unnamed town drunk.

*Note:* Four episodes of the series have been edited to form a movie called *The Far Out West*. Although it is said that Andrew and Effie are Henrietta's parents, it is not made clear how Lucy can also have the last name of Hanks (as when Henrietta married, she would have taken her husband's last name [which is not mentioned] and Lucy would have that last name). It is more likely that Andrew and Effie are her late husband's parents and that the use of "Daughter" is just a term of endearment when Henrietta is called such.

# *The Prisoner*

### (CBS, 1968)

*Cast:* Patrick McGoohan (Number 6).

*Basis:* A former secret agent for the British government is kidnapped, given a number (6), and placed in the Village, a place from which there is no escape, for one purpose: to discover why he resigned.

## NUMBER 6

*Birthday:* March 19, 1928, at 4:31 a.m.

*Real Name:* Assumed to be John Drake (from the prior TV series *Danger Man* and *Secret Agent*). Two episodes feature Number 6 giving (fake) names: Peter Smith ("Many Happy Returns") and "Do Not Forsake Me, Oh My Darling," where he is revealed to have several code names: ZM-73, Duval, and Schmidt.

*Prior Occupation:* British intelligence agent.

*Reason for Abduction:* To discover why Number 6 has chosen to resign and what he knows ("A lot of people are curious why you suddenly left. The information in your head is priceless. A man like you is worth a lot on the open market. It is my job [Number 2] to check your motives." Number 6 contends, "It is a matter of principal" (possibly due to the fact that in the last episode of *Secret Agent*, Drake allowed a scientist who invented a deadly mind reference device to escape rather than apprehend him).

*Repeated Statement:* "I am not a number, I am a free man."

*Number 6's Goal:* Learn the identity of Number 1. Number 6 uses a handmade device to study the sky in hopes of determining the location of the Village.

*Badge ID:* Reads Number 6 (left side) with his picture on the right side. He is seen wearing it only once, in "The Arrival" episode (wherein he removes it and throws it to the ground).

*Prior Car License Plate:* KAR 102C (a Lotus sedan of which Number 6 says, "I know every nut bolt and clog. I built it with my own hands"; it is seen only in the opening theme).

*Prior Address:* 1 Buckingham Place (opening theme only).

*Interrogators:* Number 2 (appearing as both men and women). Colin Gordon, Clifford Evans, John Sharpe, Peter Wyngarde, Guy Dolman, and Leo Mc-Kern were the male players; Mary Morris was the female player. They rule from the Green Dome.

*Number 6's Only Friend:* The Silent Butler (played by Angelo Muscat).

## THE VILLAGE

A fantasy-like area bound by mountains and sea from which there is no escape. Money is called "units," and store names state exactly what they are (e.g., the Café and the General Store; the name of the Village pub, however, is seen as the Cat and Mouse). The Village is identified by a nineteenth-century bicycle (large front tire and small back tire). Names are forbidden, and each person is designated by a number. Questioning other residents is prohibited (it appears that all residents are concealing something; prison is the punishment for attempting to question someone). Only Village leaders are permitted to question residents. Rules prohibit animals (although Number 6 has a cat he calls "It." The cat, which mysteriously appears, is later said to belong to the female leader Number 2). The

Patrick McGoohan. *ITV/Photofest © ITV*

leaders have instructions "not to damage Number 6 but to get all he knows. He must be won over not broken."

Rover is the large white balloon that serves as the Village sentry (it can move on its own and blocks all attempts to escape). Villagers can be seen carrying umbrellas, but only one episode, "A.B. and C.," actually shows that it is raining. The Village newspaper is called *The Tally Ho*. Although there are other publications, like magazines, they are seen only in background shots (like *The Village Weekly* and *The Village Mercury*).

*Note:* Although female characters did appear, Patrick McGoohan stood firm that Number 6 never become romantically involved. The series was filmed in the resort village of Portmeirion in northern Wales (credited only in the last episode). The British rock group Iron Maiden based two songs on the series: "The Prisoner" and "Back in the Village." In the final episode, "Fall Out," it is seen that hooded and masked delegates appear to run the Village from an underground chamber, and it contains several factions: Identification, Defectors, Therapy, Reactionists, and Nationalists.

# The Roaring 20's
(ABC, 1960–1962)

*Cast:* Dorothy Provine (Pinky Pinkham), Donald May (Pat Garrison), Rex Reason (Scott Norris), John Dehner (Jim Duke Williams), Gary Vinson (Chris Higbee).

*Basis:* Newspaper reporters Pat Garrison and Scott Norris seek the headline-making stories in the wild and reckless era of the 1920s in New York City.

## PINKY PINKHAM

*Real Name:* Delaware Pinkham.

*Address:* Room 21 at the Grently Apartments.

*Phone Number:* Skylar 2-098.

*Occupation:* Singer and dancer (typically called a "flapper").

*Business:* Owner of the Charleston Club, a fashionable speakeasy. The club is also called "Pinky's" and "Pinky's Club."

*Club Address:* East 52nd Street in Manhattan.

*Band:* The Playboys.

*Backup Vocalists:* The Girls. Cindy (Gayla Graves) and Dodie (Roxanne Arlen) play the roles, and their official name is Pinky and the Girls.

*Wake-Up Time:* 12:00 noon.

*Bad Habit:* Falling in love with men who most often have links to the underworld. The song "Someone to Watch over Me" can be heard in the background when Pinky does become involved with the wrong type of man.

*Character:* Although Pinky is beautiful and dresses like a flapper (also called "jazz babies" and referring to a girl who dances and parties all night), she is not one in the true sense. Her club is also not typical of what would be considered a speakeasy (serving illegal, homemade liquor). Pinky tries to maintain an honest operation (even sells a legitimate scotch called Highland Dew), but her club is a magnet for the gangsters, bootleggers, and crooked politicians who are also a part of the era.

## SCOTT NORRIS AND PAT GARRISON

Reporters for a newspaper called both the *Daily Record* and the *New York Record*. They are first said to earn $40 a week, then $60 a week. While their main objective appears to be getting the top stories, they also play detective and investigate the crimes to bring criminals to justice. While they do frequent the Charleston Club, they are also fond of Chauncey's, the bar located next to the Record Building (which houses the newspaper). In second-season episodes, the bar is called The Pit. The *Gazette* is the *Record*'s competition. Scott was said to live on East 53rd Street and Pat on West 41st Street. The Scott Norris character was dropped for the second season and replaced by Jim Duke Williams, a reporter who was also the city editor of the *Record*. Duke, as he was most often called, had a nose for news and did whatever it took to get the stories for his paper.

## OTHER CHARACTERS

Chris Higbee, a graduate of Cornell University, was originally the *Record*'s copyboy, then a reporter. He lived at the Hallmark Hotel. Joe Switolski (Mike Road) is a lieutenant with the Seventh Precinct of the New York City Police Department (also seen as the Bell Street Police Station); Spring 3-1000 is his direct-dial telephone number. Dixie (Carolyn Komant) is the Charleston Club hatcheck girl; Andre (Gregory Gray) is the club maître d'. Louise Glenn is Gladys, the *Record*'s switchboard operator. Wally Brown is the Chauncey's bar owner.

# *Route 66*
## (CBS, 1960–1964)

*Cast:* Martin Milner (Tod Stiles), George Maharis (Buz Murdock), Glenn Corbett (Linc Case).

*Basis:* Two friends (Tod and Buz, later Tod and Linc) travel across the country by car seeking to experience life and a place to eventually settle down.

## TOD STILES

*Parents:* Lee and Martha Stiles.
*Birthday:* March 12, 1936.
*Place of Birth:* New York City.
*Education:* Attended Yale University for three years.

*Position:* Left penniless after his wealthy father's passing (he owned a shipping company).

*Goal* (with Buz): Travel along the highway of U.S. Route 66—"We're looking for a place with a niche, a place where we can really fit in." In the episodes in which Buz does not appear and Tod rides alone, Tod sums up his situation: "I'm on some unforgotten road on the way to some little unremembered town with a road map clutched in my little hand. We [referring to him and Buz] have been through a pile of maps, and the map companies ought to give us a testimonial hamburger at any one of the stop-and-eats."

*Relatives:* Kitty Chamberlain, aunt (Beatrice Straight).

## BUZ MURDOCK

*Place of Birth:* Manhattan (grew up in New York's Hell's Kitchen). His parents later moved to Landor, Texas (311-Klondike 5-2368 was their phone number). Buz also mentions that he grew up in New York City and was orphaned and adopted by a family whose father was addicted to heroin. Buz, at the age of 15, had his first exposure to drugs when he caught his father using them.

*Job:* Worked for Tod's father on the shipping docks.

*Birthday:* September 1937.

*Social Security Number:* 100-20-0853.

Martin Milner and George Maharis. *CBS/Photofest © CBS*

*Trait:* Philosophical. He also believes he can feel hate in people.
*Relatives:* mother in one episode (Linda Watkins); father, Thomas, was not seen.

*Note:* When George Maharis left the series, Glenn Corbett replaced him as Lincoln "Linc" Case, a Vietnam War veteran (served as an army ranger) in final-season episodes. Buz was said to be hospitalized with an undisclosed disease. Linc was haunted by the war and met Tod in Texas (outside of Houston). In the final episode ("Where There Is a Will, There Is a Way"), Tod marries Mona Tiffin (Barbara Eden), the daughter of a tycoon, and elects to settle down with her in Texas while Linc chooses to return to his estranged family (also in Texas). Buz's fate is never revealed. It is also a bit unusual to see in the Linc episodes that when something gets Tod and Linc down, they tend to get drunk.

**THE CAR**
A 1960 Chevrolet Corvette. It is also mentioned that Tod inherited the car, as well as that he and Buz, who were friends, pooled their resources to buy the car. The license plate is 2D 7876 (NY Empire State is below the number; in certain scenes, it looks like 20 7876). In non-Buz episodes, the car license plate reads 1C 9-15. It is believed the Corvette is red. The program is in black and white, and the idea of its being red stems from the 1962 box illustration of the Route 66 Official Board Game put out by Transogram. A 1960 Corvette appeared in the pilot episode and in 1961–1962, the car was a light powder blue. For the remainder of the series, the car was fawn beige (although in one episode, "To Walk with the Serpent," it is mentioned as being green and saddle tan, the colors used on the 1963 and 1964 Corvette Sting Rays). The colors were chosen to photograph well for black and white.

*Note:* A revised version of *Route 66* ran on NBC in 1993. Here Nick Lewis (James Wilder) learns that the father he never knew he had—Buz Murdock—has just died and that he has inherited the perfectly preserved 1960 red-and-white Chevrolet that his father once drove. With no particular destination in mind, Nick begins traveling, stopping long enough to pick up a hitchhiker named Arthur Clark (Dan Cortese). The two become friends and begin their travels down Route 66. In the pilot episode, Brent Fraser played Nick Lewis, and Andrew Lowery was Arthur Clark.

# The Saint

(Syndicated, 1963–1966; NBC, 1967–1969)

*Cast:* Roger Moore (Simon Templar).

*Basis:* A man (Simon Templar) considered criminal by the police (a master thief known as the "Saint") uses his thirst for adventure to not only help people in trouble but aid the police as well.

## SIMON TEMPLAR

*Alias:* The Saint (considered by police to be the name under which Simon performs his criminal activities). The nickname actually came about through creator Leslie Charteris, who would use "S.T." in his scripts to indicate "Simon Templar."

*Car:* A white Volvo P1800 coupe. It was originally hoped that a Jaguar could be used, but when Jaguar refused to give a free car in return for publicity, Volvo stepped in and agreed to the terms (the publicity alone far surpassed the value of the car).

*License Plate:* ST-1.

*Credit Card:* In addition to carrying cash, Simon uses American Express and Diner's Club credit cards.

*Character:* Independently wealthy and a master among thieves. He is a handsome ladies' man and encounters the most glamorous women during his world travels. He is tall, lean, and able to take care of himself, but his voice and manners make him appear deceptively lazy. Creator Leslie Charteris describes him as "a roaring adventurer who loves a fight; a dashing daredevil; imperturbable, debonair, preposterously handsome; a pirate or a philanthropist as the occasion demands. He lives for the pursuit of excitement for the one triumphant moment that is his alone."

## OTHER CHARACTERS

Claude Eustace Teal (Ivor Dean) is the chief inspector of Scotland Yard whom Simon often helps and whom Teal would like to see behind bars. In early episodes, Norman Pitt and Wensley Pithey portrayed Teal.

*Note:* Before Roger Moore acquired the role, David Niven was considered to be the perfect Simon Templar (as his on-screen personality matched that of what Leslie Charteris envisioned). When a deal could not be worked out, Patrick McGoohan was considered but was not hired due to McGoohan's principle that he would not become romantically involved with a woman on-screen. Cary Grant was even considered for the role before Roger Moore auditioned, and Charteris wholeheartedly approved of him as the perfect Simon Templar for television (Vincent Price played Templar in the radio series, and Louis Hayward, George Sanders, and Hugh Sinclair portrayed Simon in a series of films from 1938 to 1944).

## UPDATES

Ian Ogilvy played Simon Templar in the 1979 (to 1980) CBS series *Return of the Saint*. On June 12, 1987, CBS presented the unsold pilot, *The Saint in New York*, with Andrew Clark as Simon Templar (here attempting to help a ballerina facing threats by persons unknown). The idea was revised one additional time for the syndicated (1989–1990) series *The Saint* with Simon Dutton as Simon Templar and David Ryall as Inspector Claude Eustace Teal.

# *Star Trek*

## (NBC, 1966–1969)

*Cast:* William Shatner (Captain James T. Kirk), Leonard Nimoy (Mr. Spock), DeForest Kelley (Dr. Leonard McCoy), Nichelle Nichols (Lieutenant Uhura), George Takei (Hikaru Sulu), Walter Koenig (Pavel Chekov).
*Basis:* A futuristic starship, the *Enterprise*, and its voyages through uncharted space, seeking "to boldly go where no man has gone before."

## JAMES TIBERIUS KIRK

*Nickname:* Jim
*Place of Birth:* Riverside, Iowa.
*Birthday:* March 22, 2233.
*Status:* Captain of the USS *Enterprise NCC-1701*.

*Age:* 34 and the youngest captain in Star Fleet history. He has 17 temporal violations, and, although not shown on the series, he holds the record for bringing back the *Enterprise* in one piece after its grueling five-year mission.

*Ancestry:* Jim's ancestors were pioneers on the American frontier of the 1800s.

*Education:* Although no schools were mentioned, Jim entered Star Fleet Academy in the year 2250. Four years later, he graduated and was promoted to lieutenant and in 2264 became captain of the *Enterprise* (he was promoted to admiral at the end of that five-year mission).

*Awards:* The Award of Valor, the Medal of Honor, the Prantares Ribbon of Commendation, and the Palm Leaf of the Axanar Peace Mission. He was also a major participant in the Klingon peace missions.

*Television First:* Initiated the first interracial kiss (with Uhura, his African American communications officer).

*Relatives:* Peter Kirk, nephew (Craig Hyndley).

## MR. SPOCK

*Assignment:* Science officer aboard the *Enterprise.*

*Place of Birth:* The planet Vulcan.

*Year of Birth:* 2230.

*Parents:* Amanda Grayson, a human science teacher, and Ambassador Sarek, a Vulcan diplomat. Spock's lineal Vulcan name is, as he says, unpronounceable.

*Heritage:* Human-Vulcan (his childhood was difficult, as he was torn between an emotionless and strict Vulcan philosophy and human emotions).

*Childhood Pet:* A Shelat (a bearlike animal).

*Ritual:* Spock was telepathically bonded to T'Pring, a young Vulcan girl. When a Vulcan comes of age, he or she must mate once every seven years or die.

*Interests:* Science and space exploration, music, poetry, and literature.

*Expertise:* A champion at a game called "tridimensional chess."

*Catchphrase:* "Live long and prosper."

*History:* In 2249, he joined Star Fleet Academy and three years later was a cadet under Christopher Pike, the first *Enterprise* captain. A year later (2265), he became an ensign (at the same time Kirk became captain of the *Enterprise*) and was later promoted to science officer.

*Special Ability:* The Vulcan mind meld (he can penetrate the minds of others).

*Relatives:* Amanda, mother (Jane Wyatt); Sarek, father (Mark Lenard).

## DR. LEONARD McCOY

*Nickname:* Bones.

*Position:* Medical officer aboard the *Enterprise.*

Left to right: DeForest Kelley, Leonard Nimoy, unidentified, Nichelle Nichols, William Shatner, George Takei, and James Doohan. © Paramount Pictures, Paramount Pictures/Photofest

*Education:* University of Mississippi (2245–2249) and its associated medical school (2249–2253).

*Marital Status:* He is divorced and the father of Joanna (a nurse).

*History:* Dr. McCoy enjoyed an active practice for 12 years before he joined Star Fleet (and developed a neural grafting procedure that is still used). He soon became a chief medical officer, and his first command was under Kirk on the *Enterprise.* During his Star Fleet career, he won awards of valor and was decorated by the Legion of Honor.

## LIEUTENANT UHURA

*Assignment:* Communications officer on the *Enterprise.*

*Place of Birth:* United States of Africa.

*Year of Birth:* 2239.

*Character:* Uhura is a beautiful (and sexy) African American and one of the earliest role models for girls of the same race on television. She speaks fluent Swahili, and her name translates as meaning "freedom." She can play the Vulcan harp and has a lovely singing voice. Her childhood remains a mystery, and it is known only that her mother's name was M'Umbha. She and Captain Kirk are famous for initiating TV's first interracial kiss.

## MONTGOMERY SCOTT

*Nickname:* Scotty.

*Assignment:* Chief engineer aboard the *Enterprise*.

*Year of Birth:* 2222.

*History:* Mr. Scott, as he is also called, graduated from Star Fleet Academy in 2244. During his time at the academy, he served on 11 ships. The *Enterprise* was his first assignment (2264) as a chief engineer. Scotty is proud of his Scottish heritage and sometimes wears his traditional ceremonial kilts with his dress uniform. He plays the bagpipes and is known for his beverage collection (which he acquired from all areas of the galaxy). Scotch is his favorite drink, and he takes offense if anyone negatively speaks of his "baby" (the *Enterprise*).

## HIKARU SULU

*Heritage:* Asian descent.

*Place of Birth:* San Francisco, California.

*Year of Birth*: 2237.

*History:* Called Mr. Sulu, he attended Star Fleet Academy (2255–2259) and began his career as a physicist before becoming a lieutenant under Captain Kirk. A year later (2266), he became a helm officer and worked the bridge alongside Kirk.

## PAVEL CHEKOV

*Full Name:* Pavel Andreievich Pavel.

*Assignment:* Navigator aboard the *Enterprise*.

*Place of Birth:* Russia.

*Year of Birth:* 2245.

*History:* He attended Star Fleet Academy (2263–2267) and became an ensign. He is an only child and proud of his Russian heritage (often claiming that Russia was responsible for implementing many of the innovations used by Star Fleet).

# *Supercar*
## (Syndicated, 1962)

*Voice Cast:* Graydon Gould (Mike Mercury), Sylvia Anderson (Jimmy Gibson), David Graham (Dr. Beaker), George Murcell, Cyril Sharp (Professor Popkiss), George Murcell (Masterspy).

*Basis:* The lone pilot (Mike Mercury) of a futuristic car (Supercar) battles a sinister villain (Masterspy) who has established an underworld society of villainy that poses a threat to the world. A puppet series filmed in Supermarionation.

## MICHAEL "MIKE" MERCURY

*Occupation:* Pilot of Supercar.

*Prior Career:* Test pilot. He was a part of the fledgling U.S. space program of the 1950s.

*Military Career:* Captain with the U.S. Air Force.

*Abilities:* Fearless and courageous. The only one capable of (and permitted to) pilot Supercar.

*Assistants:* Jimmy Gibson (a 10-year-old boy Mike rescued in the first episode when the aeroplane on which he was traveling [driven by his brother Bill] crashed into the sea) and Mitch, Jimmy's pet monkey.

## MASTERSPY

*Place of Birth:* Albania.

*Childhood:* Out of the ordinary, as his family appeared to earn a living through treachery, stealing, and whatever else could make them money.

*Real Name:* Alexander Slanovicz.

*Military Service:* Private in the Albanian army during World War II.

*Trait:* Cowardice (as evidenced by his inability to fight the enemy in combat).

*Goal:* To succeed in crime and eventually acquire Supercar.

*New Identity:* Masterspy. Alexander took the name "Masterspy" to form a family of criminals after the war. As he says, he is just following a family tradition.

## SUPERCAR

*Creator:* Dr. Horatio Beaker (a child prodigy who is now somewhat absent-minded; he has degrees in math, biology, and electronics) and Professor Rudolph Popkiss (a Hungarian-born scientist with degrees in electronics, aviation, and rocketry). They began building Supercar in 1955 (completed the project in 1962).

*The Car:* Hidden in a secret location at Black Rock, an elaborate laboratory in Nevada (even though the series was produced in England).

*Abilities:* It hovers above the ground and rides like an ordinary car (but on a cushion of air instead of tires); it is also capable of traveling under the sea and taking off vertically to fly.

*Innovations:* Supercar contains jets in the rear to allow lift and retractable wings to return to land and be driven like a normal car. Retro-rockets, contained on each side of the car, allow it to slow down after high-speed pursuits. The car's interior contains a special television monitor that allows it to penetrate smoke and fog for clear viewing (called a "Clear-Vu Monitor").

# *SurfSide 6*
## (ABC, 1960–1962)

*Cast:* Lee Patterson (Dave Thorne), Van Williams (Ken Madison), Troy Donahue (Sandy Winfield), Diane McBain (Daphne DeWitt Dutton), Margarita Sierra (Cha Cha O'Brien).

*Basis:* Bachelor detectives Dave Thorne, Ken Madison, and Sandy Winfield, the owners of a detective agency called SurfSide 6, solve crimes in and around Miami Beach, Florida.

*Agency Address:* A houseboat moored at SurfSide 6 on Indian Creek in Miami Beach, Florida.

## DAVE THORNE
*Character:* Dave was born in New York City and began a law practice shortly after graduating from New York University. He became a prosecutor but quit when he found that legal loopholes prevented him from getting convictions.

## KEN MADISON
*Character:* Born in Texas and a graduate of Tulane University Law School. Like Dave, Ken was disillusioned with his practice in criminal law and wanted to do more than just defend people.

## SANDOR WINFIELD
*Character:* Called Sandy, he was born in Miami Beach and is the son of a wealthy family. He lives the life of a jet-setter but feels the need to help people in trouble. He assists Dave and Ken more for the excitement their cases bring him than for the monetary rewards.

## DAPHNE DEWITT DUTTON
*Character:* Billed as the "girl in the yacht next door," she is a beautiful jet-setter and heir to Dutton Farms and Dutton Racing Stables. Daphne, called Daphe, is a friend of Sandy's and helps him, Ken, and Dave when needed. She has a horse named Par-a-kee that she raised from a colt. Raymond Bailey played Daphne's father, Reginald Dutton.

## CHA CHA O'BRIEN
*Character:* A singer and dancer who performs in the Boom Boom Room of the famed Fountainbleau Hotel, which is located directly opposite SurfSide

6 on Ocean Avenue. Cha Cha was born in Madrid, Spain, and has been singing and dancing since she was four years old. Malacy McCourt played Cha Cha's cousin, Dan O'Brien, and Mario Roccuzzo played Cha Cha's nephew, Raphael.

## OVERALL SERIES INFORMATION
Although Ken, Dave, and Sandy are from different backgrounds, they rarely argue and live well together on the houseboat. The character of Ken Madison first appeared on the series *Bourbon Street Beat*. Dave, Ken, and Sandy first work with Ray Snedigar (Donald Barry), then Gene Plehan (Richard Crane), both lieutenants with the Miami Police Department, Homicide Division. Mousie (Mousie Garner) is the Boom Boom Room waiter who supplies information to Sandy, Dave, and Ken.

# Tammy
(ABC, 1965–1966)

*Cast:* Debbie Watson (Tammy Tarleton), Denver Pyle (Mordecai Tarleton), Frank McGrath (Lucius Tarleton), Donald Woods (John Brent), Dorothy Green (Lavinia Tate), Linda Marshall (Gloria Tate).

*Basis:* A pretty, sweet, and trusting Louisiana bayou girl (Tammy) attempts to begin a new life as the secretary to John Brent, a wealthy widower and the owner of Brent Enterprises.

## TAMMY TARLETON

*Full Name:* Tambry "Tammy" Tarleton.

*Age:* 18.

*Birthday:* June 6, 1947.

*Parents:* Deceased (exactly how is not mentioned). She has been cared for by her grandfather, Mordecai, and her uncle, Lucius, since she was a child. Mordecai mentions his birthday as July 17, 18 . . . (when he realizes the year, he stops and says, "I'm gettin' to be middle age; just leave it at that").

*Ancestry:* Mordecai claims the family is one-thirty-second Cherokee Indian.

*Home:* The *Ellen B* (named after Tammy's grandmother), a houseboat docked on the Louisiana bayou in Docheau County. A land grant, issued to Tammy's great, great, great, great grandfather Sylvester Tarleton by England's King George I in 1722, ensures her family that the land surrounding the *Ellen B* is legally theirs and tax free.

*Education:* While most of Tammy's upbringing and teaching came from her grandfather and uncle, she did attend the Seminole College in nearby Boulder City for a six-month secretarial course, or, as she says, "learnin' to secretary."

*Personality:* A sweet and trusting girl who will give of herself to help others. She is full of enthusiasm and overcomes adverse situations through her philosophy of love and understanding.

*Ability:* Can type 200 words a minute. Tammy can even take dictation on the typewriter. She claims she has fast reflexes to do so—"Somethin' you're born with, like getting good at callin' hogs." She also says that she has "typing school advantage over other girls." Tammy can also add faster than an adding machine—"It sort of comes naturally to me—like smellin' to a skunk."

*Speech:* Tammy talks with a style of speech that is out of the nineteenth century. She does say that "accents don't show on type-rit letters. I can cipher and grammarize with the best of 'em. I just don't like botherin' my brain with such nonsense."

*Cooking Skills:* Tammy has been taught to live off the land (like fishing and growing her own vegetables). She is famous for her fried catfish, hush puppies, and collard greens; hog liver soup; pokeweed salad; and stuffed catfish and mustard greens. Tammy simply refers to her meals as either "vittles" or "river vittles." Mr. Brent is especially fond of her pan-fried catfish.

*Pets:* Nan (a goat; she sometimes calls her Nanny), Enoch (a mule), Alexander (a pig), Delilah (a dog), and Beulah (a cow).

*Family Philosophy:* "If we don't have anything else, we have self-respect" (referring to the fact that her family is poor). She says she learned what not to do in life from her grandfather and "a lot what to do" from her uncle.

*Place of Business:* The Brentwood Estate, which is on a plantation called the Bowers (which, as Tammy says, "is within shoutin' distance" of the *Ellen B*).

*Tammy's Nemesis:* The wealthy and snooty Lavinia Tate, who has set her mind to discredit Tammy, get her fired, and secure the secretarial job for her daughter, Gloria (in a scheme to win over the affections of John Brent for herself).

## LAVINIA TATE

*Character:* Lavinia is divorced and a member of high society. She has a dog named King Alfonse of Normandy and simply despises Tammy's "sweetness" and manner of speaking (which she calls "river talk" or "swampisms"). She also calls Tammy a "water nymph" and devises elaborate schemes to get her to go back to where she came from. She was most appalled at her son Peter (David Macklin) for falling for the very pretty but backwoods Tammy.

*Relatives:* cousin, Beauregard Bassett (Sal Ponti); cousin, Grundy Tate (Jeff York); Grundy's wife, Sybelline Tate (Bella Bruck), all of whom were an embarrassment to Lavinia, as they lacked any social graces and were, in essence, hillbillies.

## GLORIA TATE

*Character:* Lavinia's beautiful, socially inclined 18-year-old daughter who can barely type and thus lost the secretarial position to Tammy. Gloria looks up to her mother ("You're so devious, cunning, and underhanded; I'm so proud of you") and is always the foil in Lavinia's efforts to discredit Tammy. Gloria is also in a contest with Tammy to win the affections of John's son Steven Brent (Jay Sheffield). Steven is attending college in New York and is seen writing letters—to Tammy. Gloria sees Tammy as a "book out of the past" for the way she speaks.

## OTHER CHARACTERS
Dwayne Witt (George Furth), Mr. Brent's assistant, who is not pleased with Tammy as John's secretary and secretly hopes the more socially accepted and prim-and-proper Gloria Tate will become John's secretary. Cletus Tarleton (Dennis Robertson) was introduced later in the series as Tammy's cousin and moved in with Mordecai and Lucius. Cletus played the guitar, fell in love with Gloria at first sight, and made it his goal to have her. He serenades her, calls her "my darling," and "wants a kiss from her ruby lips." Gloria seeks to avoid him at all costs and calls him an "oaf" and a "bumpkin" (Cletus considers "bumpkin" a term of endearment).

*Note:* The series is based on the 1957 Debbie Reynolds feature film *Tammy and the Bachelor* (where Tammy had the last name of Tyree). Four episodes of the series have been reedited and syndicated as the movie *Tammy and the Millionaire*.

# *That Girl*
## (ABC, 1966–1971)

*Cast:* Marlo Thomas (Ann Marie), Ted Bessell (Don Hollinger).
*Basis:* A young, hopeful actress (Ann Marie) journeys from her home in Brewster, New York, to Manhattan to fulfill her dream and become a star.

## ANN MARIE
*Parents:* Lou and Helen Marie.
*Boyfriend:* Don Hollinger.
*Place of Birth:* Fenwick, New York (the family later moved to Brewster, New York, where Lou opened the La Parisenne Restaurant).
*Year of Birth:* 1945.
*Talents:* Acting, playing the violin, and tap dancing.
*Childhood History:* Ann had the nickname "Punky Puss" and would arrange her dolls by name. She was voted "Best Snowball Thrower" in Putnam County, and at Camp Winnepoo she won a medal for best actress in the camp's stage plays. Ann was—and still is—a bit mishap prone. When she was five years old, she managed to get her elbow stuck in a peanut butter jar; in adult life,

she read an article about a man bowling with his toes and wound up getting her big toe stuck in a bowling ball.

*Education:* Fenwick High School (where Ann was the class secretary and treasurer) and Brewster College. In grammar school (unnamed), she always received good grades in penmanship.

*First Jobs:* A meter maid in Fenwick, then a secretary (called "Twinkle Fingers Marie, the Speedy Steno" for her rapid shorthand skills). She taught at Brewster Elementary School before journeying to New York City.

*Address:* Ann first lived at the East End Hotel on East 70th Street in Manhattan, then at 344 West 78th Street, Apartment 4D. She later lived at 627 East 54th Street, Apartment 2C.

*Phone Number:* Plaza 3-0598.

*Rent:* $88.43 a month.

*Hair Color:* Brunette.

*Weight:* 100 pounds (later 108 pounds).

*Height:* 5 feet, 5½ inches tall.

*Shoe Size:* 6A.

*Dress Size:* 6.

*Fashion Trend:* In numerous episodes, Ann Marie did not wear a bra under her blouses or dresses (reflecting Marlo Thomas's real-life style). Unintentionally, a braless fashion style for women was created.

*Acting Classes:* Ann enrolled in classes at the Benedict Workshop of the Dramatic Arts. Billy DeWolfe plays Jules Benedict, the strict acting teacher (with a sign on his office door that reads "Never Enter Here").

*Representation:* The Gilliam and Norris Theatrical Agency. Don Penny plays her most seen agent, Seymour Schwimmer.

*First Professional Appearance:* As a mop on the kid TV series *The Merry Mop-A-Teers.*

*Game Show Appearance: The Mating Game* and *Get Rich Quick.*

*Earliest Dramatic Role:* The TV series *The Lady Killer* (where she played the "Dead Bank Teller" and embarrassed herself by opening her eyes on a live broadcast).

*Other TV Series Roles:* Doris, the ding-a-ling, a woman with multiple personalities, on an unnamed TV soap opera.

*Commercials:* Jungle Madness Perfume, No Freeze Anti-Freeze, Action Soda, POP Soft Drinks, and Creamy Soap.

*Broadway Plays: Gypsy* (a two-week engagement at a Lincoln Center revival with Ethel Merman), *The Knights of Queen Mary* (at the Empire Theater), and *The Revolutionary Heart* (starring Barry Sullivan).

*Off-Broadway: And Everything Nice* (tried and closed in Philadelphia), *The Queen of Diamonds* (in St. Louis), *Funny Man* (in Las Vegas), and *A*

*Preponderance of Artichokes*, *Honor's Stain*, and *North of Larchmont* (all in Manhattan). Ann was also the understudy to Sandy Stafford, a famous Broadway star.

*Modeling Jobs:* Miss Everything at the New York Has Everything (at the Coliseum), pajama model for Unifit, Girl Friday Productions model, Miss Chicken Big (spokesperson for the Chicken Big, Inc., fast-food chain—"We Fry Harder"), fashion model to British photographer Noel Prince, roving clothes model at Sardi's Restaurant (she performed scenes from movies while modeling dresses), and spokesgirl for the Women in Space Air Force Program.

*Magazines:* Ann also appeared "nude" in *Playpen* magazine (her face on another girl's body).

*Non–Show Business Jobs:* Ann's very first job when arriving in Manhattan was as a waitress. She was then a cosmetics salesgirl at Best and Company, perfume salesgirl at Macy's; door-to-door salesgirl for Smart and Stunning Shoes, waitress at the Cave (a nightclub), department store Christmas elf, and department store sales announcer.

*Dream:* To purchase the rights to the book *A Woman's Story* by Joseph Nelson and star in the movie version of it.

*Name:* At one point, Ann had contemplated using the stage name Marie Brewster (reflecting her last name and hometown) when it was suggested that Ann Marie was not a good acting name ("Producers ask, 'Ann Marie what?'").

*Relatives:* Lou Marie, father (Lew Parker); Helen Marie, mother (Rosemary DeCamp).

## DONALD "DON" HOLLINGER

*Occupation:* Reporter for *Newsview* magazine (located at 1330 Sixth Avenue in Manhattan).

*Parents:* Bert (also called Ed and Harold) and Mildred (also called Lillian) Hollinger.

*Place of Birth:* Toledo, Ohio (also said to be born in Shelton, Ohio, then St. Louis, Missouri).

*Year of Birth:* 1934 (making him 11 years older than Ann).

*Girlfriend:* Ann Marie.

*Address:* Apartment 1 on West 54th Street in Manhattan.

*Phone Number:* Bryant 9-9978.

*Unpublished Novel: City of Strangers.*

*Favorite Meal:* Corned beef sandwiches with a glass of milk.

*Awards:* The Humanitarian Award.

*Car:* A red Mustang with the license plate 4G82 H9.

Marlo Thomas and Ted Bessell. *ABC/Photofest © ABC*

*Favorite Eatery:* Nino's Restaurant.

*Traits:* Sloppy housekeeper; always attired in a suit or sports jacket; called "Hollinger" by Ann's father.

*Relatives:* Bert Hollinger, father (Frank Faylen); Mildred Hollinger, mother (Mabel Albertson); Sandi Hollister, sister (Cloris Leachman).

*Note:* Although Don and Ann became engaged, the series ended before a wedding occurred. In the unaired pilot version, Ted Bessell was Don Blue Sky, Ann's Native American agent and boyfriend.

# *Thunderbirds*
### (Syndicated, 1968)

*Voice Cast:* Peter Dyneley (Jeff Tracy), Ray Barrett (John Tracy/The Hood), David Graham (Gordon Tracy/Brains/Kyrano/Parker), David Holliday (Virgil Tracy), Shane Rimmer (Scott Tracy), Matt Zimmerman (Alan Tracy), Sylvia Anderson (Lady Penelope), Christine Finn (Tin-Tin).

*Basis:* The missions of International Rescue (I.R.), a global organization that incorporates highly advanced vehicles and is dedicated to saving the lives of people trapped in unusual predicaments. A marionette series produced in Supermarionation.

## JEFF TRACY
*Character:* The head of I.R. He is a former astronaut who established the organization on a remote Pacific island and named his five sons (John, Gordon, Virgil, Scott, and Alan), all members of I.R., after American astronauts.

## SCOTT TRACY
*Trait:* Jeff's eldest son who is quick thinking and fast talking. He can cope with any situation and is skilled at organizing rescue operations.

*Vehicle:* Pilots Thunderbird I, a fast scout vehicle that speeds to the crisis area. It contains a mobile control tower from which operations can be directed.

*Color:* Silver-gray.

*Abilities:* Can reach speeds of 7,000 miles per hour and can also take off vertically for speed.

*Specialty:* It has retractable wings, boosters, and downward-firing rockets, allowing it to hover aboveground or land vertically without the need for wheels. It carries a robot camera that can be guided into difficult positions where it would be impossible for a human or craft to reach (like into the heart of a fire or a narrow tunnel).

## VIRGIL TRACY
*Trait:* Reliable and steady, he closely works with Scott.

*Vehicle:* Pilots Thunderbird II, a large freighter that handles the priceless rescue equipment.

*Color:* Green.

*Abilities:* It incorporates rollers instead of wheels to allow the craft's body to set down on the ground after a flight. Telescopic hydraulic legs then lift the fuselage off the ground so that the rescue equipment can be lowered.

*Specialty:* It is the only armed craft (being slower, it is more vulnerable to attack by the enemies of I.R.). It has small rocketlike equipment that emerges horizontally and can be electronically guided to its objective.

## ALAN TRACY

*Trait:* The most romantic of Jeff's children. He has an impetuous nature and is an expert racing motorist.

*Vehicle:* Pilots Thunderbird III.

*Color:* Orange.

*Abilities:* Capable of space flight to scout situations before equipment is sent in.

*Specialty:* It possesses laser radio scanners to alert the base of its location at all times, even in deep outer space.

## GORDON TRACY

*Trait:* Young and enthusiastic and loves to joke around.

*Vehicle:* Pilots Thunderbird IV.

*Color:* Yellow.

*Abilities:* Able to travel underwater to scout for situations that may require sea rescues. It is contained in the pod of Thunderbird II (which must hover over the sea to release Thunderbird IV). To retrieve Thunderbird IV, a larger machine descends vertically, lowers the pod for it to return, settles on top of the pod, and lifts it.

## JOHN TRACY

*Trait:* The youngest of the brothers and still learning about the ins and outs of I.R.

*Vehicle:* Commands Thunderbird V, the satellite space station for I.R.

*Specialty:* Possesses the most advanced scientific equipment, the most unique of which is the Interpreter, a device that can immediately translate any language into English. It can also receive and transmit messages from all parts of the world.

## LADY PENELOPE CREIGHTON-WARD

*Position:* I.R.'s glamorous London agent.

*Trait:* Adventurous and daring (called a "female James Bond"); known for her exotic wardrobe.

*Car:* A shocking-pink Rolls Royce.

*License Plate:* FAB 1.

*Car Abilities:* Can reach speeds up to 200 miles per hour.

*Car Specialty:* The wheels rotate sideways so that it can park crabwise. The wheels also have retractable studs for travel on snow and ice and pointed end rods that shoot out to form a tire slasher (activated when Penelope pushes a button on the dashboard). The car also has bulletproof glass, a steel canopy, and a backseat with retractable handcuffs and a chest band to restrain prisoners. It has a television monitor instead of a rearview mirror, a machine gun that can be fired from the radiator, buttons to activate oil sprays and tack ejection, and a smoke-making apparatus. The car was actually submitted to Rolls Royce for its approval before being used in the series.

## THE HOOD

*Character:* The enemy of I.R., who is dedicated to discovering the secrets of its operations. He has established himself in an exotic Eastern temple and practices "Hoodoo" (places spells on people for his own sinister purposes; as he places spells, his eyes light up). He is extremely talented in disguising himself so that he can never be recognized as his true self.

## BRAINS

*Character:* The scientific genius who invented the unique I.R. equipment. He is the typical "egghead" and shy and somewhat hesitant in his speech.

## PARKER

*Character:* Lady Penelope's chauffer and manservant. He is a droll Englishman, getting on in years but young in spirit. He is an ex-con (now reformed) and has a talent for blowing up safes.

## KYRANO

*Character:* The Hood's half brother who now works as Jeff Tracy's loyal servant.

## TIN-TIN

*Character:* Kyrano's brunette daughter (in Malayan, her name means "Sweet"). When the series begins, Tin-Tin has returned to the I.R. base after being educated in America (at Jeff's expense). She is an electronics expert, and it is hinted that she and Alan are romantically involved with each other.

## GRANDMA

*Character:* Jeff's mother, who looks after her grandchildren and sees that each has a hearty home-cooked meal.

## I.R. BASE

An exotic island where nature has been adapted to aid the scenery. The cliff face moves so that I.R. equipment can enter or leave their hiding place (trees then fall back). A swimming pool can be made to disappear, and electronic devices warn of intruders. The house that accommodates the Tracy family is also unique in that it contains portraits of each of Jeff's sons that perform a specific function when "Operation Cover-Up" is enacted. The portraits rotate from the boys in their ordinary clothes to them in their Thunderbird uniforms. The eyes in each of the portraits then light up when messages are being received from them. When the message is complete, the portraits rotate back to their original position.

# The Time Tunnel
(ABC, 1966–1967)

*Cast:* James Darren (Tony Newman), Robert Colbert (Doug Phillips), Whit Bissell (General Heywood Kirk), Lee Meriwether (Dr. Anne McGregor).
*Basis:* Two scientists (Tony and Doug), lost in time, attempt to deal with the historical events they encounter while seeking a way to return to their own time.

## THE TIME TUNNEL
*Purpose:* To send a human being back in time. The project, called the Time Tunnel, was begun in 1958 and is still, in 1966, in its experimental stage. It is called a project dealing with time displacement and designed to eventually control time. The Tunnel has the ability to view the past through the person who has entered that time period (before entering the swirling maze of the Tunnel, a traveler must take a special radioactive bath [appears as a blue mist] that will enable the Tunnel sensors to pick up his signal no matter where in time he may be).
*Fault:* While in theory a human can be sent back in time, the Tunnel has not been perfected to the point where he or she can be returned to his or her own time. Experiments have been conducted with mice and monkeys, but after being sent back in time, they were unable to be retrieved.
*Cost:* Thus far, $7.5 billion.
*Secret Location:* Tic Toc Base, a secured U.S. government base in the middle of the Arizona desert. Here the Tunnel sits 800 floors beneath the surface (it takes 10 seconds to travel by elevator from the surface to the Tunnel's complex). It is here that rows of massive turbines supply the power and the most technically advanced computers control operations.

## TIME TUNNEL PERSONNEL
*Project Supervisor:* General Heywood Kirk.
*Electromicrobiologist:* Dr. Anne McGregor.
*Scientists:* Anthony "Tony" Newman and Douglas "Doug" Phillips. Tony, born in 1938, joined with Doug, who has been working on the Time Tunnel

since its beginnings, in 1965. Doug is a doctor of electrophysics; Tony is an electrophysicist.

*Supervisor:* Dr. Raymond Swain (John Zaremba), a man with the finest electronics mind in the country. He oversees the entire project but is most concerned with the history computers and tracking and freezing time (accomplished through the Tele-control, a portal through which events of the past can be viewed as they happen).

*Security Head:* Master Sergeant Jiggs (Wesley Lau).

## THE PROBLEM

The government has become disenchanted with the project and is threatening to shut it down unless it can be proved that a human can be sent through time. Believing that the Time Tunnel is capable of doing it, Tony foolishly enters the psychedelic chamber and is sent into the past (here to the ship *Titanic* on April 15, 1912—the day it struck an iceberg). When the Tunnel recorders pick up Tony's whereabouts but are not able to retrieve him, Doug theorizes that the only way to save Tony, who will become one of the victims, is to go back in time to help him. With Tony's coordinates calculated, Doug enters the psychedelic Tunnel chamber and 16 seconds later is sent back in time and to Tony's location. As disaster strikes the ship, Tunnel engineers are able to freeze Tony and Doug and send them to another time. They are safe but still lost in time, and every resend by the Tunnel could send them to "yesterday, today, tomorrow—or a million years from now. . . . It is just a matter of time" (before Tony and Doug are able to be retrieved).

*Note:* In the unaired pilot version, the second episode's coming attractions placed Tony and Doug in the prehistoric era; in the aired second episode, they became unknown passengers aboard a primitive NASA rocket.

# Voyage to the Bottom of the Sea
(ABC, 1964–1968)

*Cast:* Richard Basehart (Harriman Nelson), David Hedison (Lee Crane), Bob Dowdell (Chip Norton), Henry Kulky (Curley Jones), Terry Becker (Francis Sharkey), Del Monroe (Ski Kowalski).

*Basis:* The undersea explorations of the *Seaview*, an awesome, nuclear-powered submarine of the future (1970s).

## THE *SEAVIEW*

*Creator and Designer:* Admiral Harriman Nelson, U.S. Navy.

*Nelson's Organization:* The government-funded N.I.M.R. (Nelson Institute for Marine Research).

*Location:* Off the southern coast of California (Santa Barbara).

Seaview *Location:* 500 feet beneath the surface of the institute in a top-secret base carved out of solid rock. It is housed in Doc C-4. It was commissioned in 1973.

*Abilities:* The *Seaview* can take depths up to 3,600 feet (anything deeper strains the hull and could cause the sub to explode). It has atomic weapons and is actually called the "mightiest weapon afloat." It has an observation tower (seen in first-season episodes only), and its original eight observation windows became four as the series progressed.

*Mini-Sub:* The Flying Sub (identified as FS-1). It is yellow in color and can hold two people. It is launched from the bomb-bay doors underneath the *Seaview*. It can travel in water as well as fly in the air.

*Public Image:* That of an instrument of marine research. In actuality, patrolling the Seven Seas and battling the most dangerous enemies of humankind (which also include aliens from other planets). According to Admiral Nelson, "The *Seaview*'s job is never finished as long as there are evil forces active in the world."

Seaview *Codes:* 452 (its code to the White House) and 777 (its code to the Pentagon).

## *SEAVIEW* CREW

Admiral Nelson is in charge of the scientific projects the *Seaview* will undertake. Lee Crane is the sub's captain, a by-the-book officer who previously served with Nelson when he captained the submarine *Nautilus*. Chip Morton is the commander, Curley Jones is the chief petty officer, and Ski and Sharkey are crew members.

# *Wendy and Me*
(ABC, 1964–1965)

*Cast:* George Burns (himself), Connie Stevens (Wendy Conway), Ron Harper (Jeff
  Conway), James Callahan (Danny Adams), J. Pat O'Malley (Mr. Bundy).
*Basis:* An airline pilot (Jeff), his scatterbrained wife (Wendy), and their experi-
  ences as newlyweds living in an apartment complex owned by comedian
  George Burns.

## GEORGE BURNS
*Occupation:* Landlord of the Sunset de Ville apartment complex in Los Angeles,
  California.
*Address:* 4820 Highland Avenue.
*Apartment:* 104 (also seen as Apartment 9).
*Prior Occupation:* Former vaudeville, radio, movie, and television star. "Well
  here I am doing a weekly television series again [referring to his prior series
  *The George Burns and Gracie Allen Show* and *The George Burns Show*]. I
  didn't want to do it. I told the network [ABC] not a chance. They said,
  'George, we'll let you sing all you want.' I said, 'Where do I sign.'" (Refers
  to George's prior series, where he loved to sing but no one believed he could
  or would listen to him.)
*Ability:* George is the only one who is aware of a viewing audience. He speaks
  directly to them, relates monologues, and sings whenever the occasion allows (follows the premise of his first series). George practices singing five
  or six hours a day. ("I have to be ready in case somebody throws as party.
  I love to sing. I'd rather sing than eat. Some of my friends who heard me
  sing say they'd rather eat.") George mentions that he was originally a tenant
  and later bought the building in order to sing (as he says, "I have it in the
  tenants' leases that they cannot evict the landlord").

## WENDY AND JEFF CONWAY

*Apartment:* 17 (later seen as Apartment 217).

*Wendy's Job:* Housewife. She and Jeff are married one year when the series begins.

*Wendy's Prior Job:* Airline stewardess for TGA (Trans Globe Airlines).

*Wendy's Character:* Blonde, beautiful, and scatterbrained. As George says, "People gave up wondering why Wendy does things a long time ago. I'm glad I own the building. People can go to Wendy's apartment, get confused, and come to my apartment to hear me sing."

*Wendy's Quirks:* Always leaving notes for Jeff. She loves him very much and says, "I want him to know where I am even when we're together." (e.g., "Dear Jeff. I've gone downstairs to pick up the mail. I should be back by the time you finish reading this. Your loving wife, Wendy." She explained to Jeff that "I didn't want you to think I was out when I was gone.")

*George's Summation:* Claims that Wendy has an organized mind: "She never knows what she is going to say even after she says it." Wendy also celebrates everything: the day she first met Jeff, the day she first put sugar in Jeff's coffee, and March 23 ("The day that nothing happened").

*Performance:* In the annual airline show, Wendy and George performed the song "If I Could Be with You."

*Jeff's Job:* Pilot for TGA.

*Wendy and Jeff's First Meeting:* Version 1: Wendy was assigned to the same flight as Jeff and spent 20 minutes trying to fasten Jeff's seat belt before she figured out he was the pilot. As George says, "Having Wendy help you is like being lost in the desert for four days and then having someone hand you a glass of sand." It was love at first sight, and they married three weeks later.

Version 2: Wendy explained that she was a stewardess assigned to a Honolulu flight; Jeff was a pilot assigned to a Chicago flight. Wendy boarded the wrong plane (the Chicago flight) and met Jeff when she tried to tell him he was flying the plane in the wrong direction.

## DANIEL "DANNY" ADAMS

*Occupation:* Jeff's copilot.

*Apartment:* 19 (later seen as Apartment 219).

*Character:* A ladies' man who can't go 24 hours without being with a woman (he gets withdrawal pains; if he becomes desperate, he walks past beauty shops until a girl whistles). Danny has two dating books: The traditional "Little Black Book" and the "Red Star Edition."

## OTHER CHARACTERS

Mr. Bundy is George's apartment house janitor. He enjoys eating at Jenny's Tea Room and is constantly amazed by the antics that occur due to Wendy's attempts to help other people (something George loves to see and often complicates by adding to the situation; Mr. Bundy often becomes his dupe; Bundy continually refuses but always does so when George says simply, "Do it"). Bob Hunter (playing himself) is George's piano player (as George says, "He's out of the Juilliard School of Music. When they found out he was working for me, the next day he was out").

# The Wild Wild West
## (CBS, 1965–1969)

*Cast:* Robert Conrad (James T. West), Ross Martin (Artemus Gordon).

*Basis:* Government agents James T. West and Artemus Gordon battle evil villains in the West of the 1870s.

### JAMES T. "JIM" WEST

*Position:* Secret Service underground intelligence officer.

*Rank:* Major.

*Prior Service:* Served as a cavalry officer for 10 years before being recruited by President Ulysses S. Grant (now his superior).

*Mobile Base of Operations:* The *Nimrod*, an 1860 2-4-0 steam engine. The 2-4-0 represents the engine's wheel arrangement: 2 for the leading truck, 4 on the main drivers, and no trailing truck.

*Train Cars:* The engine's coal car and a luxurious passenger car (which doubles as his sleeping quarters and base of operations). The *Nimrod* is actually the name plate for the passenger car; the engine carries the number 3. The red marker lights on the rear car of the train serve two purposes: an alert for other trains on the same track and a signal that something is wrong (e.g., if Jim is inside of the train and needs help, he switches on the lights to let Artemus know).

*Cover:* Poses as Jim West, a big-time gambler from the East who is known as the "dandiest dude who ever crossed the Mississippi in his own train."

*Weapons:* The *Nimrod* houses rifles, guns, knives, and explosives; a secret wardrobe for Jim's undercover assignments; and a pool table for relaxation. A special pool cue contains a hidden sword.

*Wardrobe:* That of an eastern dude. He conceals pop-out guns under his coat sleeves, a tiny derringer is broken in two with one piece concealed in the heel of each boot, a skeleton key is hidden behind his coat lapel, and smoke bombs are concealed under his holster.

### ARTEMUS "ARTIE" GORDON

*Position:* Undercover agent with the Secret Service.

*Prior Occupation:* Actor.

Ross Martin and Robert Conrad. *CBS/Photofest © CBS*

*Abilities:* Can read and write in English, Latin, Greek, German, Chinese, and Braille. He can speak Russian but can't read it.

*Wardrobe:* Whatever the situation calls for (he usually gets the less glamorous assignments). He conceals smoke bombs, putty explosives, and knockout powders within his wardrobe.

*Carrier Pigeons:* Anabella, Arabella, Henry, and Henrietta are the homing pigeons Artie uses to contact Jim when he is needed. The pigeons live in a cage on the *Nimrod.*

*Favorite Color:* Red.

## OTHER CHARACTERS

Michael Dunn is Miguelito Coyote Loveless, an evil, diminutive scientist who owed his villainy "to the curse of my midget size." He believes the U.S. government took the country away from his grandmother (and getting back at the government was his main goal). Charles Davis is Tennison, Jim's manservant on the train, and Richard Kiel (as Voltaire) and Phoebe Dorin (as Antoinette) are Miguelito's assistants.

*Note:* In the CBS TV movie *The Wild Wild West Revisited*, it is the 1890s, and Robert T. Malone (played by Harry Morgan) is now the head of the Secret Service. Before being rehired as agents, Jim had retired to Mexico, and Artie began his own theater company (the Deadwood Strolling Players Traveling Tent Show; they were performing the play *The Society Lady's Revenge*). Paul Williams played Miguelito Loveless Jr., the son of their former adversary who was following in his father's footsteps.

# Index

Devery, Elaine, 120
DeWitt, Alan, 128
DeWolfe, Billy, 63, 211
Diamond, Don, 64, 74
Diamond, Selma, 130
Dick, Andy, 81
Dixon, Ivan, 111
Dolenz, Micky, 154
Donahue, Troy, 206
Donohue, Nancy, 51
Doran, Ann, 110, 147, 178, 190
Doran, Phoebe, 225
Douglas, Donna, 22
Dowling, Doris, 167
Doyle, David, 182
Dozier, William, 19
Duke, Patty, 181
Dulo, Jane, 80, 145
Dunn, Michael, 225
Dyneley, Peter, 214

Ebsen, Buddy, 22
Eden, Barbara, 117, 199
Eilbacher, Cindy, 169
Eisley, Anthony, 123
Elder, Ann, 146
England, Sue, 138
Ericson, John 115
Evans, Linda, 31
Evans, Maurice, 27
Evers, Jason, 100

Faylen, Frank, 213
Feld, Fritz, 138
Feldon, Barbara, 78
Felton, Verna, 187
Ferdin, Pamelyn, 74
Field, Sally, 73, 83, 110
Files, Gary, 46
Finer, Christine, 214
Firestone, Edie, 59
Fisher, Gail, 143
Flanagan, Kellie, 81
Flynn, Joe, 30, 144
Foch, Nina, 152

Fogel, Jerry, 155
Fong, Kam, 104
Forman, Joey, 81
Fougler, Byron, 45
Fowley, Douglas V., 191
Fox, Bernard, 27
Francis, Anne, 44, 115
Franken, Stephen, 28
Frawley, William, 172
Fulmer, Steve, 104
Furth, George, 210

Gabor, Eva, 93
Gabor, Zsa Zsa, 22
Garland, Beverly, 172
Garver, Kathy, 67
Gaunt, William, 53
Gautier, Dick, 78, 156
Gerritsen, Lisa, 70, 177
Ghostley, Alice, 30, 45
Gilford, Jack, 82
Goddard, Mark, 135
Gordon, Gale, 186
Gordon, Susan, 177
Gorshin, Frank, 22
Gough, Lloyd, 97
Gould, Graydon, 204
Gould, Harold, 110
Gould, Sandra, 27
Grady, Don, 172
Graham, David, 204, 214
Grant, Cy, 46
Gray, Donald, 46
Green, Dorothy, 208
Greer, Dabbs, 83
Griffith, Andy, 8
Gunty, Morty, 62
Guilbert, Ann Morgan, 57, 111
Gwynne, Fred, 50, 157

Hagen, Kevin, 135
Hagman, Larry, 117
Hale, Alan, Jr., 85
Hamel, Veronica, 163
Hamilton, Margaret, 6

# About the Author

**Vincent Terrace** has worked as a researcher for ABC and is currently the TV historian for BPOLIN Productions, LLC (for which he created and wrote the pilot episode for a projected TV series called *April's Dream*). The author of 37 books on television and radio history, Terrace has teamed with James Robert Parish for the *Actors' Television Credits* series of books for Scarecrow Press. He has also written such books as *Television Series of the 1950s: Essential Facts and Quirky Details* (2016), *Television Introductions: Narrated TV Program Openings since 1949* (2013), *The Encyclopedia of Television Pilots, 1937–2012* (2013), *Television Specials, 1936–2012* (2013), *The Encyclopedia of Television Subjects, Themes, and Settings* (2011), and *The Encyclopedia of Television Programs, 1925–2010*, 2nd ed. (2011).